The Civilian Bomb
Disposing Earl

The Civilian Bomb Disposing Earl

Jack Howard and
Bomb Disposal in WWII

by

Kerin Freeman

Pen & Sword
MILITARY

First published in 2015 by
Pen and Sword Military

An imprint of
Pen & Sword Books Ltd
47 Church Street
Barnsley
South Yorkshire
S70 2AS

ISBN 978 1 47382 560 4

Printed and bound in England
By CPI Group (UK) Ltd, Croydon, CR0 4YY

Pen & Sword Books Ltd incorporates the Imprints of Pen & Sword Aviation,
Pen & Sword Family History, Pen & Sword Maritime, Pen & Sword Military,
Pen & Sword Discovery, Pen & Sword Politics, Pen & Sword Atlas, Pen & Sword
Archaeology, Wharncliffe Local History, Wharncliffe True Crime, Wharncliffe
Transport, Pen & Sword Select, Pen & Sword Military Classics, Leo Cooper, The
Praetorian Press, Claymore Press, Remember When, Seaforth Publishing and
Frontline Publishing

For a complete list of Pen & Sword titles please contact
PEN & SWORD BOOKS LIMITED
47 Church Street, Barnsley, South Yorkshire, S70 2AS, England
E-mail: enquiries@pen-and-sword.co.uk
Website: www.pen-and-sword.co.uk

Contents

Dedicated to Jack, Fred and Beryl

It is not the critic who counts, not the man who points out how the strong man stumbled, or where the doer of deeds could have done better. The credit belongs to the man who is actually in the arena, whose face is marred by dust and sweat and blood, who strives valiantly, who errs and comes short again and again, who knows the great enthusiasms, the great devotions, and spends himself in a worthy cause. Who, at best, knows achievement and who, at the worst, if he fails at least fails while daring greatly so that his place shall never be with those cold and timid souls who know neither victory nor defeat?

Theodore Roosevelt, recipient of the 1906 Nobel Peace Prize, from a speech given at the Sorbonne, Paris in 1910.

ACKNOWLEDGEMENTS

I could not have written this book without the help of some truly amazing people, and if I have left anyone out please forgive me. I thank them for their support and faith in me.

The author has attempted to trace the copyright holders of information reproduced in this book and apologizes to them if permission to publish has not been obtained.

I must first express my deep gratitude for the kindness and humour shown to me by Charles Howard's son, the Honourable Maurice Howard, the archivist in the family, who has been extremely generous with his critique in the reading of my first and last draft and supported my endeavours.

I am immensely indebted to those fine people on the other side of the world who were receptive to my pleas for help: Chris Ransted and Lieutenant Commander Rob Hoole, MBA, MCMI, MIExpE, MNI, RN, thank you for all your help at the beginning of my quest, you gave me hope there would be more to find.

My warmest appreciation to John Bartleson, Jr, EOD, MNCM, CWO4, USN(ret.) and naval historian who, with his great sense of humour and remarkable knowledge of bomb disposal, has guided and supported me along the way. Steve Venus, a UK expert in German bomb fuses, too, a godsend. Thank you both for sharing your technical knowledge and encouraging someone who, before writing this book, never really thought very much on the subject.

My sincere thanks go to Clare Sergent at Radley College, and also to Miss S. Foster the archivist at Winchester College for their willingness to help in my project. I am indebted to Terry Hissey, Marion Hebblethwaite, Noel Cashford, MBE, (sadly not with us anymore) and Terry Oliver, you enabled me to gain a better grasp on civil defence and the holders of the George Cross.

John Hannaford, an ex-Second World War bomb disposal officer with a remarkable memory and a sweet heart, was kind enough to write down his experiences during those dreadful times and his remembrances of the Earl.

My gratitude goes to both Richard Hards and Eileen 'Frankie' Clark for sharing with me their memories, photographs, and documents on Fred and Beryl. I was also very fortunate to find Don Cody, Gena and Donald Brown, thank you for your efforts in helping me piece together Olaf Paulsen's life. My thanks also to Amanda Whitrod, a relative of Adelaide McColm, for sending information on Captain McColm and his family. You never met me yet you opened your hearts and that is very precious.

Credit must also go to David Sampson, the British Ordnance Collector Network (BOCN), The British Library, MoD, Swindon & Wiltshire Archives, the Australian National Maritime Museum in Sydney, John Oxley Library at the State Library of Queensland, The Imperial War Museum, the National Army Museum, National Monuments Record Centre in Swindon, the National Archives, Ken Chamberlain of the Erith Borough Historical Society, Major Emlyn Jones, CBE, MBE for his recall of that sad day, Eric Wakeling, and Eric Laureys for allowing me to use his research into diamonds, also J & J Denholm Ltd. Roy Martin, Bruno Comer, Chaim Even-Zohar and the Antwerp Diamond Bank, much appreciation for all your help.

I am indebted to Hugh Gregory for those wonderful memories of his mother who met the Earl, and to the wonderful Henry Bishop, now in his 90s, and Ken Tinker (ex-RAF, ex-RCAF) for their excellent recollections of that fateful day in 1941 (Ken Tinker, sadly, died in October 2013). To Les Cooper (who passed away in April 2012), Don Dippelsman in Australia, Alan Craxford for sharing information with me about Mimi, Chloe Howard in the US, and Dr Michael Moss for allowing me to read his father's notes on meeting with the Earl – it was a pleasure on my part to read your father's war diary.

Recognition must also go to Alastair Massie at the National Army Museum, UK, Alastair Wilson at the Army Personnel Centre in Glasgow, David Read from the Soldiers of Gloucestershire Museum, and 'Sandy' Sanderson, curator of the Explosive Ordnance Disposal Technical Information Centre (EODTIC). My warm appreciation to Pen & Sword Books for all the work they have put into this book and their faith in me.

Finally, the endless support of my family Simon, Laura and Mel, and my good friends, is beyond measure. Last but definitely not least, Julian Dickon – I would never have undertaken this mission in the first place without his help.

Kerin Freeman, 2014

INTRODUCTION

Just over 5 years ago an old friend told me of a story that caught his eye 20 years earlier in the Readers Digest. I had never heard of the man he was talking about and my friend's recollections were hazy at most. He could only remember the man was an Earl. An Earl of what he wasn't sure, but I was hooked. I began my research but ended up with very little and became frustrated. Months went by. Then one day, time worked its magic and my friend remembered – it was Charles Henry George Howard, 20th Earl of Suffolk, 13th Earl of Berkshire, GC, FRS.

Charles Henry George Howard, affectionately known as Jack to his family and friends, was a product of an ancestral family that had been for hundreds of years cloaked in an intrigue of politics, power and a nobility of spirit. He inherited a whirlpool of Jewish American and Catholic/ Protestant English blood and his mother's adventurous spirit. He also inherited the genes of his uncle, the Honourable James Knyvett Estcourt Howard, another intrepid explorer who had the misfortune of having his right foot and the fingers on both hands amputated after only just managing to survive the freezing, numbing weather of British Columbia while out hunting for moose.

On a cold wet Friday on 2 March 1906, Jack Howard came into the world in Burton Hill House, St Paul Without, Malmesbury, Wiltshire: the first born son of Henry Molyneux Paget Howard, 19th Earl of Suffolk, 12th Earl of Berkshire, and Lady Suffolk, Marguerite 'Daisy' Hyde Leiter, an American millionaire's daughter with a substantial inheritance. As it was during those rapidly changing years, roughly 500 American women married 'cash strapped' English aristocrats mainly for their title, and some for their money as an added bonus. Around 10 percent of British nobility married Americans.

When Jack's father, Henry, who was very good at sport, attended Winchester College in the late 1800s as a commoner or fee-payer at 29 years-old, he discovered he had a talent for amateur dramatics. He loved putting on lavish plays at his home and inviting his friends to act out parts he assigned to them. Henry was known to all around his Charlton Park estate as a true country gentleman with a passion for riding and owning a pack of hounds. As a Liberal Unionist, he enjoyed the creature comforts of being a titled landowner although he never allowed them to interfere with what he considered to be the most important of all – his duty to his country.

Towards the end of his 21st year, Henry was appointed *aide-de-camp* (ADC) to George Nathaniel Curzon, 1st Marquess Curzon of Kedleston accompanied him and his wife Lady Mary Victoria, née Leiter, in Calcutta and Simla in India. There he shot tigers and met and fell in love with Mary's sister, Margaret Hyde, who was known to close family and friends as 'Daisy'. She, with her mother and sister Nancy, happened to be visiting Mary at the time. Nancy and 'Daisy' became the 'belles' of Simla.

The Leiter sisters were from a wealthy family in the US – their father Levi Zeigler Leiter was a millionaire and an affluent industrialist. One of his granddaughters, Lady Cynthia ('Cimmie') Curzon, married Oswald Ernald Mosley, 6th Baronet of Ancoats, the founder of the British Union of Fascists. Lord Curzon, her father, took a while to be persuaded that Mosley was a suitable husband as he suspected that he was largely motivated by social and political advancement and his daughter's inheritance. Lord Curzon's fears turned out to be well-founded as Mosley was a cad. He had an extended affair with Cimmie's youngest sister and their stepmother. When Cimmie died in 1933 he quickly moved on and married his mistress, Diana, one of the Mitford sisters.

When Leiter's daughter Mary became Lady Curzon she was presented with a handsome dowry of $200,000. Growing up, the girls and their parents resided in a classically inspired, three floored, fifty-five roomed lavishly appointed mansion built of white brick with a red roof. It was situated at the intersection of Dupont Circle, New Hampshire Avenue and 19th Street, Washington, DC, and was considered to be one of the finest houses in the city. The family moved in a most exclusive circle of society. Daisy was tutored at home in singing, dancing, music, art, French, mathematics, chemistry, and history. She was forthright and frank and had, according to those around her, an amazing intellect. When Daisy was older her father paid for her and her sisters to attend a private boarding school in England.

Daisy was six-feet tall with a slender and graceful figure, and was considered by all to be stunning on the eye. Her first true love was Major Colin Campbell of the British Army, but her sister Nancy married him. However, the heat and lust in central India proved to be a powerful aphrodisiac and America was thrilled when they heard that Daisy was to marry the 19th Earl of Suffolk, 12th Earl of Berkshire: a man who was, one American newspaper reported, already making his mark in the world in many important positions.

Due to Daisy's father having recently died, the couple were married in a simple ceremony on 26 December 1904 in the drawing room of the family's home by the Reverend Cotton Smith in front of family and friends. For their honeymoon they travelled extensively throughout India and Africa on safaris, shooting wild animals: big game hunting being a favourite pastime of the rich and famous.

After their whirlwind tour came to an end, Henry returned to his ancestral home at Charlton Park with his new bride. Daisy settled quite comfortably into her duties as countess and proceeded to put Charlton Park in order with improvements to the plumbing and ventilation in the vast house, spending £225,000 of her own money on modernization. A trifling sum compared to her share of her father's £50,000,000.

She eventually lost her taste for the American way of life and never yearned to re-enter her home-social circle. Instead, she gained a love of speed, mainly fast cars, and travelling to exotic countries. In later years, she bought herself an aeroplane that came with an ex-RAF pilot named Stone who also chauffeured her around in her Bentley, later her aeroplane would become her passion. Her adventurous spirit would take her to a number of out-of-the-way places, including the Amazon.

Daisy's father, Levi Zeigler Leiter, had started out in life as a humble clerk in Ohio. From then on, by thrift and frugality, he amassed a fortune, and became a millionaire some five years later. In addition to being extremely wealthy he partly owned Field, Palmer, Leiter & Co., along with large areas of land, railways, mines and properties. In 1881, he sold his interest to his partner, Marshall Field, for $2,500,000. But there was one thing Leiter could not do and that was deny his family anything, so when the world famous Borghese rubies, the finest in existence, came up for sale there was great rivalry from crowned heads, princes and millionaires from all corners of the world vying for ownership of these beautiful gems. Levi's wife Mary had set her heart on them and when the hammer fell on the last bid it was she who owned the precious stones for $110,000. Levi Leiter died from a heart attack during a visit to Vanderbilt Cottage, Maine, just before his 70th birthday. Many said he was a vindictive man, an assessment borne out of years of litigious contention and squabbling over inheritances amongst the Leiter family.

The ancestral home of the Howards, Charlton Park, listed as Cereltone in the Domesday Book, sits on prime land that once belonged to the rich and powerful Abbey of Malmesbury in Wiltshire. The surrounding area is noted for high downland and wide valleys, Stonehenge ancient monuments, the stone circles at Avebury and Salisbury Cathedral. The Jacobean manor house was completed in 1607 and once housed quite an exceptional library. The Long Gallery, a most impressive feature with a handsome stone fireplace, with the Howard Lion armorial in the centre, ran the width of the house, 125ft. In an earlier time a large collection of 'Old Masters', which many claimed to have been the finest in the land, decorated the interior.

Among these was a painting of Edward Stafford, 3rd Duke of Buckingham as Lord High Steward, and one of Lord Thomas Howard – Lord High Admiral and the 'Pelican Portrait' of Queen Elizabeth I, who had presented it as a gift to her Lord High Admiral; a Tintoretto; *A Hermit Preaching to Natives* by Salvator Rosa; two Caraccis paintings – one Le Raboteur; *La Vierge aux Rochers* by Leonardo da Vinci; and paintings by Titian, Guido Reni, Sir Peter Lely, Vansomer, Kneller, Holbein and Vandyck and many more. Paintings that were not sold remained at Charlton until the end of the First World War when they were removed by Daisy when she moved to live at Redlynch House in Bruton, Somerset. Her wish, after her death, was that they be placed in the care of English Heritage.

Henry and Daisy's first born son Jack had two brothers – Cecil John Arthur born on 24 June 1908 and Greville Reginald born 7 September 1909. When Jack was 3 years-old, his parents employed a French governess to tutor him. His lessons included the complexities of the French language at which, as he grew older, he became exceedingly fluent. Later in life, Jack's knowledge of the language would be put to the test. He left the safe, secure folds of his family and governess to attend preparatory school.

At the beginning of the First World War, Jack's father wanted to join the Guards but money was short and as a result he joined the artillery and was commissioned as a Second Lieutenant and given the command of

Wiltshire Battery, Royal Field Artillery, part of the 3rd Wessex Brigade, Gloucestershire Regiment. In 1914, he sailed to India where the battery made their way from Meerut to Mesopotamia. During Henry's time away, Daisy received infrequent letters blanked out in parts, describing the difficulties they had to contend with.

Daisy sometimes read out snippets to Jack who listened avidly to his father's words as they leapt off the page. His father wrote that his battery had covered the Black Watch and had received compliments from General A.G. Wauchope who hoped his father's battery would cover them again in time of need. Jack's father, obviously charmed by the man, wrote that he appreciated his comments, and that it made his life and his efforts there worthwhile. The little boy's chest puffed with pride at his father's daring deeds.

At the first attack on the railway at Istabulet, just beyond Bagdad, on 21 April 1917, his beloved father was killed, aged 39 years-old, when a shell landed on his observation post. Before Henry's death, he had been 'Mentioned in Dispatches' and was recommended for a Military Cross. His body rested for a while in a railway culvert on General Scott's advice and was later removed and taken to Basra's cemetery.

Jack, now 11 years-old, would never forget that moment in the drawing room with his mother on that spring-like day in April when he heard a knock at the door and a man in uniform was announced. The officer spoke in hushed tones to his mother that Jack could not fully comprehend.

As the seconds passed he became acutely aware that his mother had just received news of his father's death. The never-before-questioned foundations of his world began to slowly crumble, as if in slow motion like the time when he fell off his bicycle or his horse. The room filled and hummed with white noise that sounded loud in his ears.

His eyes stayed fixed on his mother's as her features began to disintegrate. No longer able to deal with the pain he saw, he looked away and scanned the room: his eyes settling on a large opaque vase standing in the centre of a highly-polished table over by a window. With all his might he willed his tears not to fall.

It was not true, it could not be true. His father was a soldier, a fearless warrior. It was a mistake, the army made mistakes, just like anybody else. But it was not an error and just as his mother's world floundered, his altered forever. The impact of his father's death changed the way he perceived life and on placing his trust in all he believed to be dependable.

Two months later, with a heavy heart, Daisy sat down and wrote a letter to her closest friend, her niece Cimmie. It was dated 24 June 1917:

'My beloved Cimmie,

'I've been longing to tell you how I loved your precious letter but have been too weak & wretched these last few days that I could not write my Darling. [Your] Beloved Uncley's death has nearly killed me so I am less able to struggle through these cruel days, tho' I long to find courage to fight my battle as bravely as he did all of his. I wish I could tell you all the wonderful things I have heard of him. Two days ago [Major] General [Andrew] Wauchope came to see me – he commanded the Black Watch where Uncley supported them at the Battle of Mushaidie and I was very very proud while he told us of precious Uncley's magnificent work there – they were short of infantry and could get no re-enforcements & General Wauchope said it was because he knew how he could count on Uncley that they attempted what they did. Not only did he save hundreds of lives by his absolute accuracy of his fire himself to save his officers and… General Wauchope is the last man to say anything he does not mean and he could not say enough of the splendid part my Beloved played all through that terrible fighting. It is so cruel to think that it should have happened at this very (point) of that last great battle that he played so great a part in winning. I have…so much to be proud of but Oh Cimmie Darling when one has lost as much as I have nothing can help to bear the heartbreaking days that follow. I sometimes wonder if over last autumn and through his untiring efforts he achieved nothing but the greatest success all through that Dreadful fighting in Mesopotamia. He was in it all and his was the first battery to reach Bagdad. In a letter I received this week, a great friend of ours in the 14th Hussars says "At one time he galloped his Battery into action about 3,000yd from the Turks – which must be a unique experience for a Field Battery Commander in this war. I have never seen (anything like it) [seeing him] gallop into action." I'm sure you will like to hear all this, my precious, for I know how you loved him. Someday I will show you all the wonderful letters I have received – It is touching to hear that when my Beloved was hit by that awful shell he turned round first of all to his subaltern and asked "Are you hurt" – It was just that wonderful thoughtfulness for others that made everyone love him… tells me that he invariably insisted on undertaking every [kind] of danger…Yours…'

During the war, Daisy change her lifestyle and became commandant of the hospital established at Charlton Park, then later as a staff nurse at the Red Cross Hospital in Malmesbury. She also worked at the Officers Red Cross Hospital in Devizes as a commandant and received mention of her good work from King George V in 1917. Daisy was awarded the Royal Red Cross for exceptional service in military nursing.

In 1934, Daisy returned to her native country and went to live in Suffolk Hills, Tucson, Arizona, a place named after her in the area of Oro Valley. She called the architecturally designed mansion house with five bedrooms 'Forest Lodge'. In 1957, after selling her property, she moved twenty-five miles northeast and built Casa del Oro, her own private estate in Oracle, and fanned the flames of her spirit of adventure. She died on 5 March 1968, after suffering a heart attack while flying from San Francisco to her ranch: she was 88 years-old.

At the beginning of my research, Jack Howard's remarkable life was a total mystery to me. Day by day, I received small pieces of the puzzle from various corners of the globe. Stories arrived from Second World War bomb disposal men still living, from Captain Paulsen's grandson and family, Fred and Beryl's family, and more besides. But Jack was so much more than his accomplishments – it was the real man behind all those masks I was searching for.

He lived the latter years of his life under chronic wartime conditions, most of it in secret. People knew him as 'Mad Jack' or 'Wild Jack', but he preferred just Jack. He was a true scientist: open-minded, analytical, never made a rash decision or judgment, and was a creative, critical thinker. He accomplished what he set out to achieve and would not take 'no' for an answer. His top secret exploits were carried out under the radar. If he had not succeeded bringing back the whole stockpile of heavy water in the world that England and the US so desperately needed, it makes one wonder what might have happened to Great Britain if the tables had turned and it had fallen into the hands of Germany or Russia.

His nerve was sorely tested at the onset of the Second World War but, just like his ancestors, he rode fearlessly in battle. Not with steed and sword but with weapons laced with intelligence, foresight and fortitude, driving a Pickfords delivery van. He lacked the 'Tudor' Howard's gift of conspiracy, arrogant pride and raw ambition – instead, he retained their prowess of riding into the face of adversity, their loyalty to their monarch and country, and the quickness of mind and perseverance. For his actions he was posthumously awarded the George Cross (GC) for bravery. The GC takes precedence over all other awards except the Victoria Cross with which it shares precedence.

Creations:
1st Earl of Suffolk, 21 July 1603; Baron Howard of Charlton
in Wiltshire, and Viscount Andover in Southampton, 23 January 1622,
and 1st Earl of Berkshire, 6 February 1625.

Seats:
Charlton Park, near Malmesbury, Wiltshire and Suffolk House.
Charing Cross, London, (demolished in the 1950s).

THE LONG DEAD

Under their stones they lie, in great cathedrals,

dust and ashes.

But they are not there.

Under grass they lie, in little churchyards,

dust and ashes.

But they are not there.

Far in strange lands they lie, with no sign over them,

dust and ashes.

But they are not there.

Under deep seas they lie, lost in sea changes,

pearl and coral.

But they are not there...

Helen Mackay

CHAPTER ONE

Nous Maintiendrons;
Non quo sed quo modo

We will maintain; Not for whom, but in what manner
– THE HOWARD MOTTO.

A certain chain of events set in place during April 1941 ultimately led to a catastrophic date in history. Captain Kenneth Privett, Second in Command of 25 Bomb Disposal Company (25 BD Coy), Royal Engineers (RE), had just received instructions from Major Yates to stop dumping any more bombs at the 'bomb cemetery' on the Belvedere Marshes, Erith. The area was surrounded by housing and streets where children played and people went about their daily business.

The Marshes was to be ploughed up due to complaints received from local residents regarding damage to the neighbourhood, who wanted the army to refrain from using the marshes as a detonating site. In order to move bombs to the cemetery bomb disposal men had to immunize the Type 50 fuse beforehand and place a clock stopper on it, which would be removed when the bomb reached its destination. To all intents and purposes it was safe to leave out in the open. But one particular bomb had been lying around throughout winter, causing the explosives to deteriorate with perhaps some exudation.

On Tuesday 6 May, Captain A. G. Bainbridge visited the marshes and ordered Lieutenant Sprankling, the commanding officer of 25 Bomb Disposal Company (25 BD Coy), and Lance Corporal King, to take all defused bombs to another bomb cemetery at Richmond Park in London. Their orders were to leave behind any bombs still containing fuses, of which there were a few. Bainbridge made a point of referring to the 250kg SC, thin-walled general-purpose bomb fitted with a Type 17 clockwork time-delay fuse and a Type 50 anti-handling fuse that had been lying on the Marshes for about seven months. It was usual policy to avoid transporting fused bombs after an accident happened on 10 October 1940, when a bomb being carted through the busy streets of central London exploded, killing a number of people.

Someone with a macabre sense of humour had chalked 'Old Faithful' on the side of the rusty casing. Old Faithful was originally meant to be destroyed but the demolition crater in which it was lying was so full of water that to blow it up outside of the crater would cause blast damage to surrounding properties. Also it had not been possible to sterilize it by steaming out the contents due to the nearby ditch containing water too dirty for use with a small capacity boiler. However, Captain Bainbridge of the Royal Engineers had, owing to the recent dry spell they had been experiencing, made arrangements with Lieutenant Sprankling to blow up two or three 50kg bombs that had been lying around, leaving a suitable crater in which to place the 250kg bomb and detonate it.

The unfused bombs were taken away to Richmond on the 7 and 8 May, and it was on the 8 May that Lieutenant Colonel King had a conversation with Corporal Baxter and Charles Howard, who was known to all as 'Jack' or 'Mad Jack', a nickname gained during his hazardous though enterprising Top Secret mission in Paris. King mentioned the fused 250kg bomb still at Erith.

After this next assignment had been completed Jack was going to surprise his team by taking them to Charlton Park, his 10,000 acre estate, for 14 days rest and recuperation after treating his men and his secretary, Eileen Beryl Morden, to a lavish meal at Kempinski's restaurant. They had all been slogging hard, felt utterly exhausted, and deserved a break. Jack and his confidante 'Fredders' had been talking of late about what they had do after the war. They made plans to take their respective families to Australia where Jack had once owned a working sheep farm called North Toolburra in Queensland. Out there in the bush in the hot dry sun, on a horse and miles of countryside to farm, isolated from the crowds, he could hear himself think, be himself, away from England with its incessant bombing and the increasing mountain of bombs piling higher every day, all waiting to be defused. There was no doubt they would all benefit from the healthy lifestyle and it would be a wonderful place for his sons to grow up. Jack was exhausted and wished the war would let up but with Germany's need for order and supremacy he knew they would never relent.

That afternoon, on Saturday, 10 May, he took leave of his family at Charlton after spending a relaxing but brief weekend and drove back again to London, refreshed and ready for work and to meet up with his team. Even though Jack was not aware of it, Rudolf Hess handpicked that day to pilot a Messerschmitt Me 110 to Scotland for alleged peace talks. The following day Jack visited Erith Marshes, a spot beyond east London, to inspect Old Faithful. The sun was out and, if it did not slip behind a passing cloud, it warmed him. It was a habit of his to wrap up on cool days in as many layers of clothing as possible in order to heat his rheumatic bones. He set aside Old Faithful for the following day. To Jack's eye it looked corroded and dejected, it was unexploded but not ticking.

He decided on an early night because he knew the following day would be an eventful one. Once the bomb was out of the way they would drive to his favourite restaurant where he would have – chicken chasseur with rice with a nice bottle of white to help it go down – then on to Charlton for two weeks. He could not wait to spend more time with Mimi and the boys. Bloody war! Before he got into bed he looked out the window at the night sky, it was clear and dry; a good omen.

Sunrise woke Jack the next morning, he drew back the curtains to examine the view. His prediction had been right, just the ticket for the job in hand. He had telephoned Mimi the night before and the boys had become excited at the prospect of seeing their father. The afternoon turned quite warm, around 64° maybe 65°C, he hazarded a guess, and on the strength of that he left his balaclava and scarf at his apartment. Between 12.30 and 1.00pm he was back at Erith Marshes with his ear pressed up against Old Faithful's cold steel casing. Jack was not happy. He hushed his men and listened again. He was right the first time. He jumped into one of the trucks with Beryl and a driver and drove over to the Borax Consolidated Factory, 25 BD Coy Headquarters, to use their telephone.

Early that morning Ken Tinker, Borax's office boy, had peddled his weary way across Belvedere Marsh to work on the Thames embankment when he saw an army contingent of half a dozen vehicles pull away from the bomb dump as fast as their overworked vehicles would allow. He guessed another unexploded bomb had been added to the 'Bomb Dump' as the locals called it, in a locality less than 300yd from the open road, where every retrieved unexploded bomb in this area of south-east London had been gingerly lowered from the lorry that had carted it from the point of where it had been dug up. So far, approximately 100 bombs lay on the surface from which detonators had been removed. Every Borax shift going to and from the factory using bicycles or simply walking the mile from the railway station to the factory passed within a few hundred yards of the Marshes. That few hundred yards separated them from certain death if a delayed action bomb still possessed an active fuse.

It was a glorious May morning after yet another night of sirens, aircraft, anti-aircraft fire and bombs. Cycling towards the factory, Ken was glad to see it intact although shrouded in a light blue cloud of smoke. Inside the gates the still of the morning was shattered by the roar of fire pumps working on the remains of an oil bomb that had fallen at the base of the 200ft chimney. Such bombs were rarities, designed to hurl flaming masses of waste-oil products in every which way. The marsh on the east side of the factory was peppered with grey mounds of Rasorite, Borax's raw material, which had been scattered when a high-explosive bomb hit sacks of the material waiting to be processed. On the jetty, Henry Bishop had finally managed to persuade his stubborn old steam crane into action, and begun the task of unloading that same raw material from barges moored alongside.

Chaos greeted Ken in the office as the night's damage was being assessed. He reported to head office who had been bombed out of their London office, now operating from the comparative safety of the countryside in Oxshott, Surrey. The staff used Ken as a runner to collect the nightshift's reduced production figures from the shift foremen now otherwise engaged in coaxing the shattered wheels of production back to work. Back at his desk, Ken tried hard to resume his normal work but the jovial atmosphere induced by the foremen turning in reports of damage to equipment and lists of men who failed to clock-in for work rendered his routine work virtually impossible. As the day wore on, their sole contact with the outside world was the single telephone, ERITH 2163, in a kiosk beside his desk. The telephone was going mad that day as missing workers reported their lack of transportation, death and injuries to family members requiring their presence, among a dozen or so other legitimate reasons for their absence.

Ken heard an army vehicle pulling into the yard, a daily occurrence as army personnel often came to use their telephone – wireless communication had ceased to exist, or was prohibited because of security concerns. A sudden break in the general noise of loud talk caused him to look up. He walked over to join several staff members staring intently through the window at the lorry parked outside. A man bundled up in civilian clothes as though expecting a snow storm jumped down from the driver's seat and was now standing beside the closed passenger door engaged in conversation with the person seated inside. The door as with most army vehicles had no windows and it was not difficult to see the person seated inside who just happened to be female, which was quite unique because bomb squads never included ATS girls on their staff roster. Furthermore, the lady was dressed in civilian clothes which were half concealed by an army greatcoat wrapped around her shoulders. Watchers at the windows stood gawping at the unexpected appearance of an attractive young female in their rough and tumble world.

No one ever dreamt of knocking on the office door so the sudden crash of a healthy set of knuckles with two imperious thuds on the wooden door caused Ken to jump. He slid off his stool, glanced over at the clock – it was just after 1.00pm – and reached the door in short order. Upon opening it he was brought face-to-face with a handsome bear of a man with a mass of shaggy dark hair, sporting a smile that would have won any woman in an instant, and a gentle voice that belied his impressive size. He was wearing a naval duffle coat and rubber boots which reached his knees. There was no visible insignia on the coat, not even a gold-braided cap, which somehow in that first few seconds of eye contact Ken expected.

'May I use your telephone?' the man asked in a rich upper crust accent as he strode past Ken into the office, not waiting for an answer. Fred Payne the office manager and veteran of the First World War assured him he could indeed, while the office boy stood open mouthed to one side.

After that brief exchange, Ken dutifully wiped the hand piece with a clean cloth he kept handy; just before the Earl arrived the instrument had been used by a sweating barge man who was used to handling a 4in hawser and completely insensitive to the fact he was practically crushing the hand piece, shouting to a point where the telephone was hardly necessary to talk over the four miles upriver to his base office.

Their visitor was too large to enter the kiosk and close the door behind him so every word he spoke was audible to the now suddenly silent office. His opening words were very clear. 'Suffolk here, old man, we have one active so we will have to deal with it immediately. I need a Mk II magnetic-clock stopper and a Mk 2 electronic stethoscope...' The rest of his telephone conversation to Captain Kenneth Privett, RE was lost to Ken's memory as everyone rushed outside to the gate. The office manager gave the boy a stern look, and together they stayed while their visitor completed his exchange. Ken heard him explaining in calm measured tones that the mechanical clock in the 250kg bomb was running. Ken thought it had probably been jerked into life during the journey to the dump. That indicated he had perhaps hours if not minutes to extract the detonator before it exploded. The Earl ended his conversation, leant on Ken's desk and after some good natured bantering bid them a cheery 'Good day, Gentlemen,' and left the yard with his driver accelerating away at high speed.

Five minutes later Jack arrived back at the marsh and the crowd outside the factory gate filtered away, and staff in the office moved away from the windows and resumed their work.

The young office boy had never in his life met the likes of the Earl before.

Before Jack and the team got down to work they were offered and accepted a welcome brew and a genial chat with Mrs Cooper, the mother of a young boy, who lived in one of the cottages close by in a small village of seventeen cottages and a public house called The New Marsh Tavern.

Having the Earl sitting in his kitchen sipping tea with his mother brought back frightening memories for Mrs Cooper's boy of the First World War when, one night in 1914, a stick of four bombs was dropped by a Zeppelin in those same fields. His father had raced up the stairs to where his children were sleeping, grabbed them from their beds and ran downstairs again placing the young ones underneath the kitchen table. The Germans had been trying to bomb a searchlight mounted on top of residue from the Borax works in one of the fields near their cottage. While the Earl and a few of his men in the cottage were enjoying the pleasant chat, some cheeky inquisitive children had crawled through the protective fence of the marsh to inspect the bomb that was attracting so much attention. Before they could do any damage, they were seen and shouted at 'Oi, you lot, go on, get out of 'ere' by a soldier on guard duty.

Just after the men arrived back at the bomb site, Jack had a welcome visitor – his friend and mentor, his 'Master', Dr Gough, who had always been a bit nervous about Jack in his hazardous line of work. Although the Earl gave the appearance of being slap-dash at times, he knew him to be meticulous to detail. Yet for some reason he was uneasy about him that day so he decided to motor from London to see how he was getting on and found everything was as it should be. His Master found Jack going through all the motions of safety, taking every precaution he should. His Master drove back to the city completely satisfied, his worries alleviated.

Meanwhile, Lance Corporal Brownrigg, the NCO in charge of the stethoscope and clock-stopper equipment, Sergeant Cole, and Staff Sergeant Atkins had driven from their HQ at Westbury Lodge in Wythfield Road, Eltham, with the equipment requested by Jack; with the traffic being reasonably light, they arrived at the marshes around 2.45pm. Driver Sharratt drove behind them in the Guy truck carrying the heavy batteries required for the clock stopper that weighed around 81.5kg. Atkins pulled to a halt, got out of the truck, took hold of the stethoscope and then jumped into the lorry with Jack and Fred Hards and drove over to where the bomb lay. A moment later, Dave Sharratt followed. Jack, Beryl, Fred, who everybody knew as the 'The Holy Trinity', Atkins, Sharratt and the remainder of the Earl's team stood within 10yd of the bomb.

Jack and Staff Sergeant Atkins worked on the bomb for a short while as Sapper Liposta watched the Earl as he proceeded to remove the base plate of the bomb, which was usually hidden under the fins that had no doubt been ripped off when it had landed. He needed to remove it in order to gain access to the explosives which could then be steamed out. The heavy magnetic clock stopper and a stethoscope were then placed into position by the men. Nearby, Atkins was listening intently through the headphones attached to the bomb to see if the fuse was ticking. Jack told Liposta and another sapper to start filling the water tank for the steam generator, from the nearby ditch. The men were completely absorbed in their work and each one knew the odds. Although brows were deeply furrowed in concentration, their work mentally and physically challenging, they were confident. Each man had done this before, over and over and over again.

It was Jack's 35th bomb and he had, just a few months before, celebrated his 35th birthday with friends and family in fine style, his life was indeed blessed. It seemed as though he had been defusing the bloody things forever. Hopefully, one day, he would be free of it all to follow his dream in Australia. He had had more than enough of war, running all over the south of England searching for the infernal things and their fuses, and his ancestral home Charlton Park was a financial burden, but these were thoughts he kept to himself. Maybe it was just tiredness talking.

Sometimes he felt like they were fighting a losing cause because whatever they did, it was not adequate enough. The Germans always seemed one step ahead. He admired and respected his team, had every confidence in them, and he loved his country, so he was not about to give up until the enemy gave in, hence the 14 days' rest. They were a tight-knit bunch, their spirits were high, each knew what other was thinking and they relied on one another totally. Jack saw them as a well-knitted, well-loved jumper all woven together. They enjoyed being filthy, scruffy and exhausted because with that came the knowledge of a job well done. They were a good team, they laughed a lot, told each other dirty jokes, mouthed obscenities and often got drunk together.

Jack stood on the side lines watching his men hard at work, like family to him. He fixed a Dubarry cigarette into his long cigarette holder and lit it. A quick puff always settled his nerves before working on a godforsaken bomb. He patted his pocket, yes, the other holder was still there in case either one broke, it would not do being without that. The sun was out and warm on his face, bringing for Jack a sudden rush of excitement and gratitude for his life; he was looking forward to the surprised looks on his men's faces when they saw Charlton Park for the first time. Jack smiled to himself as he thought back to the other day when one of the lads, known for being nosy, asked him about his wife and his sons, and about where he had been brought up. Jack never liked talking about his private life; it was not for public consumption. But that day had been different, they had shared a few drinks after a strenuous day's work and the atmosphere had turned mellow. It seemed eons since he had been a little boy rushing around the rooms and halls of his ancestral home, or out riding his horse, playing with his dogs. Where had those years gone?

CHAPTER TWO

Before the Mast

In early autumn of 1920, while on a break from Osborne Naval College on the Isle of Wight, 14 year-old Jack Howard and his younger brother Cecil had finally been given permission to join in one of the shooting parties held at Charlton Park, with strict instructions to behave and uphold safety of firearms at all times. Both boys were excited about joining their first shoot. Due to return to school the following week they revelled in the chance to be treated like adults for a day. Jack, previously enrolled in the cadets at Dartmouth Naval College by his mother who thought discipline was the answer to his waywardness, was not looking forward to returning.

The party was in high spirits, everyone was wrapped up warmly against the cold. They chattered brightly, the air from their mouths a cold whisper in the dim morning light. Dogs ran frantically back and forth along the ground, sniffing the hard packed earth, their tails straight, ears and eyes eagerly awaiting the first sign from their masters. Extended arms and fingers pointed out birds in the air. Amongst the party were Lady Suffolk, Colonel Gillett, and Hugh Barker who were long-standing friends of the Howards. Hip flasks were brought out for a swift nip of warmth. The party walked with guns at their hips, ready for action.

Everything was going according to plan. Jack was fully focused and knew what to do, he had been shown before. He could not afford to make a blunder because he would not be asked to join them again if he messed up. Jack and his brother were climbing over a stile when it happened. Suddenly a cry shattered the peace, someone shouted excitedly and guns were aimed at the sky. The noise startled Jack and his concentration momentarily slipped. He let go of the shotgun and upon impact with the ground it fired, with Cecil on the receiving end. The whole of the charge had accidently discharged into his brother's foot. Panic ensued, a car was brought, and Cecil was packed carefully onto the back seat. The driver put his foot down on the pedal and beat a hasty dash to the local hospital where Cecil's foot had to be partially amputated. Jack was mortified and went into shock. His mother seemed understanding about the whole thing, she did not blame him, or so she said. Looking back on this accident Jack realized it was a defining moment for him, when he became acutely aware of guns and their propensity to kill. After that, he resolved to learn all there was about them and to shoot what he was aiming for; there would never be another accidental moment.

During the 1920s, Lady Suffolk, Jack's mother, who suffered dreadfully from arthritis in her back due to the freezing winters of England, took to spending them in Tucson, Arizona, at her home called 'Forest Lodge', the first home in the county to have air-conditioning installed. With his mother gone, it was the best of times and the worst of times with adolescence tightening its grip on Jack. Mood swings, attitudinal changes, personality development and surges of hormones were firing off in every direction making him ripe for college where he could lose some of that enormous energy in carving out a niche for himself. A big step towards that goal lay in beginning his sixth form education at Radley College, Oxford. Jack was now 15 years-old and it had been his father's wish he attend there rather than Eton. His father, no doubt, knew something about the Reverend Adam Fox who had taught at his old school in Winchester and was now headmaster of Radley, his reputation for fair-mindedness preceding him.

Osborne College had brought out the worst in Jack and his disregard for convention and restriction began to emerge. Radley seemed a far better fit and so began three years of study from 1921 to 1923. Radley's motto 'Sicut serpents, sicut columbae' loosely translated meant 'Be [as wise/cunning] as serpents, [and] as [gentle] as doves', and literally 'Like serpents, like doves.'

In 1827, the Reverend William Sewell was elected Petrean Fellow of Exeter College and ordained in 1830. He became a Sub-Rector of the college in 1835, and the following year was appointed White's Professor of Moral Philosophy. He founded Radley College in 1847. Sewell had been educated at Winchester College where he was awarded the Chancellor's Prize for both English and Latin essays, gaining a first in *Literae Humaniores*. His personality commanded attention, so many said – one could revere or deride him but no one could ignore him. He had been dominated by the Church's wasting disease and thought it could be strengthened by education:

'I wish to make boys – English boys – Christian gentlemen and Christian scholars; not by an artificial hothouse system of superintendence, or excitement, or formalism, or asceticism, but by the tone and atmosphere in which they lived, as in the bosom of one large Christian family, surrounded by the best society and provided with all that is needed to strengthen and enlarge and purify their minds.'

He imagined a small intimate society of devout and cultured men working for love with no thought of monetary gain. At the opening of the college and at the end of the first term there were only seven boys. It rapidly broke down leaving Sewell and his successors a large inheritance of debt.

Sewell's diary, later published and well received, was a document of extreme interest, portraying both a naïve and charming picture of an extremely novel community because it described the pattern Radley was to follow. The Fellows would be devoted and worldly men, sharing their leisure with their students and keeping a watchful eye on their table manners. The boys would be full of health and good manners, show respect for their fellow man and be neat, tidy and clean. The students were to pay £100 per annum with every tenth boy receiving his education for free.

Punishment varied, and apart from 'rowings' and lectures there was detention, impositions, extra prep, lines, solitary confinement, submission to a very 'simple diet' and beatings of every degree. Singleton's 'rowing' always resulted in tears.

During the 1920s, when Jack was a student, apart from the traditional three 'Rs', the college encouraged the boys into sports, debating, chess, bridge, singing and drama which involved sketches and dramatic extracts. But it was cinema, jazz music and dancing that held the boys' attention the most, especially if they brought in girls on a rare occasion from another school. Gramophones were imported in large numbers, and the school's jazz band's melancholy strains could be heard throughout the school. In the winter months, impromptu dances were frequently held in the hall on half-holidays with the boys as well as the Wardens participating during the get-togethers.

A new reform was introduced – a cooked meal for tea in the hall, in addition to the bread and butter they had been served for a number of years because a well-known parent had officially complained that the boys were being fed on 'train oil and muck'. Reverend Fox had been the Dean of Divinity at Magdalen College, Oxford, and later became Canon of Westminster Abbey where he is buried at Poet's Corner. He followed no accepted model in his manner and bearing in his position. His methods were often surprising and original. All human relations in his practice were based on simple, open-minded friendliness. He liked to see other people happy, yet a disciplinarian lurked underneath – he could be stern and angry when the need arose. Possessed of a lively and rather cheeky wit, based on acute observation, Fox made a strong male role model for young Jack.

The Earl discovered himself gradually being drawn towards the more practical topics the college had to offer. Rather than sitting in some dark dusty corner slaving away over the unyielding pages of mathematics and history, his passion took on a more creative bent. He revelled in working with fine grains of wood and learning automatic welding which had been introduced the preceding year. By integrating the use of arc voltage and bare electrode wires, Jack learnt how to repair and work metals, though chemistry and engineering and, given his wit and love of mimicry, the odd spot of drama also remained at the top of his list.

Science became more and more popular amongst the boys at Radley and lectures were well attended. In Jack's day some lecturers feared that science may or may not teach only the rudiments of the future profession and held a strong belief the 'Classics' was a better option, teaching them how to manage men and that each man was a law unto himself. Others said science might well be useless and even harmful. But most believed that the state of the world was largely one of misery and that corruption came not from without but from within, and the benefits gained from science were prosperity, additional leisure and advanced culture. The world would be in a bad way without the comfort science would bring.

Radley teachers found Jack surprisingly intimate with the tales and trails of the American 'Wild West', not surprising seeing as his mother was born in that country, but quite unreceptive to Latin verbs. Sitting in a classroom trying to conjugate verbs, inflect nouns and translate English into Latin, Jack wondered what use, if any, was a 'dead' language. None that he could think of, his mind stayed blank no matter how often he repeated it. He found, though, to his increasing enjoyment and passion, he excelled in outdoor pursuits where he learned to ride and sail and delight in the freedom and the feeling of having the elements envelope him. He also enrolled as a cadet in the Officer Training Corps.

Radley's values no doubt played a great part in shaping Jack into the man he would later become – sensible, tolerant, friendly, and also easy to deal with, but he was no man's fool.

Jack had changed from the slightly built, unhealthy boy who left preparatory school for Radley, to an inquisitive, strong young teenager. As usual when he was home on a school break, he would make his way over to Charlton's forge where the blacksmith was only too happy to teach the boy: he believed he could knock some of the aristocratic arrogance out of him. Nothing like getting one's hands dirty, learning a trade. From a young age the man had always seemed mighty to Jack: his arms and back muscles taut and bulging, his hands large and sinewy. He once told the boy that the forge was the heart of the blacksmith's shop, the anvil its soul. It was laborious work, fire, smoke and sweat and gradually he learned how to work the forge and the bellows, growing hale and hearty, revelling in its formidable heat and smells.

Not one for being inactive for too long the intricacies of plumbing also caught Jack's overactive mind, and he was not amiss to the odd spot of idling away his time but was always at his happiest when getting his hands dirty. Not far off his 18th birthday his health was pretty good apart from the odd ache in his joints. On his doctor's orders he was supposed to keep a check on exerting himself because, as a boy, he had fallen victim to rheumatic fever. But poor health was never going to rule his life. He was young and impetuous with a mixture of adventuring, buccaneering Howard and Leiter blood running through his veins. His mother was at a loss to know what to do with Jack, but do something she must. So she invited an acquaintance of the family, Captain M.C. McColm, master of the *Mount Stewart*, to Charlton Park to discuss Jack's future. It was decided that her son would, with the full consent of his mother, give up the comforts of home, his title and the country he loved on condition he attend Oxford on his return, and set his sights on lands further afield – Australia. He was itching to experience life far beyond the constraints of family and privilege.

He joined the merchant ship, the steel-hulled clipper *Mount Stewart*, known only to the crew as Jack Howard; he was one of nine cadets on board and would receive no distinction. For this his family paid a premium. Jack received his apprenticeship papers from the owners of the ship, Donaldson Rose & Co of Aberdeen, stating they agreed to teach him seamanship and navigation. As cadet, he had to live in the half-deck amidships on board. It was a known fact that cadets were considered the lowest of the low and would constantly be chivvied. They would mix with the crew and be given all the dirty work of the ordinary seaman and be expected to stand their watch. Cadets could be sent aloft although it was up to the officer of the watch as to whether he would allow Jack the opportunity.

The *Mount Stewart* and her sister ship, the *Cromdale* (launched 26 May 1891), were the last two sailing ships built especially for the wool trade to carry large cargoes. Both were the last of the big windjammers – hard ships to sail thus needing a hard crew. The *Mount Stewart*, registered at 1,903 tons (gross), was launched on 23 April 1891. It was the latest development of the square-rigged ships featuring a short poop and a long main deck. Despite their cargo capacity, these two ships were the fastest colonial clippers, capable of sailing an average of 300 miles a day. The ship carried general cargo to Sydney and returned to London with wool and grain. The vessel was fitted out for carrying passengers, and often carried a number of them on both outward and homeward bound voyages.

The Earl arrived at the bustling Liverpool docks in the chauffeur-driven family car, bringing with him a grand-looking sea chest; after all, he was leaving England for who knew how long. The chest was crammed full of everything he thought he might possibly need for the long trip to Australia. With a smile on his face and impatience barely concealed, he gave his mother and siblings a hug then turned, picked up one end of the chest and dragged it towards the steep gangplank. Jack struggled to gain any headway and kept slipping back. Help was at hand – one of the crew, a young, hard-faced rough-neck called Tom, from Manchester, appeared. He was a senior cadet for that voyage but was dressed like a tramp in filthy overalls. Unaided, he slung the trunk on his back, as though it were a bag of potatoes, and bounded up the gangway.

The masts and yards of the *Mount Stewart* towered high above Jack, and he felt his legs tremble as he peered up into the vastness of the rigging that seemed to almost brush the grey clouds. Any view from that height would be very impressive.

The chief officer, dressed like any other member of his crew, greeted Jack on deck. The officer held out his hand and welcomed him aboard, saying he hoped his stay would be a good one. He pointed out that he would be shown no leniency because of his title and would be known as Jack Howard from here on and treated like any other cadet. Once the pleasantries were over he was shown to his quarters.

Coughing harshly as he entered, the dense clouds of tobacco smoke made it difficult to see but once he got used to the atmosphere he saw he was not alone. Six boys around the same age as himself all wearing dirty overalls, were sitting at a long table that stretched the length of the deck. There were bunks that looked reasonably comfortable, though Jack thought they had the appearance of coffins, on each side of the area. Everything was painted either white or a dull grey. The only illumination came from six grimy portholes and a gimbaled oil lamp suspended from the deck head.

Jack's 'good morning' was treated with silence. He found a bunk and pulled his chest up to the end and began rummaging through to find something more appropriate to wear. He had brought with him underclothes and ordinary clothes. His working clothes consisted of oilskins, a heavy overcoat, sea boots, an old pair of shoes, overalls, jumpers, an oilskin hat and one other hat which he would wear every day. He also had writing pens, pencils and paper, also *Norie's Nautical Tables* and *Nichol's Seamanship & Nautical Knowledge* in two volumes. It was here all the cadets would sleep, wash, dress and eat.

Before arriving at the *Mount Stewart*, Jack had been told something about the people with whom he would be sailing. Most of the officers held a Masters' Ticket. The young master, Captain M.C. McColm from Kirkcudbright, Scotland was a quiet, unassuming man but a strong, no nonsense, hearty seafarer, he had been with the ship since 1907: first as mate then, from June 1909 as master. He had sailed the ship throughout the First World War and travelled to various ports around the world in the sixteen years he lived on the ship. For twelve of those years his Australian wife, Adelaide (née Lewis) born on 6 February 1879 in Brompton, Adelaide, South Australia, travelled with him along with their two sons Donald and Malcolm, who had been raised on the ship. Both boys had sailed round Cape Horn; Donald nine times and Malcolm seven.

The *Mount Stewart* had also been home to the sailmaker for sixteen years and the cook had lived on the ship for eleven years. There were the two mates (First and Second), three, sometimes four apprentices, the bosun, the lamp trimmer or bosun's mate, the 'chippie' (carpenter), the sailmaker, some twelve seamen, a cook, deck boys, and the 'donkeyman' who looked after the boiler. Also setting out on this arduous journey were people who aspired to set up home in Australia.

There was not much of a fanfare as *Mount Stewart* left Liverpool docks. His mother and his brothers stood on the quayside waving anxiously; Jack saw his mother quickly dab her eyes with a handkerchief. He watched as they slowly became tiny dots in the distance, but was far too excited and busy imagining the adventure ahead of him to think about what he was leaving behind. The ships' mates began to give orders to the crew: 'Stand by Forrard', 'Stations Forrard', 'Stations Aft'. Jack looked puzzled not having a clue as to what was going on. There was a lot of whistle blowing between the ship and tug. The captain on the poop deck began shouting instructions – 'Leggo Forrard', and men lifted off the heavy hawsers and the *Mount Stewart* was free at last. The muffled sound of the tug's hooter sounded further and further away, and the gap between the ship and Liverpool became wider and wider. It took some time to get out into the seaway – at least an hour by Jack's reckoning. Then as the tug disappeared, and with her topsails set, the ship glided silently and smoothly across a calm sea. Without warning, Jack felt a slight sinking feeling in the pit of his stomach, probably just a twinge of homesickness.

The young Earl's first task at sea was to clean the 'heads' which was much worse than any task he would be later given. He was also put in charge of the pigs and chickens onboard, quite a pleasant job after the reek of where he worked before. The first weekend in he helped wash down the paintwork of the main deck. Other menial tasks on his journey included cleaning out the ship's bilges, tarring down, chipping, scraping and painting. He had thought himself fit before he arrived but now everything ached, even muscles he did not know existed.

The *Mount Stewart* began to gather way using the power of the wind for the first time, with topsails, lower topsail, main and mizzen set. The first days and nights that followed the majority of new boys, including the Earl, had no idea of what was required of them. It appeared he had been thrust into madness, but madness with a semblance of organization. Ropes were quickly thrust into his hands for him to haul on. He was instructed on how to turn the handles of and load the winches for the halyards, braces and sheets.

Jack loved standing on deck in the pitch blackness of a night sky that sparkled full of bright stars; they shone more brightly than he had ever seen at home. He still had not been seasick, and maybe he would not if his luck held. For two weeks the ship had wandered around the Irish Sea looking for a fair wind: they had tacked ship so many times Jack lost count. He had never in his life experienced that kind of tiredness before; the type of tiredness that seeped deep within his bones, and none of the young newly joined cadets had either. So tired were they, they failed to glory in the pyramids of gleaming sails billowing above them.

When engaged at all hands on deck, Jack was the sleeping dead, forever catching a toe on a ringbolt. The main meal was usually a stew made up from various ingredients, depending on the cook's mood at the time. Bully beef was a favourite ingredient. Whatever they were given it filled them up but it did not satisfy and it certainly was not gourmet. Tea was available all the time; and the coffee made from inferior beans always tasted burnt. Also available were biscuits, but these were also invariably burnt.

The first time Jack steered the ship was from 10.00 to 11.00pm one evening during which he received a drenching. He was alone for only a few minutes, but in that time he allowed the ship to swing 22° off course, from north-east to north-north-east. The officer of the watch received a 'roasting' from the captain for allowing him to go on the wheel alone on a dark night so early in to the voyage.

One day Jack heard, for the first time, the tremendous roaring sound of a strong wind blowing through the rigging and saw the steep Atlantic waves threatening to swamp the *Mount Stewart*. Another time, when on deck during a raging storm, he saw a huge wave rear up over the ship when from aloft came the horrifying cracking sound of canvas, the crashing of block and chain-sheets as the ship turned into the wind. He spent the next hour soaking wet under tuition from a seaman called Jarl who kept telling him he was 'no focking good.' In stormy weather, the ship rolled and plunged violently; they saw nothing but the sky above and the sea below, as though every wave would make each of them a grave. There were many times when the night was so black that they could barely see one another. There were other times when the wind blew so loud they could not hear one another speak. Jack realized that the sailor's instinct in these hardy men, even when sleep, was so sensitive to the motion of the ship that the slightest change or sudden movement woke them into action.

Jeremy Pitshank, a young crew man fell into the empty hold and landed on the keelson, 20ft below. He broke a number of bones and was put ashore the first opportunity to receive treatment. His recovery took several months.

Due to not having any communication from ship to shore, Jack was blissfully unaware that his mother had been thrown by her horse near

Tetbury, Gloucestershire, and broken her leg. If he had known, it would have unsettled him and would have demanded to be dropped ashore at the first possible port.

After twenty-two days at sea, the crew began stowing the storm sails in order to preserve them, and began bending-on the old sun-bleached fair-weather canvas. At thirty days into the voyage, the crew was woken at 3.00am by a series of loud bangs; the sound of six sails blowing out as tornado-strength winds hit the ship. The noise on deck was appalling: a howling wind and the loud beating of the canvas and the roaring of the steep waves. Yet the following day a large brilliant yellow sun appeared, the sea was calm and all seemed so peaceful. There was no other noise except the hypnotic sound of the sea rushing past the hull. Toward evening the breeze picked up, and the calm waters began to break lifting the ship in the swell. By midnight, *Mount Stewart* was running at 13 knots and pushing out a 60ft bow wave.

Jack worked hard on that voyage. He painted bulkheads and washed endless cooking pots and dishes for the cook. Food was becoming scarce as they neared land, a situation not helped by an expert thief from Liverpool who tried to steal as much food as he could. For fun the men played cards, drank, listened to the gramophone, told stories, read, and sang songs; some found a quiet space in which to concentrate on making model ships they then would sell on land. The vessel passed Cape Otway at 1.00am on 27 November 1923, and from there made a fast passage through the Bass Strait, due to a fair southerly wind, to round Wilson's Promontory, Gippsland, Victoria, after 125 days at sea.

At the beginning of the voyage Jack, along with his fellow younger crew mates, at first loudly cursed the voyage, complaining all the time. But towards the end, without knowing, they developed an unspoken but deeply felt sense of achievement and an affinity with the *Mount Stewart*. What struck Jack was the immense power of the ship, which was entirely dependent on the crew to achieve maximum performance. This demanded strenuous teamwork by them. He would feel a sense of great loss, of companionship, when he left, especially for Captain McColm who had become his friend.

What surprised Jack most of all was that he never encountered all the bullying, the harrying, or was forced to climb to the top of those towering masts that he expected when boarding the ship in Liverpool. Added to his amazement was how quickly he had been accepted and fallen into the ship's routine. The *Mount Stewart* was one of the last and finest of a long era of great sailing ships and crewed by men who picked the windjammer over the despised kettles of boiling water, the so-called steamers. They were the best, the most highly-skilled, handpicked seamen and proud of it. From the captain to the lowest deck boy, or 'Peggy' as he was known, they were a team whose lives would depend on the man standing next to them. Their ship was no ocean greyhound but a swift and consistent passage maker. If you had asked them about Jack they would have said, 'Who? That apprentice lad? A focking good pully haul, if you ask me. He'll do just fine.' It had not taken them long to realize the boy had a good memory for the complex and complicated rigging, and a quick brain that mastered the mysteries of spherical trigonometry, the sextant and celestial navigation. The dock workers were very impressed with his command of elaborate profanity which he could utter brilliantly in six languages.

Under the watchful eyes of the master and the chief officer, he had been eased aloft, just the once, until he was at home up there as he was on deck. On deck it was the bosun, an older man who knew seafaring talent when he saw it, who taught him the art of knot tying, splicing and other rope work. At first, Captain McColm was doubtful about the young man he had been pressed to take on but having kept an eye on his new cadet, he not only grew to like him but, and this was very unusual for a man of his rank and position, befriended him. The lad was bright, brainy and showed courage and also a sense of humour. By the end of the voyage, Jack could out-drink and out-swear even the hardest of the seamen on *Mount Stewart*.

In 1923, a well-built, healthy young lad wearing a blue shirt arrived in Australia at the helm of the British clipper, had his photograph taken by the Australian press when it docked. Jack was asked by a reporter for his thoughts on the voyage: he readily admitted that even though he felt compelled to see out the time he had actually, towards the end, revelled in the experience. But he realized it was not the life for him. With his title and inheritance waiting for him, he felt impelled to persevere, mainly because he did not consider himself ready enough, at that moment, to manage his legacy. He also admitted that he would not be ready until he had experienced what the everyday, hardworking person had to go through to survive in the world.

Captain McColm, having taken the *Mount Stewart* safely through the many dangers of the First World War, finally hauled down his flag at Nantes, France, in the summer of 1925 where the ship had been sold to the breakers. He had served 17 years on the vessel. When the *Mount Stewart* was finally laid up at Nantes, the men whose home was the ship became very emotional. Captain McColm had never lived in a house ashore, but after much deliberation he chose to spend the rest of his days with his family on a farm he had purchased some years earlier in Maitland, New South Wales. He later became chairman of the council for the Shire of Allora.

After his time on the *Mount Stewart*, Jack spent time voyaging from Australia via Chile, South America, on a ship carrying a cargo of nitrate bound for Nantes. Now 18 years-old, Jack had grown a splendid bushy beard and was the proud owner of a parrot. On 2 November 1924, after the grueling trip, he arrived in Paris for a holiday with his shipmates where they made the most of the bars and clubs in the city and Jack gave them a taste of his awful dancing, sparkling wit and terrible piano playing. He enjoyed regaling his friends with crude jokes, stories of his Howard ancestors' love of adventure and intrigue. Although he spoke French remarkably well, he also enjoyed demonstrating his talent for various dialects and other languages. He wandered down the many alleyways talking to fellow seamen about their adventures, then stepped into a seedy looking, dimly-lit, tattoo parlour that came highly recommended by his fellow seamen. He laughed as he explained to the French tattooist that he wanted snakes, women and skulls tattooed on his arms and back.

Jack loved his freedom, but Charlton Park, Oxford University, and his aristocratic legacy became dark clouds looming on his horizon; without doubt he had to return home. He had been away too long and his mother was becoming anxious. As for university, well, that could wait.

CHAPTER THREE

Changes in the Air

Instead of enrolling at Oxford as he had promised his mother, and having served as a former cadet, he signed up, on probation, with the Scots Guards. One morning in March 1925, a letter arrived for him from the General Officer Commanding, Brigade of Guards. He had been accepted on the Supplementary List of the Regular Army Reserve of Officers, Scots Guards, as a Second Lieutenant; the notification would appear in *The London Gazette*. The letter also mentioned he would be required to undergo probationary training for a period of twenty-six weeks which would, if successful, count as part of the two years' attachment to a regular unit. At the time of joining Jack was very fit, if a little thin, due to a shortage of ship's rations towards the end of his last voyage. He was almost 6ft tall and weighed 154lbs. His certificate of moral character supplied to the Guards was signed by Major Nycee, the Sub Warden of Radley College, and Captain McColm of the *Mount Stewart*.

As a young boy, Jack always wanted to follow in his father's footsteps but sadly this was not to continue. On 30 October 1925, Jack tendered his resignation in a letter to his officer commanding. He appreciated the honour they had bestowed upon him but was resigning because of 'private affairs'. And even if he wanted to he could not afford to stay. He may have been an Earl but Charlton Park was a huge financial burden. Any monies they did have came from his mother's inheritance and she was very frugal with her finances. Jack informed his regiment that he would also refund the £75 uniform allowance that had been granted to him on joining. Also he gave his assurance that he would not enter the service of a foreign power within five years of his resignation without consulting and obtaining permission of the Army Council. His 'private affairs' turned out to be chronic rheumatic fever that would plague Jack for the rest of his life. Nevertheless, even if he had not developed this illness he probably would have left the army at some other time: soon after he had joined he realized the Scots Guards were far too disciplined and structured for his liking.

On numerous occasions he would arrive late for morning parade due to his preoccupation with other matters, and would be forced to remain in the Mess that evening. The sergeant major shouted at him in the exact same way he shouted at the others, but always adding 'sir' at the end of it, much to Jack's mounting frustration and the enjoyment of his fellow officers. He was never one to dwell in the past and this particular setback made him even more determined to find another challenge. As a result, the eligible young Earl left the country in 1926. He chose to sail again for Australia under the name of Jack Howard on SS *Ruahine*, of the New Zealand Shipping Co, taking with him nothing more than his parrot and a duffle bag. The ship, built for the NZ Shipping Company, was a new luxury liner over 580ft long which carried some 300 passengers and had a crew of 200. Sailing from Southampton it transported passengers to New Zealand via the Panama Canal to Tahiti then on to Wellington. He was following in the footsteps of Lord Hobart, the son and heir of the Earl of Buckingham, who was now working in Queensland.

In early February, Jack Howard was met off the ship by his ex-captain William McColm and taken to the family's farm in Kendall they had purchased the previous year. The McColms had also purchased the IXL Timber Mill, not far from the farm on the Camden Haven River, seeing as the timber industry was booming in the area and had been for many years. Jack did his fair share of work around the farm and was happily accepted by the workers. Sometime later, the mill burned down so Jack with McColm and his family left the area in search of work. This they found at a saw mill situated inland from Port Macquarie. Jack could now add crosscut sawing and wielding heavy axes to his growing list of skills. After a short time they left to tend cattle and perform other duties on horseback (cow punching) at another station. Moving on towards Kempsey, New South Wales, and after staying only briefly, they eventually made up their minds to go into partnership and purchase, with the view to Jack setting up residence, North Toolburra – a freehold sheep farm – from the Union Trustee Company (UTC), some 8 miles from Warwick, Queensland. There was mention that the previous owners, the Swinburne Estate, had not kept up their repayments, so the property was sold to them on terms either under a contract or by way of a mortgage. If repayments were not kept up the UTC were entitled to repossess the property and sell it in order to recover the amount they were owed.

North Toolburra station was well-known in the area, being the first property to have been settled in Warwick. Built in the late 1850s on Darling Downs, southern Queensland, the property overlooked the Condamine River, and had panoramic views out over rolling pasture-covered hills. Long stretches of crisscrossing roads, bushy ridges, winding creeks, woolsheds, wind-powered water pumps, and lush pastures were ideal for stock during eight months of the year. Some acres were prime alluvial flats, while others were covered in Lucerne [animal fodder plant], and all irrigated by water from bore holes or a large, dammed lagoon. What added to its appeal for Jack was a 4,900ft airstrip adjoining the property.

The two partners purchased the 9,600 acres and worked it themselves along with several share-farmers. The demanding hard labour and the dry heat reaped good reward on Jack's health. Although his mother in England was often heard to say that he suffered dreadfully from rheumatism and even though he was often in great pain he made light of it, never letting it interfere with his work unless the pain became crippling.

Australia and Jack were meant for each other, they got along famously. People knew him only as 'Wild Jack' or John Howard, 'that crazy Englishman'. His 'cobbers' voted him a fair 'dinkum' bloke, his unaffected manners making him very popular in the district. If someone went looking for him at Toolburra and could not find him, their next port of call would be the golf links at the Warwick Club where he was often seen playing a round, which concluded with a much needed drink in the clubhouse bar.

Peter Cooper and his family, who ran a 200-acre property adjoining North Toolburra, were Jack's nearest neighbours. They also grew wheat on Toolburra land. Cooper's son, Les, a healthy 9 year-old, enjoyed spending his spare time in the company of the Earl. Les knew that everyone called the Earl 'John', and the Earl, cheekily, always called his father Peter, 'Pedro'. To Les, the man he knew as John was a slim, jovial, flamboyant character completely without pretention, and often seen smoking cigarettes through a long holder. He was also seriously interested in explosives and had felled many trees around the area with that material.

In 1931, Jack and the McColms decided to take an active part in the development of tobacco growing in the district; they put aside twenty plots of land near the Condamine River. The land had been inspected and described as ideal for tobacco growing by purchasers from Texas, their company agreeing to provide storage facilities and curing plant. The total cost of the irrigation plant, mainly manufactured in Queensland, was over £1,000. They used a novel method of irrigation which involved 1,450ft of 5in-bore piping being laid from the river. Connected to this were 750ft of movable spray piping. Twenty tobacco growers had set up quarters in a 'tent town' at one end of the estate and were given 5 acres each. Wheat growing was also carried out by the share farmers on the estate and harvesting operations on 1,500 acres were in full swing. However, tobacco growing eventually proved to be non-economical and was quickly abandoned.

Les Cooper thought all his birthdays had come at once at North Toolburra. One day his hero, Charles Kingsford Smith, flew in and gave the locals joy rides for 10 shillings. Kingsford Smith was well-known to everyone as the aviator who, in 1928, flew from Australia to London in a new record time of 10½ days.

A newspaper editor in London heard that the Earl was living in Queensland and speedily sent out a reporter, an inexperienced horseman, from Sydney to the harsh conditions of the outback to interview Jack. Much to his own great amusement the Jack spent the entire day with the poor unsuspecting reporter riding the land in the fierce midday heat, finally coming to a halt in the middle of nowhere. Turning in his saddle towards the reporter he said, 'You know, you came on a really bad day because on Saturdays his lordship's always dead drunk and you can never find him till he sobers up.'

The reporter returned to Sydney the same way he came – with nothing.

Loving nothing more than getting on his horse and riding his estate, it did not take much encouragement from the locals for Jack to take part in pole bending races and other riding events in competitions throughout the area. Captain McColm's son Malcolm also competed in various riding and rodeo competitions with the Earl, and they were reasonably successful in the Warwick Gold Cup at the local rodeo. A newspaper reporter at the time described the Earl as a tall commanding figure with a small black moustache, who was generally looked upon as a good mixer. To the amazement and the amusement of the locals who had never seen the likes before, the Earl took to mustering stock on his property in his large and prestigious Vauxhall 30/98 OE Velox sports tourer motorcar. His love of speed saw him drive the car, always at a furious pace, along local roads.

When the Earl's 21st birthday arrived he commemorated the day in his own way on the other side of the world. However, in England it was an entirely different celebration: a meeting of family and friends toasted his coming of age with food and the bottles of champagne that his parents had laid down for this occasion when Jack was born. In Australia, he partied with his newly-found friends in the way he had become accustomed – with bottles of champagne and fine food at expensive restaurants. He was often seen in Australian society wearing snakeskin shoes and a roll-collared Byron-style shirt which set many a heart fluttering, as mothers with daughters cast their speculative glances at the Earl. Many hostesses in the Warwick district were startled out of their complacency by his unconventional appearance and behaviour.

His love of the outback and the ability to ride his horse on the vast open land added to the charm and attraction of the wild country. He was, he admitted, very satisfied. He adored animals and when asked his views on hunting, he replied that he just did not care for it but had no objection to those who did.

Now Jack had come of age he was eligible to take his seat in the House of Lords, but that fact hardly bothered him. Indeed, it was the last thing on his mind; he had all the time in the world to wrestle with who he was and the type of man he wanted to become. Not aware of it at the time, later on in life his love of Australia would influence him into thinking it would be a perfect place for himself and his family to settle down. For now he was content to join the forces of nature and be with his friends.

Meanwhile, Jack's mother, Lady Suffolk was fast becoming exhausted by her family's dramas, especially those caused by her brother. In the USA, she had been drawn into a fierce courtroom battle by Joseph over the management of the Leiter fortune. Mary, Levi Zeigler Leiter's widow, and Nancy his third daughter, had relinquished their Power of Attorney to Joseph, and with him being the only son he assumed management of the estate and ran it for eight years. Lady Suffolk and her brother-in-law Lord Curzon were much opposed to her brother's governance;

some of his projects had not been successful and income for the estate had dwindled. Joseph had also purchased a lake in Wyoming in the hope it would be used to irrigate estate lands and make them profitable, thus allowing him to sell water to neighbouring ranches, but that also failed. Culmination of these events was the filing of a law suit to evict Joseph, accusing him of inefficiency and gross mismanagement. Figures produced as evidence revealed that when Levi Leiter died the estate was valued at $14,000,000, and was now only worth approximately $8,000,000. What, Lady Suffolk wanted to know, had happened to the rest of the money? What, speculated The New York Times, was happening among the Leiter clan?

Cook County Superior Court ruled Leiter had acted in good faith in managing the estate and refused to remove him as trustee, although he was required to pay back a large sum of money to the estate for investments he had made without proper authority. The ruling was upheld on appeal. Following the settlement of the suit in 1931, both Mary and Nancy Leiter and also Lady Suffolk resigned as trustees, leaving the management of the estate to non-family members. On 11 April 1932, Joseph Leiter, a horse-racing enthusiast who had owned a $5,000,000 stable in his later years, died in Chicago of complications resulting from a cold he caught while attending the races in New Orleans.

Between 1927 and 1928, Jack's grandmother, the Dowager Countess of Suffolk and Berkshire, died; a very sad loss for him as he had been very close to her. A well-known English newspaper reported her death in November 1928 and also drew the reader's attention to the present Earl, now 22 years-old, a handsome and eligible bachelor. To those around Jack who knew him well he was a determined character and a stranger to conformity, whose zest for life matched his persona. He loved people and thrived on good company and conversation, and his opinions, according to most, were way ahead of his time. Like bees to a honeypot, people were attracted to Jack. He possessed none of the expected interests of a titled landowner such as hunting and shooting, and other such pastimes. They did not feature on his 'Things to Do' list because of their unappealing nature. His American heritage impressed him far more than his British Earldom.

CHAPTER FOUR

Smitten

Due to the financial effects of the Great Depression, Jack and William McColm had trouble keeping up repayments on North Toolburra, mainly because they lacked any practical experience of the specific problems presented by Australian farming. In the late 1920s, anyone wanting to buy a rural property in Australia would be hard pressed to cope with the collapse of market prices in the early 1930s. People living in the area, including McColm, believed Jack was returning to England to ask for financial support from his mother to keep the farm going. But Jack had not realized just how much Charlton Park was becoming a massive burden on the finances of the Howards. In the 1930s, North Toolburra would be repossessed and Jack would never again return to the land he had grown to love.

In 1933, after spending seven hard years in Queensland, Jack and Adelaide McColm and one of her sons left Australia on the SS *Mariposa* bound for England. Jack had every intention of returning with them later. Recently his mother had become very ill in Florida, so he decided it wasn't the right time to ask for money. Instead, he stayed with her until she regained her health then returned to England to run the 10,000 acre Charlton Park estate. He expressed his wish of letting Charlton Park for the first time to his mother. His mother had spent £250,000 over the last thirty years on improving the house, and felt the time had come to find a smaller residence nearer London.

Feeling rested and fit, Jack enthusiastically took on the mantle of country gentleman, which included participating in the usual round of parties, theatre, shows and clubs. He also learnt to play the ukulele and the saxophone (he could already play the trumpet given to him by his godfather Lord Curzon), which allowed him to take a prominent part in entertaining his long-suffering friends.

Seen by those unused to his sublime disregard for established customs, Jack often came across as very intimidating and yet extremely waggish. There was a certain dashing Elizabethan air about his sweeping bow that informed all present a gentleman had entered the room. His interests encompassed everything that was new, and his ability to swear was indeed spectacular: he could issue forth deplorable oaths for at least ten minutes and never repeat himself or insult the ladies – a splendid feat. And this he did with such composure and smoothness of manner it completely absolved him of any vulgarity. A visiting Frenchman once scoffed at the British people's love of fiery English mustard, so Jack calmly leant over the table, picked up the mustard pot and consumed the contents with a spoon, then wiped his mouth delicately with a napkin and smiled.

It was only a matter of time before Jack became restless and sought other challenges that country life could not possibly provide his eager, untiring spirit. His analytical mind and restless hands needed to be kept active so he decided to return to his love of science and enrolled at the University of Edinburgh. However, before that happened he thought carefully as to the future of his ancestral home, the bailiff's house and three cottages, as well as the excellent hunting facilities and trout fishing. Due to the poor state of the British economy in 1933, he made the difficult decision and set about letting the property for the first time.

Harry Barnes, a foreman on the Charlton Park estate, found himself in a serious predicament; his son Peter had become very ill. Harry spoke to the Earl who immediately visited the boy. When Jack saw that the boy was gravely ill, he called the doctor who arrived somewhat later. The doctor was blunt in his assessment. After examining Peter he told his father that his son had pneumonia and would be dead by morning. Harry looked at Jack who was watching in silence from the foot of the bed as the doctor carried out his examination.

Jack asked the doctor, 'Why not try one of those pills – penicillin? You've told us he'll die so you've nothing to lose, have you? Just try half a tablet.'

The doctor looked at Harry and then back to Jack before reluctantly granting his request. Harry's esteem of the man grew to a new height: he had saved the life of his son.

While the Earl was contemplating his future, another person's career was beginning to blossom and reach its peak. Minnie Mabel Ford Pigott, known to everyone as 'Mimi', was born on 21 December 1897 in Holloway, London. Her father, Alfred G. Ford Pigott, had been the stage manager of the Alhambra Theatre for some years and had given Mabel an unquenchable thirst for the stage at a very young age. The Alhambra was a very popular music hall in its day, staging the usual musical hall acts, including Jules Léotard who performed an aerial act above the heads of diners, patriotic demonstrations, ballet and the can-can. Classically trained as a dancer and singer, Mabel used 'Mimi Crawford' as her stage name – a tribute to the Craufords of the Britannia Theatre. She first began acting and dancing on stage in 1909 at His Majesty's Theatre. In 1910, she went on to work with Sir Herbert Beerbohm Tree's Theatre Company. By now Mimi Crawford had acted and danced in numerous plays such as *Sitting on Top of the Word*, *Alice in Lumberland* (as Alice), and *Sentimental Me* alongside Cyril Ritchard, also with Fred Astaire in *Stop Flirting*. In January 1925, she appeared in *Meddlers* at the St. James's Theatre; and completely dazzled by the audience's reaction to the play. It was unusual to receive a curtain call but they achieved one that night.

Her name often appeared in many advertisements for health and beauty products, and her smiling youthful face could be seen on advertisements posted on the sides of buses. Women admired her and wanted to emulate her and men just liked looking at her. Her musical repertoire included songs from Richard Addinsell, George and Ira Gershwin, also Lorenz Hart and Richard Rogers. She was asked to perform with Basil Howes in *A Venetian Wedding*, a delightful ballet, and also in *Vaudeville Vanities* at the Vaudeville Theatre, with scenery painted by the grandson of Sir Henry Irving. A self-professed workaholic, Mimi acted in *In the Looking Glass – A Day-Dream*, *The Return of Columbine*, and A. A. Milne's *When We Were Very Young*.

The daily newspapers adored her and fought to interview her. In August 1928, the *Daily Mirror* asked her opinion on the rewards of working and dancing with the view to keeping slim. The real reason why she kept so slim, she said, was work and worry. She took her profession very seriously, even to the point of worrying about it, but it kept her brain alert, her thoughts clear, her cells refreshed and her body young. All it was, really, was a triumph of mind over matter. Her slimness, she believed, was due to her restless nature and always being on the go, always exercising.

'The trouble is,' she told the reporter, 'you seldom realize when you have had enough. You go on until you are ready to drop.' She did think, however, that her own system of keeping slim was not for everyone. Mimi was a household name and women hung on to her every word.

In 1929, she starred in a short film called an *Old World Garden*, the supporting film to Alfred Hitchcock's *Blackmail*. In April 1929, Mimi Crawford was selected to appear for the *Co-Optimists* variety review at the London Hippodrome alongside Stanley Holloway. Her career was riding high, and the crowning point came in 1931 when she was chosen to be the first English artist ever to dance the famous Blue Danube waltz in *Die Fledermaus* at The Royal Opera House, Covent Garden before King George V and Queen Mary.

Mimi became one of Jack's closest friends. They had met during his social rounds and, much to his mother's annoyance and disgust, he began hanging around like a stage-door 'johnny' in the hope of seeing her. Lady Suffolk made it very clear she did not care for her son spending time with an older woman. Mimi was eight years older than Jack and, according to his mother, came from less respectable stock. His mother forgot, or maybe she had not, of her own father's humble beginnings as a clerk. Jack confided in the actress of his long-standing ambition to make a career for himself in science, which he had aspired to ever since his school days.

'There's nothing to stop you, so why do not you just do it,' she encouraged, believing that you made your own luck.

It was largely due to Mimi's advice that, in 1934 aged 28, Jack became an undergraduate at Edinburgh University. He found lodgings at 49 Moray Place and began studying under Professors Kendall and Clark, and quickly became a highly intelligent asset to the university.

Jack and Mimi frequently spent time visiting Professor James Kendall's house, whose 8-year-old daughter always looked forward to their visits. One lazy summer's afternoon Jack unexpectedly arrived in his car while her father was out in the garden cutting the hedge. Jack had been visiting relatives nearby and in the back of the car was a stack of fifty or more rabbits which he had shot because they were pests and were ruining the land. He jumped out of the car full of *joie de vivre* – unshaven, wearing a bright blue sweater and a wide black hat, looking more like a gangster than ever, demanding of Kendall, 'Now, do I get a degree or not?' Professor Kendall, his daughter, and Mimi, like most people, were not immune to his audacity, believed he would have made an excellent actor.

Jack revised hard at the Faculty of Science studying his chosen subjects in Natural Philosophy, Chemistry, Zoology, Physiology, Bacteriology and Pharmacology, applying himself diligently. He was as devoted to his studies as he was to shooting, swearing and the odd piece of gambling. A paper of his had been well received in the *Quarterly Journal of Experimental Physiology and Cognate Medical Sciences: Pharmacological Actions of Acridine Derivates with Especial Reference to Those of Acriflavine and Atebrin* in August 1938.

While studying the intricacies of pharmacology, chemistry of another nature finally laid claim to him. After working hard one day Jack decided to take time off for 'good behaviour', and called a friend who agreed to a night at the theatre. They were there to watch Mimi, society's darling and cause of gossip at the time, dancing in her most vivacious manner. During the interval, a 'thunderbolt' struck him out of nowhere. He turned quickly in his seat to his friend and told him he was going to marry the girl. His friend laughed and replied, 'Steady on, old chap. What's got into you?'

After all the time Jack had spent enjoying her company he suddenly realized that he wanted to keep her in his life. His mother, of course, would be furious but that could not be helped. He had seen Mimi perform on stage many times before but tonight was different. He admired her intellect and kindness, and found her stunning, stimulating and mesmerizing on stage. The one thing Jack had certainly inherited from his ancestors was their stubborn streak.

Pulling out all stops to impress her was not as easy as he first thought even given his rakish charm. Mimi had spent her whole life in the theatre and was used to all its 'drama'. She decided for a while to wait and see what would eventuate. She knew of his magnetic appeal to women, she had seen its effect with her own eyes and was smart enough to realize that his true 'colours' would reveal themselves in the fullness of time. She liked him well enough and loved being in his company, but did she love him enough to marry him? Was she ready to take on the role of Countess and would it force her to give up the stage? She had to admit she had been delighted when he asked for her hand in marriage. Mimi was very non-committal but his persistence never lessened: she eventually agreed to marry him in 1934. It came as a shock to Lady Suffolk but not to their friends, for they had seen love blossoming long before it was acknowledged by the happy couple.

In February 1934, the *New York Times*, and a number of US magazines who had a stake in the matter, also the English daily newspapers, proudly announced the engagement of their much loved Lord Suffolk to Mimi Crawford. At the time Mimi was living with her mother, Louise Caroline Bryant, in Highgate Hill, London. Her father, who had died in 1929 aged 83 years-old, would have been impressed with his daughter's choice of husband who was the grandson of the late multi-millionaire Levi Leiter. The news of Jack's engagement certainly surprised Captain McColm in Australia when he read in the press the announcement that Jack had taken out a licence to wed Mimi. McColm was under the impression that Jack would be returning to Australia. The captain had once met Mimi in London and his lasting impression was that she was a pretty blonde of medium height with a lively personality.

On 7 March 1934, the 20th Earl of Suffolk, 13th Earl of Berkshire married his bride in a quiet ceremony at St Luke's Church, Chelsea, London, and not in the family chapel at Charlton Park as was usual. His mother did attend, but entered by the back door to avoid unwanted and unwelcome publicity. The couple decided to keep it a private ceremony with just thirty friends attending to witness their betrothal. Mimi was given away by her uncle, Lord Robert Chalmers, 1st Baron of Northiam, the late Governor General of Ceylon. The bride looked an exquisite vision of radiance and loveliness wearing a long gown of shimmering yellow satin trimmed with sable, appearing like an iridescent buttercup on a summer's day. On her beautifully coiffured hair, sat a yellow picture hat.

After the ceremony, Jack hosted a luncheon for twelve of their closest friends, after which he whisked away his new bride, the Countess of Suffolk, on a honeymoon through the West Country.

CHAPTER FIVE

Beryl

After swopping her role as a dancer who was used to accepting rapturous applause from her audience for one that held the title of Lady Suffolk, Mimi's new position took time to adjust to as it was a dramatic change from being in charge of her own future on the stage, such was her popularity at the time.

To combat any fears that her new title may bring she decided to look upon it as just another role in to play, she had always been good at that, despite the fact her mother-in-law Daisy was making life increasingly difficult for them because Charlton Park now had two mistresses. Jack, however, would not allow his mother to unsettle his new life. His mother's anger knew no bounds; she auctioned off items in the house on the lawns so that Jack was forced to buy back his inheritance. The newlyweds realized they could not stay at Charlton Park any longer, and he being too much of a gentleman to fight with his mother, they decided to move to Edinburgh where they found a mews flat in Murray Place.

When asked about her life in Edinburgh, Mimi often said that Jack worked very hard and because of that they both preferred the quiet life. Watching him take a splinter out of his hand was like watching an artist at work she told a friend. He had extraordinary sensitive, nimble hands in any practical experiment. When the caretaker hurt his back, Jack massaged him and soon got him back on his feet again. The man was so grateful he presented him with a Dalmatian they called 'Noogie' who adored his master. Jack's love of animals meant he could never bring himself to dissect them.

On 27 March 1935, Mimi gave birth to their son, Michael 'Mickey' John James George Robert, in an Edinburgh nursing home. But even though the tiring restraints of parenthood, finding the right nanny and university placing high demands on them, they still managed to find the time to squeeze in a busy social schedule.

Jack became very ill with rheumatoid arthritis in June 1935; he was taken for treatment to the Westminster Hospital, London, and for the rest of his life walked occasionally with the aid of a stick.

A year later, on 3 November, their son Michael received a 'present' from his parents – a brother named Maurice David Henry. Agnes Moffitt, their 14-year-old under nurse, witnessed continually the deep affection between Jack and his wife. She also noted how the Earl never made much of his title. One day he decided to wear a sombrero, she could not help but laugh, he looked so funny. Children in the street took to hanging around the mews where the Earl parked his car. Occasionally, he would whisk them away into town where he bought them tea then drove them to Woolworths and bought each of them a bag of toys. Not once did Agnes witness the domineering ways of his mother, and if anyone on the staff became ill they went to the Earl who would do all he could to help them get treatment.

In 1936, Jack decided to sell Garsdon Manor, which had 1,110 acres and included seven dairy farms. Garsdon, two miles east of Malmesbury, was a typical North Wiltshire hamlet of old stone-built houses, cottages and farm buildings. It had once been the early home of a member of the Washington family from the Northamptonshire branch descended from George Washington. Sir Lawrence Washington had purchased the manor from the Moody family in 1641 and built the manor house at the farm. Sir Lawrence died in 1643, so the house passed by marriage into the possession of Sir Robert Shirley, the first Earl Ferrers. Eventually, Garston became incorporated in Charlton Park estate. The following year, in 1937, an advert appeared in a local paper stating that Charlton Park was again to let.

Professor Emeritus Neil Campbell, OBE, admitted a profound astonishment, which his colleagues shared, when it was announced that the Earl of Suffolk intended to study for a science degree at Edinburgh University. Campbell's first impression of Jack was of a tall, striking looking, bold, adventurous looking man, more of a hero type in a rollicking historical novel than an undergraduate about to endure the drudgery and hard work necessary for a serious degree in science. The Earl's many ancestors had led wild and exciting lives, and Queen Victoria was often heard to declare during her reign, 'Those mad Howards!' Jack's reputation as a deckhand on a sailing ship, a Second Lieutenant in the Scots Guards, a sheep rancher in Australia, along with other exploits distinctive of an *enfant terrible*, had already reached the university. Naturally, his tutors and lecturers regarded the decision of a restless wanderer becoming a scientist as little more than a passing whim of the aristocracy.

Nevertheless, Jack was made of sterner stuff and set about studying scientific methods for large-scale farming. In 1937, he was elected a Fellow of the Royal Society of Edinburgh, proving the doubters all wrong. So wrong, in fact, they had to eat their words. In 1938, Jack graduated in Pharmacology as a Bachelor of Science (BSc) with first-class honours, the first person ever to win such a distinction at the university. Professor Kendall, whenever he was asked about Lord Suffolk, said he was practically a reincarnation of that fictional hero, the elusive 'Pimpernel'. Combining a charming manner and the easy courtesy of a nobleman, Jack showed the most astonishing versatility in the assumption of other roles. It was by mutual consent the titles of Professor and Earl were both forgotten during his time in the Chemistry Department.

Jack was filled with hope for the future. By his side was his supportive, intelligent wife and healthy sons – the family lineage safe. His degree would no doubt have the world clamouring at his feet, and his gift of 'perpetual gaiety', as Johnson said of Falstaff, gained him many friends in the student fraternity. Seen as tall and commanding it was difficult to judge just how tall Jack was because he constantly stooped, like his father. His warm enigmatic charm made it effortless for him when making friends within the aristocratic or the working class, as he slotted easily into either niche. With a demeanour born for a tuxedo or the sweaty, grimy clothes of a working ranch-hand, his good looks could often change in an instant when putting on a piece of mimicry, something he excelled at, when delighting people with anecdotes. His pose was that of a dilettante with his always present cigarette holder which he held with the grace and dexterity of an artist.

One never knew whether they had been on the receiving end of his jokes or witticism. He was not intentionally unkind but could uncannily navigate to the heart of someone's gross stupidity or pomposity. In that regard he was very much his father's son, in that he had a remarkable capacity or plasticity to change according to his circumstances. Jack would actively explore the world around him rather than merely absorb its spoon-fed lessons.

Now that his studies at university had come to an end for the time being, planning later to carry on in his subject matter to Ph.D level, Jack decided to return to Charlton Park in order to manage the estate because his mother had elected to live in Somerset. He had a family to look after and wanted to concentrate on his experiments in his home laboratory.

He took time in exploring his career options, and after thorough deliberation he finally decided to take up a position at the Nuffield Institute of Medical Research in Oxford as a research chemist where his chief interests lay in high explosives and poisons. He was unable to rejoin a front-line regiment because of his frequent bouts of rheumatism and had refused several offers of staff jobs. The last thing he wanted was to feel claustrophobic and trapped behind a desk. He told a friend that he was not going to sit behind a desk and issue orders for the discomfort of the 'poor bloody infantry.'

It was while working at Nuffield Institute that he was introduced to his new secretary, Miss Eileen Beryl Morden, a meeting that would change the course of both their lives. Beryl, as she preferred to be known – she always hated being called Eileen – was 5ft 7in tall, attractive, with brown hair, and a fresh complexion, with fun and mischievousness written in her playful grey-blue eyes. Her face beamed constantly with a smile that could light up the Blackpool Illuminations: nothing dampened her spirits. Imaginative, exuberant and untidy in her habits, she retained one great fear, one she did not like to express openly, and that was losing her independence.

She was born in Leytonstone, East London on 19 October 1912, and enjoyed a happy childhood, being one of four siblings. She had been offered a secretarial position at the Nuffield Institute of Medical Research and had accepted it with alacrity, the job being too good an opportunity to miss, and became exceedingly efficient in her work. Just before the outbreak of war, Beryl's life became even more eventful when she and her boyfriend became engaged. Her life was perfect until the war when her fiancé, a RAF pilot, was sent abroad to Malaya, never to return.

A working rapport and respect for one another quickly developed between Beryl and the Earl. She was very proficient and soon became indispensable. After losing her fiancé she decided to bury herself in her work. Eileen Clarke, Beryl's niece, was only 4 years-old when Beryl used to visit her home. She eagerly looked forward to seeing her vivacious aunt, a larger-than-life type of girl who lived each moment to its fullest, bringing sunshine into Eileen's life. Sometimes a man paid them a visit and stayed for the odd weekend; she was even allowed to call him 'Uncle Charlie' or sometimes 'Jack'. As she grew older she often heard her aunt and other family members talking about the exciting things her aunt and 'Uncle Charlie' did, leaving an abiding impression on her. She knew Grandma Morden never liked Jack because in her mind's eye she thought him far too dashing for his own good.

The Earl spoke only once in the House of Lords, and that was his maiden speech. Thirteen days after his 33rd birthday he took part in the second, hotly debated, reading of the Cancer Bill. Jack was in good company: Earl of Donoughmore, a patron of homeopathy; Viscount Trenchard who had been to India like Jack's father, and known as the 'Father of the Royal Air Force'; Viscount Samuel, the High Commissioner for Palestine; the Duke of Devonshire; Lord Balfour of Burleigh, and Earl Stanhope, the Under Secretary of State for War.

Lord Balfour of Burleigh moved an amendment regretting that the Bill had not contained enough provision for increased research into the cause and treatment of cancer. He mentioned that some of the methods tentatively being used at that time to help cure cancer were radium treatment and X-ray treatment.

Lord Donoughmore spoke of the definite improvement and increase of knowledge in the treatment of the disease, and asked them to remember when cancer was a sentence of death. They could now, he said, take courage in the continuing attack on this problem, because there was a definite improvement seen in using these treatments to date. He was surprised that people researching cancer were not in touch, nor co-operating with, clinicians and vice versa. One of the reasons could be that cancer treatment was spread over twelve hospitals in London and some twenty-two regional centres.

Donoughmore proposed that a diagnostic centre for cancer, manned by a surgeon, a physician, a radiographer and possibly a physicist, be set up. He also proposed that after-care and patient management remained with the local clinic, and that treatment should only be carried out at large hospitals. He stated it would be a crime to let X-ray apparatus be used by inexperienced hands because gamma rays, which came from radium, could penetrate lead up to 4½in thick and even penetrate a brick wall. He also reminded them of the tremendous importance in keeping adequate records of cases, both administrative and clinical.

The Earl supported the amendment because he himself was in the pursuit of research, though probably not cancer, but realized the financial problems people in research met during the course of their work. He was fortunate enough to be working under the benefaction of Lord Nuffield, and was in the happy position of not requiring outside help, though many laboratories were working at the present moment under very difficult financial constraints. He mentioned that he had spoken with a friend who was engaged in research into chemotherapy and was told that it was successful in ten diseases. It also showed remarkable promise in laboratory trials at the Fulham Cancer Hospital under Professor Kenway and his team. They had discovered a compound which, when injected, would reduce the size of a tumour to the size of a small pinhead. To date, it had not been trialed in clinical medicine but would be shortly. Jack had no doubt it would be a marked success. Definite experiments in new processes to treat cancer were being extremely hampered by lack of funds, and he expressed his hope that the government would make more money available.

The Earl noted that his noble friend Lord Balfour of Burleigh had the day before adopted the metaphor, 'that it was not worth spoiling the ship for the sake of ha'p'orth of tar'. According to the Duke, 70,000 people died of cancer every year, and he would like to bring those two points together. Was it worth buying tar for a ship whose seams leak to the extent that 70,000 people may be drowned in falling through those seams? Was it not better to buy something better than tar, something that would close those seams? There was no specific cure at present, but Jack was in possession of information that enabled him to believe they were within a short distance of getting something specific that would close up the 'leak'.

Viscount Trenchard supported the amendment. Research, he pointed out, was the most vital factor in the struggle against cancer. Lord Balfour of Burleigh said the money required for research was so infinitesimal compared with the amount the government was spending on treatment.

He knew they were providing £600,000 a year for treatment and an additional £500,000 to purchase radium.

To establish a research unit such as the Medical Research Council had in mind would cost somewhere around £30,000 a year for ten or fifteen years. He appealed to the Leader of the House to give an assurance that he would support an application for the necessary funds. Viscount Samuel added his view on the subject stating national health was at least as important as national defence, so should receive great sympathy and attention from the government.

It was during this industrious time in Jack's life, his brother Cecil John Arthur Howard, who had attended Eton, was himself very busy falling in love and marrying someone who would later become a Second World War pin up and actress in the USA. Frances Drake, the name created by Paramount Studios, was born Frances Dean on 22 October 1912 in New York, was a slim 5ft 2½in, dark haired, wide-eyed beauty who had started her career as a dancer in a London nightclub. She was the daughter of Edwin Morgan Dean, and had been educated in Canada and Great Britain.

In 1934, Drake returned to the USA and began studying with Marguerite Namara, the classically-trained soprano and actress who also was a close friend of Isadora Duncan and Howard Hughes. From 1934 to 1940, Drake appeared in *I Take This Woman*, with Spencer Tracy and Hedy Lemarr, *It's a Wonderful World*, *Mad Love*, *Les Misérables*, *You Cannot Have Everything* and *Bolero*.

Cecil Howard, despite living in London, travelled regularly to the USA. In July 1937, when recuperating from an illness in California, he met his bride-to-be. Cecil was around 6ft tall, and described his occupation as 'salesman'. After marrying on 12 February 1939 in Tucson, Arizona, at the Dowager Countess of Suffolk's house, the couple went to live in Beverly Hills.

Frances decided to retire from performing shortly after her marriage although she must have been popular because there is a star in her name embedded in the Hollywood Walk of Fame. Cecil Howard died in 1985, Frances Drake died on 18 January 2000 aged 91years-old in Irvine, California.

Greville Reginald Howard, born 7 September 1909, was Jack's youngest brother. Also educated at Eton, he attended the Royal Military College, Sandhurst. In February 1938, he enrolled in the Royal Naval

Volunteer Reserve (RNVR) and was attached to the London Division. During 1939, he was promoted to the rank of Lieutenant Commander. From 1940 to 1944, he served on HMS *Cape Howe*, a special service vessel; on the destroyers HMS *Punjabi* and HMS *Malcolm*, and then commanded the frigate HMS *Nith*.

In November 1945, Greville married his sweetheart Mary Ridehalgh and the marriage produced one daughter, Caroline Margaret Howard. He was elected Mayor of Westminster in 1946-7 and served until 1950. From 1958 to 1964, he served as a permanent RNR officer, on the Unattached List. In 1966, he was elected as the Conservative Member of Parliament (MP) for St. Ives, Cornwall, but later switched his allegiance to the Liberal Party. The Hon. Greville Reginald Howard died, aged of 78 years-old, on 20 September 1987.

CHAPTER SIX

1939

Jack Howard's work as a research chemist was short-lived; for some time he had been worried by growing nationalism in Germany which had led to the invasion of Poland. On 3 September 1939, Britain and France declared war on Hitler's Germany. Many politicians reflected the sentiment of the day, 'We're all middle class now' because of the blurring of differences that distinguished the various tiers of British society. People came together from vastly different regions and cultural backgrounds, something that had not happened during the First World War, which separated the officers from other ranks. What was to come – the common threat of invasion and bombing, rationing, evacuation of children and conscription of men into the military – would bond the populace together whether they were of noble or common birth. London was taken by surprise when the first air-raid siren wailed out on that sunny, sultry day in September. It turned out to be a false alarm but frightening nonetheless, triggered by the unscheduled arrival of a French aircraft – it would be the first of many alerts.

Churchill called it the 'Twilight War', comedians aptly named it the 'Bore War', borrowing the phrase from a US senator named Borah. But to most, between September 1939 and April 1940, it was the 'Phoney War'. Inactivity eroded morale and very few British people were even aware of events taking place in other parts of the world.

The French government was involved in secret peace negotiations with Germany, and Churchill decided to send William Stephenson, MC, DFC, a Canadian soldier, airman, inventor, businessman, spymaster and the senior representative of British Intelligence, to the USA on 21 June 1940. His task was to set up the British Security Co-ordination (BSC) to direct operations should Great Britain be invaded by Germany.

Winston Churchill made his morale-boosting message to the nation:

'... let us to the task, to the battle and the toil. Each to our part, each to our station, fill the armies, rule the air, pour out the munitions, strangle the U-boats, sweep the mines, plough the land, build the ships, guard the streets, succour the wounded, uplift the downcast and honour the brave. Let us go forward together in all parts of the Empire, in all parts of this island. There is not a week, nor a day nor an hour to be lost.'

Chamberlain thought it a strange war, rather like a siege, and he did everything possible not to antagonize Hitler. President Roosevelt, concerned that Chamberlain might negotiate peace, speedily made contact with Churchill. Rumours and uncertainty flourished. RAF pilots carried out 'bombing' raids over Germany, dropping propaganda leaflets to persuade the German people of Hitler's folly in pursuing an unnecessary war. People picked up the leaflets from the streets, their gardens, and read about the evils of Naziism and how susceptible they were to bombing raids. This massive amount of paper could, if needs must, supply the German people with toilet paper for a number of years. Kate Phipps, a Red Cross worker, stated: 'Will that have any more effect than if they dropped them on us? We would just burn them. No doubt they'll do likewise.'

Poland collapsed and was being partitioned or plundered by the Soviets and Germans. By the end of September 1939, the country had been divided up. Chamberlain made a broadcast to the people of Great Britain and the Empire, talking of hardships and inconveniences and what measures to take against air attacks even though there had been none. It would not do, he said, to be found unprepared, because if that happened the people could rightly blame the government for neglect.

Chamberlain met with Hitler three times and in 1938 returned with a signed undertaking which would, Chamberlain stated, 'offer peace in our time'. Six months later, when Germany invaded Poland, he announced to the nation:

'...unless we hear from them [German Government] by 11 o'clock that they were prepared at once to withdraw their troops from Poland, a state of war would exist between us. I have to tell you now that no such undertaking has been received and that consequently, this country is at war with Germany.'

Germany began the war in earnest, with military sites, docks and railway stations the main targets. Civilian casualties mounted, but the first 'victims' were the poisonous snakes in London Zoo that had to be destroyed in case they escaped into the population. Britain's first civilian casualty was Jim Isbister who was killed in March 1940 during an air raid on the Orkney Islands. The first unexploded German 50kg bombs, which had penetrated the earth to a depth of 6 to 10ft, were retrieved from the Shetland Isles in November 1939. The fuses were sent to the Research and Experimental Branch of the Ministry of Supply (MoS) where it was discovered they were of the electrical-condenser resistance (ECR) type. This dedicated group's work, apart from finding out how each new fuse worked, was to develop a method of defusing, designing and organizing the manufacture of specialist equipment, so that men working in the field with unexploded bombs (UXBs) would not have to improvise. It was soon realized that any bomb dropped in an urban area would have to be made safe and removed.

The 'Blackout' immediately transformed life. Illuminated signs and advertising were switched off, as was street lighting which required cars, trucks and public transport to use masked headlights. The intense darkness caused numerous accidents; people fell down stairways, walked into walls, or were involved in road accidents. Pedestrians began walking along the white lines painted in the centre of the roads, becoming a menace to those driving almost 'blind'. During the first four months of the war, a total of 4,153 people were killed on the roads, of these 2,500 were pedestrians. The king's surgeon pointed out to him that the *Luftwaffe* was able to kill 600 British citizens a month without ever taking to the air. In November 1939, Churchill noted that in Paris the lights still shone and that the citizens could drive around in ease, whereas in Britain the blackout was causing so many problems.

CHAPTER SEVEN

Ministry of Supply

Jack Howard received a crushing blow when told he was classified as unfit and rejected for military service due to his earlier illness. He had hoped they would make an exception seeing as war was imminent. Arthur Vesey Meade, 5th Earl of Clanwilliam (now a Whip in the House of Lords), once an extra ADC to Lord Curzon in India, was talking to Jack over drinks at the Carlton Club. Arthur could see that Jack could barely hide his frustration, he was impatient and wanted to put his scientific knowledge to good use now that war was on the horizon. Lord Clanwilliam patted him on the shoulder and told him not to worry, to leave it with him, telling him he had would do whatever he could for the son of his dearest friend.

He visited Herbert Stanley Morrison, Minister of Supply, at his ministry and recommended the Earl who held a science degree and had great knowledge of poisons and explosives. On the strength of that, Morrison summoned Jack to London for a secret meeting shortly before France fell on 14 June 1940. Jack's subsequent interview convinced Morrison that his talents would be very useful to the government. It was rumoured that he would make the ideal candidate for a sensitive position that had just become vacant. Morrison described Jack to anyone who asked as one of the most remarkable young men employed by them.

Jack's file was placed on the desk of Dr Herbert John Gough, the Director General of Scientific Research at the Ministry of Supply

(MoS). Born on 26 April 1890 in Bermondsey, London, Herbert Gough was the second son of Henry James Gough, a civil servant in the Post Office, and Mary Ann Gillis. His thorough and accurate manner was inherited from his father who, although having a lively personality, was precise and meticulous in his habits and work. He was the first member of his family to show an interest in science and engineering.

Growing up, Herbert Gough attended university. Soon after, he became an apprentice at Vickers Sons & Maxim Co. Ltd, followed by a year as a design draughtsman on naval and military weapons and other armaments with Vickers. In 1914, with his BSc (Hons) degree in engineering he joined the scientific staff of the engineering department at the National Physical Laboratory at Teddington where he began his first studies into metal fatigue. His main interests remained in this area of science.

At the outbreak of the First World War, Dr Herbert Gough, MBE, PhD, IMechE, FRS, joined the Royal Engineers (Signals), rose to the rank of captain, and was twice mentioned in dispatches. After serving in Cologne with the Army of Occupation, Gough was demobilized in 1919, and helped run a school of further education in Germany for officers and men until demobilization. Re-joining the staff at the National Physical Laboratory, he continued his research into metal fatigue. In 1938, he was appointed Director of Scientific Research at the War Office and was directly responsible to the Director General of Munitions for the production, general direction and organization of research work for War Office purposes. He advised on the programme of research work to be undertaken, wrote proposals for specific research, and checked the efficiency of the organization and experimental procedures of various departments in the War Office. In 1947, he was decorated with the Medal of Freedom with Silver Palm by the US government for his meritorious service in the field of scientific research and the development of ground forces weapons, and aiding the US in the prosecution of the war against the enemy. His other responsibilities included the Chemical Warfare Establishment at Porton Down, near Salisbury; the Radar Research Establishment at Malvern, and the rocket research establishment at Aberporth, Wales.

Gough was now suddenly faced with a heavy responsibility and with his knowledge and technical skills he had no room for hangers on. He contemplated the name of the man, who held an honours degree, on the paper in his hand. The Edinburgh degree impressed him considerably but still he retained some qualms. He was concerned at being landed with a titled member of society that he knew so little about. Such work as theirs could carry no one who was not there on technical merit. He refused to be stuck with some 'snooty' aristocrat. In that frame of mind he decided to interview the Earl of Suffolk. And thank goodness he did. The Earl pleaded with Gough to employ him, his enthusiasm was tremendous, and before long his infectious personality, intelligence and buccaneering spirit won the scientist over completely. Gough employed him, and explained him that he was sending him to France as his personal representative.

While this was taking place, another figure appeared in the background, one who would make just as much impact on the war years – Arthur Douglas Merriman. He took up a position with the Directorate of Scientific Research and became a 'backroom boffin'. Caught up in the war and eager to play his part he became a Senior Experimental Officer working in the directorate, and although he was supposed to be a part-time experimental officer with office-based duties, he strayed into the world of bomb disposal. All members selected for the Scientific Research Department were volunteers and very much the fourth arm of the services, recovering new fuses and explosives also co-ordinating research and development.

An early example of Merriman's work came in November 1939 when he recovered the first German electric fuses and bombs at Sullom Voe in the Shetland Isles. On 28 July 1940, he removed three fuses from 50kg bombs dropped on Great Yarmouth and over a period of ten days, he defused seventeen bombs from as far afield as King's Lynn and Bristol. In one day, he removed ten fuses from bombs in a crashed Luftwaffe bomber at Southampton. When he was not defusing bombs he served as joint secretary with Captain A. Hamilton on the Unexploded Bomb (UXB) Committee. Arthur Douglas Merriman was awarded the George Cross for conspicuous bravery in bomb disposal, and added OBE, DFC, MA, MEd, DSc, CEng, CIMechE, FRSE after his name.

The MoS was also responsible for the building and running of the Royal Ordinance Factories which produced explosives and propellants, they filled ammunition and constructed guns and rifles, and supplied tanks and other armoured-fighting vehicles. The MoS arranged for the labour force and construction of a large number of satellite factories that were run on its behalf by private companies, such as Nobel Industries.

The MoS had been formed in 1939 and was based at Shell-Mex House on London's Strand, headed by a government minister; its primary purpose was the provision of equipment to the army, although it also served the Admiralty and the Air Ministry where there were common needs. Dr Gough's responsibility was to oversee research, development, assessment of bomb disposal methods and specialized equipment for the three services.

Herbert Morrison, standing before the House of Commons, informed them of the extensive powers given to him under the defence regulations as Minister of Supply. His chief responsibilities were raw materials. Under the act, setting up the ministry and duties regarding stocks of various essential commodities were transferred to him. The purpose of his duties, with regards to raw materials, was to see that supplies of the materials were made available and used to their best purpose for the essential needs of the country. When supplies were not being replenished by normal processes of trade, it was his responsibility to ensure other steps were taken to provide them at reasonable cost. Gough informed them he had found it necessary to set up a number of organizations to control the supply of iron and steel, timber, copper, lead, zinc, aluminium, even wool, paper, leather, and many other vital commodities.

Action taken was varied. He first needed to make sure any shortage or difficulty was to be expected and then see what was available. An element of control was to be applied lightly in the first instant without disturbing the usual commercial channels. One of the functions of the control organizations would be to supplement and replace ordinary means of maintaining supplies of materials while utilizing to the full the men in the industry who had made a lifetime study of these particular commodities.

On 21 September 1940, describing the task in hand for the MoS, Winston Churchill said:

'The rapid disposal of unexploded bombs is of the highest importance. Any failure to grapple with the problem may have serious results on the production of aircraft and other vital war material. The work of the bomb disposal squads must be facilitated by the provision of every kind of up-to-date equipment. Priority A should be allotted to the production of the equipment and to any other requirement which may come to light.

All members selected for the ministry's Scientific and Research Department were volunteers and very much the fourth arm of the services. All practical safety precautions were taken but hazards were unavoidable and accepted.'

Promoted by Dr Gough, the Earl's position was now that of Liaison Officer. He came under the wing of the Department of Scientific Research, consulting between British and French scientific organizations. Jack was under no illusion that it was mostly due to his expertise in a number of areas that he was given the position by the British government. His tremendous love of adventure was no fantasy but it was the dreams that fantasies were made of for young boys of his generation. And of course, Jack had the added advantage of being a Howard – a social position he was not afraid to take full advantage of.

His office was to be in Paris where he would render indispensable service to his 'Master', Gough, who did not doubt for one second the suitability of his choice. His mission was vital and to be kept 'Top Secret' – his task was to identify people and items of value to the British war effort. Jack's responsibilities lay in the actual collaboration between British and French research laboratories that had been accomplished by a generation of diplomatic official exchanges.

Once he was in Paris, once he had found his feet, the responses Britain would receive from him were often described as a fascinating mixture of scientific data, political and personal gossip, and much profanity. His reports were delivered to London and Oxford, and on more than one occasion language experts had to be brought in to interpret the involved cursing to scientists not well versed in such language. One report they received showed his outright disgust of the French government. He wrote that '... they had met with nothing but a most obstructive and defeatist attitude from the higher members of the Bordeaux Government.'

Jack took with him his trusted secretary Beryl Morden, mainly because of her understanding of engineering terms and being very familiar with his eccentric ways. Beryl was eager to go in order to do her 'bit' for her country. Also part of the mission was Major Vautier Ardale Golding, of the Royal Tank Corps, who had studied military and mechanical engineering and was member of the British security service, along with his secretary Miss Marguerite Nicolle. In 1938, Major Golding had visited Berlin to report on Hitler's army and reported his findings back to government his findings. Beryl received her passport on 28 February 1940 from the Foreign Office, informing her it would expire on the 28 March. It was stamped by an official '2 March 1940' upon entering France with the Earl. She also carried on her person a visa from the French Ministry of Armaments allowing her to carry out duties for the Earl while in Paris. Her French Ministry of Armaments' identity stamp was not issued until 5 April and her *carte d'identité* (identity card) stated that she was employed by the Scientific and Technological Research Service. Beryl and the Earl were now to all intent and purpose working with the scientific elite of France.

Jack Howard's mission had the hallmarks of tight, long-term planning stamped all over it. Everything had been concisely fitted together. Known targets showing an advanced knowledge of the possibility of an atomic programme were kept 'Top Secret' by an exclusive group of intelligence personnel and scientists. Paris for Jack was not just an adventure for the elite, although there was a high element of that in the prospect.

A few months before Russia and Germany divided Poland, scientists at the Kaiser Wilhelm Institute in Berlin bombarded the uranium atom and split it, achieving nuclear fission. The Russians too were concentrating hard on the same work. William Stephenson, senior officer in British Intelligence, reminded Churchill that atomic research required heavy water, and all the world's heavy water was in Norway. It was imperative, he said, they stop Germany's progress. One of the world's leading atomic scientists Niels Bohr, in Copenhagen, had split the uranium atom with a release of energy a million times more powerful than conventional high explosive; the Russians were also aware of this. England could not, would not, consider even for one minute that the atomic bomb would fall into the hands of their enemy. In October 1939, Stephenson contacted Alexander Sachs, the New York financier and mathematician who, in turn, visited President Roosevelt, handing him a letter from Albert Einstein and other atomic scientists warning that the dictators could build the new bombs. Roosevelt was forced to take action, and he did. He contacted his ally Churchill.

Towards the end of November Russia invaded Finland, putting the bordering countries of Norway and Sweden in jeopardy. On 16 December 1939, Churchill required naval intelligence's support for STRIKE OX, so-named after Oxelsünd near Stockholm, where there were tons of Swedish iron ore, which, if the Germans failed to get their hands on it, would leave Hitler with only enough to keep the Ruhr steel industry supplied for another nine months. This was his argument for sabotaging the loading facilities of the port. What he did not say was that he and only a handful of scientists knew that the heavy water also travelled this route from Norway to Germany, it could even reach Russia if they were not careful.

Through various channels Stephenson let it be widely known he was on a sabotage mission in Sweden. Swedish counter-espionage picked up these reports which duly became known to German agents, informing them that a Canadian industrialist had plans to destroy the port owned by his friend Axel Axelson Johnson. Johnson was a major stockholder in iron-ore mines and owner of the railway from the mines to Oxelsünd, and it was extremely doubtful he would agree to blow up his own property. This was all pure deception. It came to the knowledge of King Karl Gustav V of Sweden who urged King George VI to halt the madness. Lord Halifax, who did not want to antagonize Hitler, strongly asked for it to be stopped. King George IV remained silent but STRIKE OX was cancelled.

Germany, now satisfied that the plan had been terminated, left Stephenson in peace to visit his Swedish friends, allowing him to gather a network of friendly Swedes about him to discuss how the mines could be sabotaged. He then travelled to Norway to talk to Professor Leif Tronstad, a chemical engineer who knew the layout of Norsk Hydro plant at Rjuken that produced the heavy water. Tronstad handed over a copy of the plant's layout and warned him if the Germans captured the plant they would have to destroy it.

Stephenson began making plans so that the heavy water could be re-routed to France. By early 1940, there was proof that Nazi funds were supporting research into all possible approaches to the control of nuclear fusion. In March 1940, the Frisch-Peierls's memorandum, (Dr Rudolph Peierls, a German scientist who worked at Birmingham University, was attempting to derive the critical mass of a block of uranium) informed British defence chiefs it was possible to construct an atomic bomb using isotope U-235. Einstein had written to Roosevelt several months previously about extremely powerful bombs of a new type. In Great Britain, atomic research was proceeding apace at laboratories in London, Oxford, Cambridge and Liverpool. There was absolutely no way Germany would be allowed to obtain supplies of these valuable commodities.

This very secret mission, to bring the heavy water to Britain, was no spur-of-the moment exercise because it was remarkably well executed. The British government decided that Jack was the only person for the job mainly because of his scientific expertise, his knowledge of chemistry and explosives, and also his knowledge of the French language. It suited the government's propaganda purposes to send a British nobleman, who no one would suspect, to France to bring off this most daring mission.

CHAPTER EIGHT

Paris –
The French Effort

Leaving behind England's bone-chilling weather in February 1940, the temperature almost the same in Paris, the Earl, Beryl Morden, Major Golding and his secretary Marguerite Nicholle arrived at their destination eager to commence work. They had been booked in at the Ritz hotel but were graciously offered, and happily accepted, rooms at the *Ministère de l'Armament* with the compliments of the French government.

Over the next few weeks Dr Gough became bombarded with letters written in an Elizabethan-style scrawl advising him on items including anti-allergy treatment to mine detectors. His replies to the errant Earl were laced with rebukes, reminding him he was a British government agent and to keep his reports on the business at hand and not on dealing with requests from Vickers and other such things.

In April, Jack accompanied the South African zoologist Sir 'Solly' Zuckerman and the British scientist Desmond Bernal, who was a communist, political activist and physicist, around the French capital. Zuckerman was testing chimpanzees, as surrogates for humans, on the effects of bomb blasts. Both men finally concluded that there was more likelihood of surviving an explosion than first thought. Bernal and Zuckerman had arrived in Paris to discuss scientists' comparable studies and once completed they were in the willing hands of the Earl who showed them how Parisians really lived – by wining and dining and exposing them to high society's glitter and glamour.

Jack and Major Golding spent much of March and April gathering contacts and beginning preparations of what was to be a massive undertaking. Jack contacted his master with his concerns about Major Golding, because he was making much of evacuating staff while Paris was calm but becoming anxious; he was even talking of cancelling the mission. His anxieties, however, were soon allayed. Their mission solely depended on them both remaining alert. Jack and Golding visited the *Collège de France* where they met with the physicist Jean Frédéric Joliot and his team of scientists and talked about all matters nuclear. Besides being responsible for more actual collaboration between British and French research laboratories and gathering numerous French scientists and secret documents together, Jack and Golding also liaised with the French ministry of armaments. Golding's task was to secure those armaments and prepare them for transportation back to England.

Joliot was an assistant to Marie Curie at the Radium Institute, and fell in love with her eldest daughter, Irène Curie. Soon after their marriage, in 1926, they changed their surname to Joliot-Curie. Frédéric Joliot-Curie, at the insistence of his wife, obtained a second *baccalauréat* and a doctorate in science, his thesis being the electro-chemistry of radio-elements. He collaborated with his wife in the research of the structure of the atom, particularly the projection of nuclei – the essential step in the discovery of the neutron. In 1935, the couple received the Nobel Prize in Chemistry.

The French Minister for Armaments, Raoul Dautry, a reserve officer drafted by the French Ministry of Armaments, was considering whether or not to send Lieutenant Allier of the *Deuxième Bureau*, the French secret service, who was a senior official of the *Banque de Paris et des Pays-Bas*, (the *Banque* co-ordinated the French holdings in Norsk Hydro), with a team of French agents on a covert mission to Norway. Their sole purpose was to negotiate the loan of the entire stock of heavy water from Norsk Hydro. He had already spoken with his government and his request had been cleared. After realizing the importance of the mission Allier readily agreed. Frédéric Joliot spent time briefing him on certain technical precautions he must take when transporting the heavy water to Paris. It was decided to have the canisters fabricated from aluminium because of its weight. Most importantly, if Allier should fail his mission he was to do his utmost to ensure the existing stocks of heavy water, whether at Ryukan or on the way to Paris, were contaminated and made useless to the Germans.

At the end of February 1940, Allier left by train for Amsterdam and after a tense journey he arrived in Stockholm on 4 March. In Oslo, he met with the French Ambassador who made arrangements for somewhere for him to stay without revealing his true mission. From a telephone booth on a nearby street he made contact with the general secretary of Norsk Hydro, agreeing to meet him on a specified street corner.

Sitting in the headquarters of the Director General of Norsk Hydro opposite Axel Aubert, Allier discussed heightened German interest in buying up heavy water stocks held in Norway. He was very concerned about his perceived sympathies of Aubert who might prove neutral in his dealings with Germany, but there was nothing to worry about. Aubert was totally devoted to the Allied cause.

Negotiations continued and were completed on 9 March. Aubert agreed to lend France the entire stock of heavy water, 185kg (410lb), for the duration of the war. He also assured Allier that France would have priority claims on production in the near future. It was not until the end of negotiations that Allier revealed the military implications of the transaction. At midnight, on the same day, the heavy water was poured into twenty-six 5ltr aluminium containers. These were off-loaded with considerable uneasiness in Oslo and stored in a house belonging to the French Embassy. Unfortunately, the property next door belonged to the *Abwehr* (German Military Intelligence) which remained brightly lit all night.

How was it possible to get the containers out of the country? That was the question. In the end, by air seemed the only possibility. They booked airline tickets for three consecutive days for the two scheduled flights out of Fornebu Airport to put the *Abwehr* off their scent. One was bound for Perth in Scotland, the other for Amsterdam and both were due to depart at around the same time early on that morning. Allier and his travelling companions repeatedly went over their movements late into the night before they left, keeping a close watch on next door.

·   On the morning of 12 March, two airliners were parked side by side on the apron, the day was bright and clear; a good day for flying. Inside the main building, Allier and his companion openly made arrangements to book on the flight to Amsterdam, and then went back outside. At the very last moment a taxi drove up, after the driver had made an anxious fuss at the gate to be allowed entry. The vehicle stopped between the two aircraft, out of sight from the terminal building. The cases containing ten canisters, were placed on the Perth-bound plane and Allier and his companions boarded with seconds to spare before the passenger door was closed. A British secret service agent had organized clearance at the airport and assisted in handling the bulky cargo. The remaining sixteen canisters were taken out by other members from Allier's team in another direction.

Lieutenant Allier and one other secret agent accompanied the canisters on the flight to Scotland. It was said that the unpressurised aircraft flew so high that Allier passed out while resting on the cargo. When the pilot realized this he quickly lost altitude and Allier regained consciousness.

Both teams met up later in an Edinburgh hotel and then caught a train to London with their precious cargo in the overhead luggage rack of their compartment. On arrival, personnel from the French military mission assisted in transferring the cargo on to a train bound for Paris, and the party continued on their way home to France. On arrival, Jean Frédéric Joliot accepted receipt for the cargo and safely locked it in the cellars of the *Collège de France*. Hans von Halban (born in Leipzig 1908, had come from the laboratory of Niels Bohr and harboured no love for the Germans. He had come from the Copenhagen laboratory of the nuclear physicist Niels Bohr.), and Lew Kowarski (born in St Petersburg 1907, a naturalized French physicist of Jewish Russian-Polish descent, was a talented musician but he had an impediment – his fingers grew too large for the piano keys. At the age of 27 he joined Joliot-Curie's group after gaining a degree in chemical engineering and a PhD.), suddenly appeared with their families from their three weeks of enforced holidays, just as the cargo was being locked away.

At the beginning of April, Lieutenant Jacques Allier visited Paul Reynaud, the Finance Minister. At the meeting he described to Raoul Dautry, the new Prime Minister of France, Frédéric Joliot's nuclear energy initiatives. The new leader promised him state support as there was considerable enthusiasm for the French chain-reaction effort among high-level government officials – Dautry and Henri Laugier, the first director of *Caisse Nationale de la Recherche Scientifique* (later to be renamed *Centre Nationale de la Recherche Scientifique* [CRNS]), and their subordinates – although there was some confusion as to its primary goal. At any rate, Joliot's team now had the heavy water. Not enough to operate a nuclear reactor but enough for preliminary experiments on homogeneous and heterogeneous mixtures of deuterium and uranium oxide. The sheet aluminium required to fabricate the canisters, was not so easily available in France. Joliot tried, with some urgency, to persuade Dautry to organize a supply of the material.

Regardless of these frustrations, Halban, Joliot and Kowarski managed to keep a scientific programme running at Ivry, measuring neutron-diffusion rates through paraffin and delayed neutrons after fission. The latter measurements brought them, unknowingly, tantalizingly close to an *experimentum crucis* of bomb production.

Raoul Dautry dispatched Allier on a mission to London, and on 10 April 1940 he arrived with a letter of introduction from Paul Montel, the director of the Franco-British mission in the *Ministère de l'Armament*, addressed to Dr H.J. Gough at the War Office. The letter detailed further collaboration between Britain and France in uranium research. Allier reported that the situation regarding heavy water in Norway was looking more ominous by the minute. He then shared the progress being made in nuclear physics by French scientists. Later, he passed over a list, drawn up by Joliot and his colleagues, of leading German scientists to be watched.

From Allier's perspective the British meeting was only moderately successful. French scientists were anxious to locate more sources of deuterium and even though the British had searched at home and abroad, there was scarcely a kilogram to show for their attempts.

CHAPTER NINE

Mad Jack

Two men dressed in dark clothes stood hunched together, whispering, on the steps to the *Oberkommando der Wehrmacht* in the blacked-out Bendlerstrasse in Berlin. Hans Oster of the *Abwehr* said quietly to the other, 'The invasion is to begin.' *Fall Gelb* (Case Yellow), the German offensive against the Low Countries and France, would start at 5.00am the following morning, 10 May 1940.

The next morning Prime Minister Neville Chamberlain who, for two years had been trying to appease Hitler, resigned. King George VI speedily sent for his First Lord of the Admiralty and after greeting him graciously, the monarch regarded his visitor for several moments: 'I suppose you do not know why I have sent for you?'

Adopting his most capricious mood Winston Churchill replied, 'Sir, I simply cannot imagine why.'

Amused, King George laughed at Churchill's dry wit. He explained he wanted him to form a government and Churchill eagerly accepted the challenge. Over the next hour, the two men discussed the bleak war. Churchill had been a politician for forty years, and without any hesitation, he plunged himself fervently into his new role with his usual vigour. Good sense told him there was nothing he could do at such short notice about the situation across the English Channel.

Exactly on schedule the *Blitzkrieg* began, advance units of an army of 2,000,000 armoured, airborne and motorized infantry troops poured across the borders of Holland, Belgium and Luxembourg. At the same time, hundreds of *Luftwaffe* Stuka dive-bombers and low-level bombers swept in over airfields and communication centres in northern France.

Long before dawn, 150 miles of the borders of Holland and Belgium were aflame. In a single day, the armies under General von Bock broke through all the outer lines of the Dutch defences. It was swift and devastating. Four days later, the Commander-in-Chief of the Dutch forces still holding The Hague ordered a general ceasefire.

Unknown to the French and the British, the German attack through the Low Countries was only a feint. Army Group A, commanded by General Karl Rudolf Gerd von Rundstedt, was set to deliver a deadly blow through the Ardennes Forest in southern Belgium, spearheaded by 1,806 tanks and supported by 325 Stuka dive-bombers. They crossed the Meuse and were now forging their way through the French countryside. Three brigades of French tanks tried to halt the advance but were easily defeated. The following day, the first German assault boats crossed the river Meuse into France between Namul and Mezieres.

Early in the morning of Saturday 15 May, Churchill, in his sleeping quarters at Admiralty House, received a telephone call from the French minister, Paul Reynaud. The clearly distraught man blurted out, 'We've been defeated,' in clear English. 'The front is broken near Sedan, they're pouring through in great numbers with tanks and armoured cars.' He was beside himself. Churchill, now fully-awake, managed to say, 'surely it cannot have happened so soon.' He then tried to pacify the man, he reminded him of the dark days in 1918 when all turned out well in the end. But Reynaud remained distraught, ending as he had begun: 'We are defeated; we have lost the battle.'

In the spring of 1940 the French police urged the Earl, after he had been attacked in a pro-Fascist newspaper, to accept an official bodyguard. Thanking them for their interest in his wellbeing Jack declined the offer. Instead of relying on someone else to look after him he acquired two of the largest pistols he could find and wore them with great aplomb, christening them 'Oscar' and 'Genevieve'. He also hired his own bodyguard.

'Mad' Jack, the nickname given to him because of his approach to his mission, drove around the streets of Paris at break-neck speed in a large open car, paying unexpected calls on jewellers and bankers. By his side was his trusty bodyguard, his 'Man Friday', in the shape of a stocky, ex-sailor with battle scars and a fearsome reputation that followed him as a knife-fighting specialist. Their arrivals and departures were as good as any theatrical routine one would find anywhere in the world. Whenever they arrived at a destination the sailor was first to step onto the street or into a café. He would glance up and down, around and about, a few times and when he was certain it was all clear, he would shout: 'Okay, Monsieur Jacques, allons!' and Jack would appear in his black, wide-brimmed fedora. An English officer stationed in Paris at the time commented that you risked your life if you tried to see Jack: 'his Man Friday certainly had a deep seated persecution complex as far as Jack was concerned, and you could not reason with the fellow because he did not seem to understand any of the known languages.'

Jack and 'Man Friday' became an inseparable pair. Jack's wayward spirit would not, could not, be tamed by the dreary middle-class conventions of the Baldwin-Chamberlain era. He was a typical Englishman in that he was so untypical in every respect. His love of England ran surprisingly deep, burning like a red hot flame inside him, like a Drake or Raleigh. He wanted to amass fortune and success and lay them down at the feet of his second love – his homeland. The French government conceded and agreed wholeheartedly with him that certain key scientists should go to Bordeaux to await *'le Comte de Suffolk et Berkshire'*.

Late morning on 15 March, after consulting with Major Golding, Jack reached the conclusion that the situation was sufficiently grave enough for them to proceed to Bordeaux. They reported to the *Ministère de l'Armament* at 56 Rue du Commandant Arnould where they assisted in a meeting with Dautry. In view of the gravity of the situation, Dautry declared he would try his utmost to save everything he could from the clutches of the Germans. There would be two missions composed of General Martignon and General Blanchard travelling to the USA.

During the course of the conversation, Dautry decided that the MoS in London was in dire need of technicians, but since telephone and postal communication were in a state of utter chaos there was no possible chance of confirming this, so he chose to proceed on his own initiative. Jack requested all armament experts and scientists Dautry could spare, and to this he agreed willingly, at the same time offering them as many machine tools as they could take away on a ship. Dautry then instructed Captain Henri Bichelonne, his *Chef du Cabinet Technique*, to smooth the process and hasten arrangements to the best of his ability.

That Sunday, Dautry telephoned Joliot and ordered him to remove the canisters locked in the cellars of the Collège de France, as fast as humanly possible, and take them to a place of safety. Their research had come to an abrupt end. When he had finished speaking to Dautry, Joliot telephoned Henri Moureu, his trusted friend and sub-director of the chemistry section of the *Collège de France* laboratory.

'Henri, you must come immediately,' he instructed.

Moureu lost no time, and the two men sat down to talk. Dautry impressed on him that the heavy water must never fall into German hands. It had to be evacuated to some safe place in the centre of France.

'I give you the job,' said Joliot simply, 'absolute secrecy. You have a free hand.'

Moureu made numerous telephone calls and found that a branch of the *Banque de France* at Clermont-Ferrand, 200 miles to the south, was willing to store the unexplained containers in the vault. People had already begun to flee Paris in large numbers and time was of an essence. Moureu had the twenty-six containers loaded onto a lorry the same evening, and he left for the south at around midnight. On Dautry's suggestion, Moureu was joined by Halban, their mission papers authorized Moureu to carry arms.

However, that Sunday evening the Reynaud cabinet fell and the acts signed by Dautry were null and void. At 2.30am, Paul Reynaud was abruptly awakened with news that the Germans were rapidly advancing and that the government must prepare to evacuate Paris. Churchill decided to fly to Paris to pay a visit to Quay d'Orsay, the French Ministry of Foreign Affairs, where he found utter dejection on everybody's faces. Already they were burning files.

Despite these events, Jack and Major Golding, aided by Captain Bichelone, carried on amassing as many armament experts and scientists as they could possibly find amid the turmoil, and commenced loading machine tools onto a lorry. Frustratingly, they were met with nothing but the most obstructive and defeatist attitude from the higher members of the Bordeaux Government. Nonetheless, demands made to Marshal Pétain by Jack in his most authoritative manner allowed them to extract his permission to embark the technicians and scientists. He then set about locating the SS *Broompark*, the ship which was to be made available through a Mr Irving, the Commercial Attaché at the British Embassy.

In England, Churchill requested Neville Chamberlain to study the problems which would arise if it became necessary to withdraw the British Expeditionary Forces (BEF) from France.

Moureu and Halban arrived in Clermont-Ferrand at 5:00am on 17 May, and 'Product Z', the codename for their secret cargo, was manhandled into the bank vault. Moureu returned to Paris immediately while Halban continued on to nearby Mont Dore, a sleepy little place except for the fact that some members of the French cabinet were already installing themselves in the town. When he arrived, Halban's Leipzig accent and general demeanour sparked a small frisson of suspicion in the mayor of the town, a former general, but fortunately nothing happened.

Halban began setting up an improvised laboratory in a villa on Rue Étienne Dollet in Clermont-Ferrand. Confidently believing that a victorious military counter-offensive would halt the advancing German forces to the north as had happened under Marshal Pétain in 1914; it was taken for granted that Joliot's team would continue its research in this quiet retreat. The University of Strasbourg also had similar plans to relocate to Clermont-Ferrand, a place which would eventually become an important centre of the French Resistance.

Riom prison later acquired fame as the place where Daladier and Reynaud were imprisoned until they were brought before the Supreme Court of Justice at Riom near the end of 1941, accused by the Vichy Government of having inadequately prepared the country for war.

The military situation worsened by the hour and the local bank manager was growing more and more agitated, ranting on about them taking 'Product Z' out of his vault. Moureu stepped in, and then the minister himself. It was eventually moved – first to the women's prison in Mont Dore then to the Central Prison in Riom, near Clermont-Ferrand, where the containers were hidden in an isolated cell reserved for dangerous criminals.

The following day nine Panzer divisions swept towards Amiens and Abbeville. Because of the military disaster unfolding in France, the supreme commander was dismissed and Weygand was recalled from Syria to replace him, which he did, the next day. At the War Office in Great Britain, they discussed the probability of evacuating their troops from France, but still with no great sense of urgency. The Ministry of Shipping felt there was plenty of time to assemble the number of vessels that might be needed. The ports of Calais, Boulogne and Dunkirk would all be used. There were three phases to their plan: 20 May, all 'useless mouths' would be shipped out at a rate of 2,000 a day; 22 May, some 150,000 service personnel would leave, followed by the hazardous evacuation of the very large military force.

On 20 May, two divisions of the XIX Corps commanded by General Heinz Guderion began rolling west from Péronne. By 10.00am, they were advancing through the town of Albert where a party of untrained English territorials tried to hold them back with a barricade of cardboard boxes. The following day, in Great Britain, things were rapidly changing – the emergency evacuation of a very large force now gained top priority. Two days later everyone knew the drill by heart – be quick and be flexible. Everything that could float would be used.

On 23 May, Churchill again contacted Reynaud, informing him of the British intention to evacuate and strongly urged him to issue a corresponding order, but because French communications were badly disrupted, vital messages were delayed, not sent, or were missed completely. Operation Dynamo was planned to commence on 26 May at 18.57pm. Churchill flew to Paris and met Maxime Weygand. His first impression of the man was one of energy and bounce; like a rubber ball. Weygand's thinking paralleled Churchill's own. The Frenchman wanted eight divisions from the BEF and the French First Army, with the Belgian cavalry on the right, to strike southwest the next day. That evening Churchill cabled Gort his enthusiastic approval. Henry Pownall's response was, 'the man is mad,' when the message reached General Lord Gort's command post on the morning of 23 May because the situation was worse than ever.

On 26 May 1940, the Germans broke through Calais-Nord, splitting up the defenders into two pockets of resistance. The next day disturbing news reached the French: the British were considering evacuating with or without the French. The following day General Weygand was first told of the British plan even though, on 23 May, orders had been sent. To add to the chaos that abounded, on the 27 May, *Luftwaffe* pilots were given a massive shock, they no longer had control of the skies – suddenly large numbers of RAF Hurricanes and Spitfires began a furious defence – a completely new situation to the German pilots.

When General Gort was told of the British evacuation plan, he was horrified. He had not heard anything, mainly because either Weygand had not passed it on to him or it had been lost. General Blanchard decided to leave the army in the Lille area, which left Gort exasperated beyond belief. Finally, Belgium surrendered unconditionally on 28 May. General Blanchard remained completely disillusioned with the British.

During the day and night of 28 May, some 17,804 were evacuated, twice as many as the day before, and the following day saw over 47,000 men taken off the beach, although only 655 were French. Bad weather followed, but between 31 May and 1 June the weather became fine and evacuation went well. Apart from his own men, Churchill wanted as many French troops out as soon as possible.

The next day blew in bright and clear when Churchill flew to Paris with a hope of clearing up any misunderstandings with the French. He met with Pétain and Weygand: they sat on one side of the table, the British on the other. Weygand was not averse to showing his anger, unhappy that the British had not taken off more French from Dunkirk. Churchill calmly stated that equal numbers of men were to be recovered. They all waited while Weygand made a decision.

On 3 June, the *Luftwaffe* made plans to bomb Paris. The Germans were by now two miles from Dunkirk. Operation Dynamo, the 'Miracle of Dunkirk' had come to an end. A total of 338,226 fighting men had been evacuated. The next day the Germans captured Dunkirk and the Nazi swastika flew over Paris in the mid-morning breeze. Hitler ordered the destruction of the Royal Air Force, a prelude to the invasion of Great Britain, thinking it would only take four days to achieve his goal. Great Britain suffered one of its worst military disasters in history, standing alone in the fight against the military might of German that was now deployed along the English Channel coast in France, Belgium and the Netherlands. Churchill confided in an aide nearby his feelings on the situation:

'If they come, we'll have to hit them over the head with bottles! That's all we've got to fight with!'

Jack Howard was very much aware of Operation Dynamo, making it imperative he succeed in his mission. The French, too, were understandably concerned about the evacuation – British soldiers and civilians were being evacuated but what about the French? The Admiralty simply assumed that British troops would be taken off in British ships and French troops in French ships, each of the allies conducting their own retreat to the coast, but the French military, at that time, were not even thinking about evacuation. On May 27, they finally faced reality when the British were already leaving.

In Paris, time was passing faster than a speeding bullet. The French government had departed the city to join the flood of refugees blocking up all roads leading south. At the *Collège de France*, Joliot and Moureu, practically the only ones left, were preparing to leave after Paris had been declared an open city. On 11 June, the last load of scientific equipment, including electroscopes, ionization chambers, galvanometers, even lead bricks, left by lorry for Clermont-Ferrand. Technical documents were destroyed. Joliot and his wife Irène also left for Clermont-Ferrand in their Peugeot 402 motorcar taking with them platinum, some gold, and the gram of radium given to Marie Curie by the Women of America – all of which was placed on the back seat in order to minimize any possible danger from radiation. Moureu followed close behind in his own vehicle. The following day the Germans crossed the Marne at Chateau-Thièrry, some 50 miles distant.

Kowarski, having sent his wife and 4-year-old daughter to Clermont-Ferrand by train, set off for the south with a convoy of trucks loaded with the bulk of the consignment, including the deuterium oxide. They met up with Halban in Clermont-Ferrand. Their orders were short and to the point – go to England in a ship allocated to a Lord Suffolk who had been given the use of it to evacuate scientists and material destined for Great Britain. The two scientists were to put themselves and the heavy water at the disposal of British authorities and observe absolute secrecy.

The sky was black, darkened by smoke rising from blazing fuel tanks along the Seine all the way to Rouen. Two days later, German troops goose stepped down the Champs Élysées as Nazi swastika flags were hoisted on the Arc de Triomphe and Eiffel Tower. Indeed, a sad day in the history of France.

The Joliot-Curies joined Halban and Kowarski at Clermont-Ferrand on or about 6 June. Their very make-shift laboratory was up and running, there was running water and some equipment which had been cleaned by army engineers. On the 16 June, they awoke to a beautiful clear Sunday, feeling they deserved a small lunch in honour of what they had been through. Having just strolled into town and sat down in front of a small café to have breakfast, a Simca motorcar drew up outside and out stepped Allier who hastily took Joliot aside. Joliot then called for Moureu to join them. The Allied armies were in full retreat and the government had ordered that the heavy water be sent to Bordeaux and then on to Great Britain.

Allier's orders called for Halban, Kowarski and Joliot to accompany the heavy water. Joliot agreed that his companions should go, although he could not reach a decision on his own actions. Events in Paris had escalated much faster than Joliot could have predicted. That evening

Paul Reynaud and his cabinet resigned and his successor, Marshal Pétain, asked Hitler for an armistice. Raoul Dautry had already fled with the remnants of the Third Republic to Bordeaux and then on to Provence.

The following day, Allier and Halban returned to the prison in Riom. The governor was in two minds whether to hand over the heavy water but soon came to a quick decision when Allier drew his revolver and threatened to shoot him. He acceded, and ordered prisoners serving life sentences to carry the containers out of the cell to the waiting vehicle. Once completed, Halban and Kowarski sped towards Bordeaux as fast as their vehicles could take them with their heavy load of wives, children, and baggage. They carried with them a multi-stamped pass to forestall any trouble. Their trip was difficult as they had to cross countless north-south roads which were congested with evacuees from Paris.

They arrived in the dead of night and were greeted by Jean Bichelonne, Dautry's chief-of-staff. He tore a sheet of paper from a schoolbook lying on the ground and scribbled an order for the party to board the SS *Broompark* that was moored in the estuary near to Bordeaux docks. When they arrived, to their utter surprise, they were welcomed by a very unlikely-looking character of dubious appearance who would, they were told, escort them and their varied cargo across the English Channel.

CHAPTER TEN

Escape

One of Raoul Dautry's last acts before the Reynaud cabinet fell was to scribble a few words of recommendation on the back of one of his visiting cards and hand it to the Earl of Suffolk. It would provide him with all the authority necessary to cajole or threaten difficult bureaucrats when they tried to thwart him. Mayors and industrialists eventually ended up surrendering their property to him and obeying his orders.

More often than not the Earl's persuasive charms usually worked, but if the visiting card or his charisma failed to achieve his expectations he resorted to using the traditional method of the ancient buccaneering pirate – his two most trusted and valued friends – 'Oscar' and 'Genevieve', the automatic pistols he kept in his shoulder holster and could fire with deadly effect. His brother Greville had seen him on several occasions shoot a sixpence off a tree trunk at 25yds, firing from the hip. France, apart from feeding Jack's love of adventure, gave him the opportunity to revel in giving public demonstrations of his ability to use them. One of the most spectacular was in front of the Dôme café, when he shot the necks off six champagne bottles from ten paces. Staying longer than he should have to entertain the outdoor café patrons he threw small saucers, on which drinks were served, into the air and shattered them as they dropped.

As France fell no one in England had heard from the Earl for some time, due to the fact that he was kept extremely busy gathering up a most bizarre collection of baggage – one being the most closely guarded secrets of the war. In the beginning when it had been requested that Jack travel to Paris to secure certain vital French patents for the British Government, he felt he had not been given much of a job but he came to realize it had given him an excellent excuse and opportunity to sample France's exquisite culture, especially Montmartre and the Left Bank.

He had been informed that large stocks of diamonds had arrived in Paris from Antwerp, Brussels and Amsterdam, and discovered where the bankers were hiding their precious jewels. He also realized they had every intention of keeping them in Paris.

After Germany attacked Poland during 'The Phoney War', Great Britain had refused to supply Belgium with industrial diamonds in case they fell into enemy hands, so they initiated control agencies. In Amsterdam, Antwerp and New York similar controls had also to be established. The British had contractually promised to prioritize supply to Antwerp but at the onset of war they were no longer bound by the agreement. For the Diamond Corporation (Dicorp) which Forminiere and Beceka, *Société Minière du Beceka*, the Belgian company later known as Sibecka were contracted to, it meant the contract was broken. De Beers feared it would be very difficult to reinstate the contract in its original form. Now Beceka could develop the mining of unlimited quantities of industrial diamonds.

They were assisted by specialists from the sector who checked all deliveries from London before they reached the client. In Belgium, that was the Committee to Protect the Diamond Trade and Industry, located in the offices of the *Diamantklub* in Pelikaanstraat, Antwerp.

Dicorp demanded serious safety mechanisms and so, from September 1939, technical committees were established. The director of the Committee to Protect the Diamond Trade and Industry in Belgium was Félicien Cattier. Paul Timbal became vice president, John C. Williams was head of administration and Antonius Oldenburg was elected *chef du bureau* – all three were co-workers of the Antwerp Diamond Bank (ADB).

Desperate Jewish diamond merchants lobbied van Antwerpen to help them escape from the Germans but alas, on 19 June 1940, when the news of the Franco-German armistice broke, it became clear to them they had to look elsewhere for help, and they chose Great Britain.

When bankers remained stubborn and would not comply, it was as though a red rag had been waved in front of Jack's face. The diamonds were going back to England for safekeeping come hell or high water.

Jack and 'Man Friday' frantically travelled the streets in his motorcar collecting untold wealth in the shape of bags filled with diamonds and other valuables. And if the vaults did not open quickly enough he invited a quick reaction from the staff by showing them his pistols. When arguments arose, Jack simply carried the bags out of the open bank vaults while his bodyguard kept personnel at bay. Some important Paris jewellers did accept his offer to evacuate their stock to England, and his collection increased by substantial voluntary contributions. In every instant he left a receipt.

Knowing full well the Germans were only a few steps behind, Jack toured laboratories searching for scientists, research data, and rare chemicals, which had been transferred to Paris from famous laboratories in occupied countries. He visited factories for machine specifications, designs and armaments, and also the offices of the 'boffins' to pick up technical secrets, all of which would be of immense importance to the Germans. Within a few hours he had managed to stockpile all valuable papers in his motorcar. He completed his final round up with a number of eminent French scientists with whom he had been working and sent most of them off to Bordeaux, assuring their anxieties that he had arranged passage for them to England. The others he directed to Bayonne and were to remain hidden until a ship came to collect them.

Early on 10 June, Major Golding and Miss Nicolle left Paris by the Porte de Versailles, just an hour before the arrival of the Germans. It was slow progress and they were continually caught up in air raids and military convoys. The next day they carried on in their car to Orleans passing refugees and vehicles clogging the roads while Major Golding shouted at people to move out of the way. They travelled on towards Tours and the British Consulate, and found food and rooms at the Hotel Univers.

After a good night's sleep they continued their journey via Bourges to Mont Dore. On Wednesday 12 May, Major Golding, exhausted from all the driving and the stress, and Miss Nicolle rested for the night in a Chateaux run by monks. On Saturday 15 June, the situation was alarming: Paris was now occupied by the Germans so they hurriedly left for Bordeaux.

For days and nights the Earl, with Beryl in the passenger seat and the Gorilla sitting behind Jack perched high on an unbelievable fortune, made a slow tortuous journey along the teeming highway massed with panic-stricken people. People ran hither and thither, desperate to

86

leave, terrified and crying, with harried looks etched deeply in their faces. Children clung to their parents' limbs and each human being clung tightly onto their slipping sanity and meagre possessions. Baby carriages were stuffed with as much of their belongings as they could hold, as well as their babies. Rough sacks and battered suitcases were being dragged along by exhausted people wearing as many clothes as possible, using their cases for their personal belongings which would, hopefully, fetch money. The Germans were only hours away.

More than once Jack and his group only just managed to evade roadblocks set up for him by the Gestapo who were in hot pursuit. They backtracked and drove through abandoned fields and made their way to Bordeaux, a distance of 496km from Paris, while the mad ex-sailor kept continual watch for German scouting parties and patrolling aircraft. All roads, it seemed, were jammed with distressed people. It was often necessary for Jack, who was still wearing his black fedora, and his teeth still clenching a long cigarette holder, to walk in front of the car to clear the way through the misery by waving his pistols high in the air and shouting as loud as he could in French while Beryl drove with intense concentration, her shoulders hunched tightly over the steering wheel. The first day's travel took them to Orléans. Only 121km stood between them and the Gestapo.

They slept in the car, taking turns to stand guard. On the second night they travelled a distance of 98km to Tours after spending the whole day being harried by German aircraft and, on one occasion, quickly driving off-road through open fields in order to hide their car in farm buildings as the *Luftwaffe* patrolled the skies overhead. On Wednesday 12 June, Major Golding and Miss Nicolle caught up with Jack and Beryl in Bourboulle. They stopped to see how the Earl was getting on, only to find that his car had been taken from him and Jack raging and ranting at French incompetence. Major Golding managed to save the day by driving them all back to Mont Dore to find the Earl a lorry, which they rescued from a back street. Jack piled in his luggage, along with Beryl and the sailor, then headed off to Bordeaux.

In Tours, they found themselves in the middle of a heavy air raid and spent precious time hiding in a bombed-out building along with local people. While listening to the radio they heard disturbing news – German troops had entered Paris. It was Friday, 14 June 1940.

The Germans could so easily overtake them. It was then Jack made the decision that in order to arrive as quickly as possible at their destination, they would travel by both day and night. They made a large detour, almost 423km, taking them south, almost to Toulouse.

A French patriot who arrived in London months later revealed that it was probably this manoeuvre that saved them from capture, because as soon as the Germans arrived in Paris they were immediately informed of the Earl's activities by French quislings. The enemy tried to intercept the group, and for days all vehicles travelling south from Tours were stopped and thoroughly searched. They arrived in Bordeaux at 2.00am on Sunday 16 June. On reaching the city, Jack changed his name to Charles Henri because his suspicious mind knew the enemy would try everything in their power to recover his precious cargo. He needed to conceal his identity until he left them far behind.

They city of Bordeaux was packed with refugees. Food and water was scarce and its population had swollen from 300,000 to 900,000. Millionaires who had hurriedly left their villas in Paris a week before were camping out, starving and smelling from days without washing, in the public square. There were ladies intent on saving themselves and their precious pet dogs along with poor artisans bent double under the weight of their meagre belongings, all trudging along the roadside, desperate to put distance between themselves and the Germans. Only one thing was on people's collective minds – escape. Civic authority had given way to martial law, and General Maxime Weygand was now in command of the city.

Jack parked the lorry outside the British Consulate and asked a harassed official where one could hide a few diamonds and other valuables. He received no answer which irritated him greatly. The best thing to do, he decided, was to park in a deserted side street and sleep in the car.

The following day they went searching for Weygand to enquire about the ship, because Jack was not sure whether the ship the British government was sending had arrived. He forced his way, none too gently, past protesting sentries and struggling humanity into the presence of a distasteful-looking soldier who appeared to list Englishmen among his aversions. Jack found, without his help, who he was searching for and began commiserating with them on their defeat. The grating voice and bushy moustached Marshall Pétain was also present. Jack told them he needed a ship to get to England, but it did not quite work out the way he planned. Weygand instantly took a great dislike to the Englishman confronting him with his demands. The pompous general told him he was opposed to any French scientist leaving France, but he could not care less if any Englishmen got away. Barely hiding his distain, he declared coldly: 'I prefer Hitlerism to French Socialism,' while Pétain nodded in sycophantic agreement in the background.

Reporting on this scene later, the Earl said, 'I was never so disgusted and angry in my life. That just goes to show what they were, the rats. Imagine Englishmen welcoming an invader! I did a thing I never did before – I gave them the raspberry! I would not take their help even if they wanted to give it to me.' The two French officers were already scheming with the enemy who were less than 160km away. Jack decided there and then it was best to keep secret the diamonds and chemicals he was transporting in case they were confiscated.

A German radio commentator, after hearing news of Jack's escapades, referred to him as, 'The Earl of Suffolk who liked to hide his true activities behind pistol acrobatics in Paris cafes.'

CHAPTER ELEVEN

Haste

Source notes on our *'Flight from France'*
(Marguerite Nicolle).

Much to his relief Jack found Major Golding and Marguerite Nicolle waiting for him at the docks. They, too, had survived their arduous journey.

On arrival at the docks the Gorilla bid his fond farewells to the Earl and disappeared into the crowd. The city was in absolute black-out though no one could understand why. They had difficulty finding the Prefecture, but were eventually guided there except they were refused entry on their first attempt. On their second attempt only Major Golding was allowed to enter. He returned later with letters finally enabling them to check-in at the Chapon Fin Hotel. It was around 3:00am and they were utterly exhausted. The next day, Miss Nicolle was given the near impossible task of finding a large suitcase for the Earl in a town seething in turmoil. After rushing madly from shop to shop she, at last, succeeded.

Jack cashed in a personal cheque at the British Consulate for £1,000 and set about finding a French skipper willing to be bribed into taking them and their cargo back to England or, failing that, to gather together a crew and seize one of the ships in the harbour. Haste was the word of the hour. Jack had been promised the SS *Broompark* but there was no sign of the ship.

For three days, Jack wandered the docks dressed as a French sailor. In and out of waterfront bars, appearing more haggard by the minute, he tried desperately to find a ship that would get them out of this hell. He did, however, manage to arrange a deal with the skipper of a small vessel secretly embarking on a similar voyage. But before the planned date the vessel had struck a mine in the harbour entrance and was blown to smithereens. Everything that could float had already been sent to ports in the south of England. By this time the German troops were less than 160km away at La Rochelle.

Finally, not knowing what else to do and throwing all caution to the wind, he took into his confidence a French Admiral who became captivated by his tale; so enthralled was he that he loaned him a lorry, some Bren and Lewis guns, rifles and hand grenades and a naval crew. Quite by chance Jack and Major Golding discovered some 700 tons of recently delivered US-supplied heavy-machine tools that had been left in railway wagons in the quay area; by arrangement with the Consulate and helped by the French, they loaded them onboard the lorry taking up precious time.

On the last day, an employee of the Ministry of Aircraft Production arrived with two light trucks containing special machine tools which had been loaned to the French. With no time to waste Jack and Golding drove the lorry at a hazardous speed to the small port of Bayonne where they left what they could not take onboard ship, issuing orders to the French scientists who were already there not to panic and remain hidden, with Jack promising to send a ship for them.

On Sunday 16 June, the SS *Broompark*, a coal-fired steamer of 5,136 tons, built by J & J Denholm Ltd., Glasgow, flying the British ensign sailed slowly up the estuary. To Jack, the ship's presence was like the first sightings of the albatross that appeared before the dazed eyes of the shipwrecked mariner. Without any delay and with the help of Mr Irving, the Commercial Attaché, he took command of the situation, and once the captain realized that the Gestapo were only a few hours away, there was a sudden urgency to load the ship and depart. Captain Paulsen walked to the consulate and was introduced to Mr Irving who in turn introduced him to the Earl and Major Golding. Paulsen seemed very impressed with the fact that Jack Howard had once been an apprentice on the *Mount Stewart*.

The leaders of the mission boarded at 11.30pm that night. Beryl Morden and Marguerite Nicolle were shown to their temporary quarters, and all the women passengers were told not to leave the ship. Joliot and Moureu had also arrived in Bordeaux after leaving Joliot's wife and children behind in Clairvivre, as she was sick with tuberculosis and waiting to be admitted into a sanatorium.

First impressions are always the most vivid and this was true of Joliot and Moureu's initial encounter with a tall heavy set, dark haired, bearded man standing before them on the dock wearing an impatient expression on his face. Dressed in a grubby shirt, with rolled-up sleeves showing his bare arms covered in tattoos, the man's face carried the swarthiness of an Italian and the edgy demeanour of a Mafioso. He wore two revolvers in a shoulder holster and was impatiently swinging a heavy hunting crop by his thigh. This man, they were told, was the legendary 34-year-old 20th Earl of Suffolk & Berkshire who was fully aware of the importance of the twenty-six containers of heavy water being loaded on the ship.

By the evening of Tuesday, 17th June, it was becoming very apparent to the scientists that their presence in Bordeaux was known to fifth columnists as there had been an unsuccessful attempt to bomb the ship; whether they had been the target or not, it was unsafe to remain in port. With this in mind, they kept loading machine tools until 5.00am on the Wednesday morning when they decided, for the safety of all present, it would be wise to depart. Exclusive of the cargo of machine tools and eminent scientists and armament specialists, Jack had been entrusted by Mr Irving to take with him a parcel containing diamonds worth £3,000,000, together with three gentlemen in whose custody this consignment was placed. The diamonds were highly sought after by the Ministry of Economic Warfare.

If Joliot had boarded the ship, he most probably would have been detained and ended up in England along with Halban and Kowarski. He could easily have gone to the USA with the other French scientists and played a relatively greater role, than actually was the case, in the wartime development of the atomic bomb project

Joliot was frantic, he had no idea what to do, and when he and Moureu ran into Jack, the Earl grabbed hold of Joliot's arm and attempted to pressure him into accompanying him to England, promising he would personally look after Joliot's wife and children. Joliot impatiently shook him off saying very little in reply, and left in search of Halban and Kowarski, desiring one last meeting with his colleagues before returning to Clermont-Ferrand. But the ship was not where he thought it was. He paced up and down the wharf searching for it, panic all the while building inside of him but still he could not see the ship. The *Broompark* had been moved to a safer berth south on the Gironde after an air raid earlier that day.

An utterly exhausted and dejected Joliot sat down on a packing case and discussed his predicament with Moureu. He told his friend that

France and French science needed him more than ever before, also that his children and his wife needed to be considered and therefore had decided that he was going to remain on French soil.

Meanwile, Halban and Kowarski, onboard the SS *Broompark*, repeatedly implored Jack to give them permission to go ashore for one last talk with Joliot. Jack, feeling time slipping through his fingers, answered it was up to the captain but permission would probably be denied as the ship was preparing to sail.

Paul Timbal's journey, which came to an end on Bordeaux docks, had been every bit as arduous as Jack's and the scientists. Like so many others, Timbal scarcely believed the French army could be defeated. The French presumed the Germans would never cross the Meuse, nor did they realize the *Luftwaffe* could act as flying artillery. When the French, Belgian and British armies were cut off and unable to be supplied, all that was left for the British and the French to do was to make a hasty retreat towards Dunkirk. Throughout this time, Paul Timbal, a patriotic man, had faith in the Allied armies. He had been optimistic that Paris would be safe, but over time his confidence had eroded.

At the beginning of the war, a large number of the Antwerp Diamond Bank's clients withdrew their cash and purchased diamonds which added to the large stockpile of diamonds already in the vaults of the ADB after Germany bombed Warsaw. Paul Timbal, Managing Director of the Antwerp Diamond Bank, relieved of his duty to report for military service, foresaw the diamonds were not safe and believed the best place for them would be at the National Bank of Belgium in Brussels. He purchased a battered old lorry, which rarely went faster than 30kph, and loaded the diamonds onboard. He drove his Panhard motorcar in front of the vehicle in order to hear any enemy aircraft, while four armed bank employees travelled in the back of the lorry. They made good time to the Willebroek canal before enemy aircraft caught up with them, causing everyone some very tense moments. Luck was with them because the only minor damage they sustained was a small amount of damage to the bodywork of the lorry. After an arduous journey they reached Brussels.

On 12 May, Timbal met with the representatives of the *Générale, Banque de Bruxelles*, and *Kredietbank* to discuss the destiny of foreign stocks, shares and bonds held by Belgian banks, and what would happen if they fell into Germans hands. One suggestion was to stamp all securities with the words 'Belgian Property', but that was thought to be pointless. Paul Timbal knew the diamonds were special and could not be destroyed and that no duplicates could be made. The only alternative was to take them to Paris to the *Banque Transatlantique*, one of ADB's shareholders. Because the diamonds would be crossing the border, Timbal had to contact the Minister of Foreign Affairs who gave his agreement as long as he was accompanied by an official: André van Campenhout, head of the ministry's legal department. Each of them carried a revolver, and safe within Timbal's jacket pocket was a letter of safe conduct from the French Embassy. The various official stampings would open any door they needed in the coming weeks.

They drove south with their precious load amongst nightmarishly heavy traffic and columns of refugees. Water shortage was everywhere, making their boiling hot journey an absolute nightmare. They passed frightened people in cars with mattresses tied on top in an effort to protect them from strafing attacks by the *Luftwaffe*. Timbal's large Panhard motorcar carried them through the back lanes through farming countryside, kilometre after kilometer, while they constantly scanned the sky for enemy aircraft. The only high point of their trip was to stay in expensive hotels courtesy of considerable financial resources at Timbal's disposal, but even with the limited money available there were only the barest of necessities.

They reached Compiègne but could go no further due to the blackout that night. An empty cell in the local police station was found for the diamonds once Timbal produced his official letter. The cell was closely guarded by two policemen who spent the night playing the French card game Belote. Meanwhile, Timbal and van Campenhout lodged overnight in a luxurious nineteenth century hotel. During the dangerous days ahead, Paul Timbal or van Campenhout remained in the car while the other went out searching for food and water. Come what may, the car and the diamonds would never be left unguarded.

The following day they reached Paris and found the *Banque Transatlantique* without any mishap. An exhausted, grateful Paul Timbal handed over the diamonds. At that point, Timbal still planned to organize the diamond trade from Paris, believing the city would always be safe. But before driving back to Belgium, he went south to spend a few restful days with his wife wife, Barbro de Jounge, and his very young twins in Cannes. He had become so attached to his Panhard that he often found himself speaking out loud to it, his lengthy trips reminding him of the intimate relationship between man and horse.

Heavy rain clouds gathered on the horizon. Timbal thought of Cannes and how close it was to Italy and Mussolini. He and his family would have to leave soon; he would take them further inland, near Languedoc-Roussillon.

During the middle of May, he made his way back to Paris where he received bad news from the front. The French army had scattered and people were panicking. The *Banque Transatlantique* decided to transfer the diamonds to Cognac.

Timbal rapidly drove the 402km to Cognac, arriving on 20 May to a deserted town. Five days later, he was granted an unlimited extension of his military leave to organize the diamond situation. He now understood how hopeless his idea to set up a diamond centre had become in a country about to be occupied. The Belgians capitulated on 28 May which did nothing for his confidence because, like every other Belgian, he was met with hostile reactions from many French people. Paul Reynaud called the surrender by King Leopold III a cowardly act. Affected by the defeat, Timbal returned to Paris.

At the beginning of June, the British Consul General in Bordeaux asked him to travel to London for talks with the British government about the future of the diamond market. On 8 June, after receiving permission to leave from the Belgian government, Timbal was flown to London in a military aircraft from an emergency airfield. Setting up of the diamond industry in Great Britain was already being discussed by the chairman of De Beers and Ernest Oppenheimer. Paul Timbal was given the task of negotiating with the Belgian government, which by now had fled to France, how to ship the diamonds to England. On 13 June, while waiting for his flight back to France, Ernest Oppenheimer telephoned him to say he had approval from higher authority to take the action they had discussed. Oppenheimer also authorized Timbal to officially advise the Belgian government of the British proposal.

Timbal flew back to France, again in a military aircraft. On 14 June, while having lunch at Poitiers with the Minister of Foreign Affairs, who looked far from happy and distant throughout their meal, Timbal was told that the French government was considering a negotiated surrender to the Germans. That night Paul found it very difficult to sleep.

Paris was going to fall. An official car was placed at the disposal of Paul and van Campenhout; they set off for Tours, but the roads were filled with fleeing refugees so that the car had to be abandoned. On foot they saw a French military lorry pointing in the direction of Tours. Inside the vehicle were four very drunk French sailors lying on many bottles of 1928 Pommery Grenot champagne (this champagne would later be used onboard the SS *Broompark* as a cure for seasickness).

Panic was rife and the *Banque Transatlantique* refused to return the diamonds because they thought the French army would prevail. Even Charles van Antwerpen, president of the *Diamantklub*, would not sign them over for the very same reason, while Reynaud still believed in victory. Antwerpen stuck to his guns because he was certain the Belgian was seeking to profit from transferring the diamonds to England. They almost came to blows. Luckily, help arrived in the guise of Mr van Campenhout. At last, Paul Timbal had the diamonds and a written agreement from the Pierlot and British government in his hands.

The Belgian government, having arrived, finally, in Bordeaux, met with an exhausted, pale and unshaven Timbal at the Belgian Consulate. Time was running out. It was Tuesday 18 June. He had been outside the Consulate, guarded by British soldiers, for hours waiting for it to open at 8.30am. British citizens came and went but he was refused entry. At around 10.00am, a French naval lieutenant, who served under Admiral Darlan, arrived and Timbal was shown inside where he was told to wait for the attaché, Mr Irving. Timbal's frustration mounted by the minute and he became very uncertain as to whether he and his family, who were waiting in a taxi outside, would be allowed to leave Bordeaux. Finally, an hour later, Mr Irving appeared and told Timbal the SS *Broompark* was still in port, complete with the diamonds and van Campenhout, and was waiting at the docks for him. With his passport stamped and embarkation papers for five people, he and his family thankfully boarded the SS *Broompark*.

Mr Irving explained to Timbal that he and his family would have to sleep on the metal deck when on the ship, and suggested he buy pillows and also food for five days. Before leaving Mr Irving, Timbal earnestly requested he provide embarkation papers for all the diamond people arriving from Paris, and enquired as to why the diamonds had been placed on a cargo ship rather than a destroyer or cruiser. The destroyer, he was told, was at the disposal of the Ambassador but he was not yet ready to leave France. Timbal would, however, be provided with a British military guard and an anti-submarine gun, and anti-aircraft machine guns for the trip back to England.

CHAPTER TWELVE

Infested Waters

On the way to the ship, Timbal raced from shop to shop hastily purchasing numerous bottles of Evian water and cheap red wine for himself and his wife. It was close to 12.30am when they arrived at the ship; some of the crew, who were from Antwerp, helped the family up the almost vertical gangway. Once onboard, Timbal hastened to find Captain Paulsen and van Campenhout. The diamonds had already been secured in a cabin next to Captain Paulsen's, the door had been locked and an armed guard placed outside throughout the voyage. To their great relief, Timbal and his family had been given a cabin with two small bunks.

Various people arrived during the afternoon – civilians and soldiers, French and Polish officers, and a detachment of the RAF ground personnel with anti-aircraft machine guns placed under the command of Major Golding. An anti-submarine gun had also been obtained and mounted on the aft deck on the orders of a colonel in the French reserve.

Late in the afternoon of Tuesday 18 June, Timbal was introduced to the Earl of Suffolk & Berkshire who told him that he had been ordered to evacuate certain French engineers, technicians, managers of munitions factories who would be useful to the British war effort. These included Hans von Halban and a Mr Kowarski, and a 'priceless' commodity: the twenty-six containers of heavy water that had been already been placed in the cabin alongside the diamonds.

Miss Nicolle recorded in her notes that other passengers were beginning to board. The captain's intention was to take 500 refugees, which she relayed to the the Earl and Major Golding. Both Beryl and Marguerite made their way to the British Consulate only to find a huge crowd outside waving their passports. Inside chaos reigned, but there was no sign of their bosses. After that they visited the hotel and a restaurant, still no sign. When their car broke down they were given a lift to the *Ministère de l'Armement* and finally tracked down the two men and told their tale.

The crew of SS *Broompark* began making ready to sail. From Bordeaux it was 98km, in a northerly direction, along the Gironde to the Atlantic Ocean at Royan. Any swift advance of the enemy might jeopardize their departure. On the quayside, having arrived only a few days earlier from the USA, were several railway wagons loaded with aircraft engines destined for the French military. Jack and Major Golding, without any permission or hesitation, ordered them to be loaded on the ship.

Seeing as there was no food or water, the captain assembled a consultative committee composed of Major Golding, the Earl, von Halban, Mr Kowarski, the French colonel, van Campenhout and Timbal. Each would take responsibility for a certain number of passengers, draw up a list of their names, verify their identities and find somewhere for them to sleep. The French colonel and Timbal's wife, ventured into Bordeaux to search for supplies. Later that day, Timbal met with Paulsen and asked whether he had been contacted by a certain Mr Armand de Haan, to which Paulsen replied that he had and was given a sealed envelope containing diamonds. This he handed over to Timbal who locked it in the cabin along with the other diamonds.

It was around 7.00pm when the colonel and Timbal's wife returned laden with packages of food. The following morning people were woken by the sound of the ship's engines, they were on their way at last and entering the Gironde. It was mid-morning when they reached le Verdon sur Mer, the weather was calm and warm, and Royan on the north side of the river was bathed in sunlight. The mouth of the Gironde was packed with large and small craft, flying British, French and Dutch ensigns lying at anchor.

Jack, concerned there could be a mutiny if food supplies ran out, went to find Timbal and explained why he was going into Verdon. The Belgian thought it rather odd after hearing that it was impossible to embark anyone from Verdon. The Earl and Major Golding spent two hours ashore in the village and returned with supplies and more ammunition for the anti-aircraft guns. They had also made one final effort to collect more scientific personnel.

It was then, unexpectedly, that shore-based anti-aircraft batteries began firing. Frightened passengers on the *Broompark* heard the now familiar drone of German aircraft flying at high altitude which were invisible in the hazy heat of the day. Minutes ticked by and still nothing happened, and the droning faded away into the distance.

Then out of nowhere, a tremendous explosion shook the air; a two-funneled, 15,000-ton ship, anchored to starboard, was hit and began to sink. Had it been a bomb or a magnetic mine? Had a submarine slipped into the bay? People continued to eat their lunch and gaze at the ship slowly disappearing beneath the surface of the Gironde, until all that remained of the ship were a few lifeboats and floating wreckage.

French and Polish officers on *Broompark* were counted: among them were colonels, majors, captains and lieutenants. Each man, armed with a revolver, would take turns in guarding the cabin containing the precious cargo.

While taking a walk round the deck, Timbal noticed two 75mm anti-aircraft guns, 9mm Hotchkiss machine guns, and a 9mm Hotchkiss anti-aircraft machine gun. When he reached the after deck, he examined the 120mm anti-submarine gun. It was elevated to permit a range of around 5 to 6km. What would happen, he wondered, if a submarine surfaced at a distance of 2 or 3km? The French colonel who had personally supervised the mounting of the gun happened to be there at that moment. Timbal questioned him, then informed the colonel that he was a reserve artillery officer and that the gun was not in a position to fire at an enemy vessel at a range of less than 3km without hitting the superstructure of the *Broompark*.

The colonel became extremely agitated and said it was none of his business and stormed off. Sometime later, Timbal returned with Major Golding and introduced him to the pompous French officer as the man in charge of the diamonds. Timbal completely ignored the colonel's diatribe. Instead, he turned to Golding and told him that he had no reason to grumble at him because he was not the person who had placed the gun in that position. He should, however, reprimand the person who had. Major Golding tried his best to hide a smile that was threatening to escape. By late afternoon, the superstructure that would have hindered direct fire had been removed.

The weather became hotter by the minute on 20 June. Timbal could not stop thinking about the diamonds and heavy water in the locked cabin. What would happen if a bomb or a torpedo struck the ship? The items were very heavy and difficult to move. Perhaps they could be kept in a lifeboat; in an emergency all they would have to do was lower the boat. Just after sunrise Timbal spoke to the captain who confirmed his apprehension. However, they only had two medium-sized lifeboats which would not even hold all the women and children. What about rafts or lifebelts, Timbal enquired? There were no rafts and only a few lifebelts, he was told. Timbal, van Campenhout, von Halban, the captain, Jack and Major Golding met that morning to try and solve the problem.

Above all else, the safety of the passengers was paramount. They removed the tyres from a number of motor vehicles, took out the inner tubes and, when inflated, they were to be used as lifebelts. By the afternoon, every passenger was given either a lifebelt or an inflated inner tube.

It was Timbal's suggestion they build a raft for the diamonds and heavy water containers and Jack wholeheartedly agreed. Captain Paulsen allowed them use the ship's carpenter and the wood from the hold. Hans von Halban set about calculating the amount of wood required to build a raft to carry the diamonds and heavy water and maybe Timbal and a few other passengers.

Paul Timbal took his coat off in the sweltering heat and got down to work. Jack took peeled off his shirt to reveal, to the complete surprise of many, the tattoos that adorned his arms and back. Timbal never forgot this initial impression of Jack. Before him stood a 'pirate' who spoke fluent French with an atrocious accent. He shouted orders, cracked jokes, cursed in various languages, sat astride the raft which was taking shape and handled the hammer with strength and accuracy. To his amazement the man was smoking two cigarettes at the same time in a purpose-designed holder.

The raft was so heavy that even with the help of several crew members it could not lifted. No one had given it much thought when they began building. They could use the cargo-loading derricks, but after a discussion it was decided to leave it where it was built. It could not have been in a better place: just in front of the bridge, next to the closed hatchway. Access to this part of the ship would, from now on, be forbidden to passengers: only crew members on duty were permitted.

The two crates of diamonds were placed in the centre of the raft since they were the heaviest part of the cargo. Next were the heavy-water containers. Jack asked the captain for some old sacks in which each container was placed and firmly tied with rope. With the aid of more rope these were tied to the beams of the raft: if the ship sank the precious cargo would float.

Timbal estimated the value of the diamonds to be around £1,000,000, it could be even more. The heavy water according to von Halban, was worth, at the very least, £2,000,000 – almost the price of a warship! There was no way this cargo could be allowed to fall into enemy hands

Hans von Halban, van Campenhout and Timbal spoke to Jack and Major Golding about the idea of attaching the raft by a strong cable to one of the gangways of the ship. They agreed that the man guarding the raft should have an axe at his disposal in order to cut the cable in the event of an emergency. If the ship was hit by a bomb or struck a mine, he would cut the cable. But if the ship was torpedoed by a submarine, the cable would not be cut and the raft would go down with the ship. The idea was thoroughly approved.

To cover their responsibility, Campenhout drafted a memorandum detailing every measure they had taken so far, which was then typed by Beryl Morden. Each man signed the document and given a copy for safekeeping. If anything did happen there was a possibility that one of them would be saved. None of them had been issued with a lifebelt: in the event of a sinking they would have to swim and try to get hold of the raft.

The ship was still very near the French coast although they had been steering northwest since their departure. The further north they sailed toward England and safety, the nearer they came to the coast of Brittany at Isle de Sein and onward to Ushant where the Atlantic met the English Channel, some 250km from the mouth of the Gironde. The Germans were probably there already.

CHAPTER THIRTEEN

Skull & Crossbones, Snakes and Women

Captain Olaf Paulsen, master of the SS *Broompark*, was a native Norwegian. He had left home at 14 years of age with only a smattering of English, and made his way to Leith in Scotland where he began working for Christian Salvesen & Company as a ship's cook, working his way up to gain a masters' ticket. Paulsen was a polyglot, able to communicate in several languages since he often had to secure local labour in the ports of various countries for cargo handling, or when speaking with customs officials. He was a heavily-built man with a gruff voice and a thick accent and always seen smoking his pipe. He was known to be very dedicated and generous with his family.

Underneath the quaint mixture of showman and clown, Paulsen had a humorous exterior, intense drive and dedicated to his duty as a seaman. These traits would stand him in good stead when later faced with the outspoken, devil-may-care attitude of the Earl.

In his slightly broken accent, Paulsen often gave vent to the most outrageous utterances, and was always trying to impress the owners of the ships he sailed, with the most bizarre measures to effect economy. His personal expenses, while in port, he reduced to the bare minimum. The ships' ledgers were carefully written up and all monies accounted for; and because of this, other masters in the company disliked being in port at the same time as him. While in command of SS *Briarpark* in the 1920s he sailed from Leixões in Portugal to the USA and ran short of fuel, the voyage having taken them forty-two days against head winds. They had to rig up tarpaulins to act as sails to assist the vessel into Baltimore. When Captain Rickard, then in command of SS *Mountpark*, asked him why he had strayed so far south covering excessive distances, he replied that it was far too costly for the owners to sail in a great circle in the North Atlantic as in the colder weather on the northern route the crew ate too much food.

The SS *Broompark* was attacked at 11.38pm on 21 September 1940 by U-48 and struck, amidships on the port side, by a torpedo. The impact killed two of the crew; the master and a crewman. The ship remained afloat long enough for those left onboard to abandon ship. HMCS *Brandon* (a Flower-class Corvette) picked up forty-five survivors from the crew of forty-nine in 'seas of considerable height'.

Another time, when Olaf Paulsen was asleep in his cabin and before he could reach the bridge to take over control, a large number – forty of the forty-eight crewmen – had abandoned ship in the lifeboats. An escort arrived alongside to rescue the remainder. It was at that time Paulsen's sterling qualities as a seaman took charge. He shouted frantically to the escort to bring his crew back at once – telling them that it was impossible the ship would sink as it was loaded with timber. Only the chief engineer and seven crewmen remained; following Paulsen's instructions, they commenced the dangerous procedure of pumping ballast into the bilge tanks on the windward side just enough to lift the lee gunwale clear of the sea. With the crew returned, Paulsen then resumed his course and continued the voyage. On nearing the coast of Scotland the ship was strafed and bombed by a patrolling *Luftwaffe* Focke Wulf Fw 200 Condor. The attack was driven off by the anti-aircraft guns on SS *Broompark* and supporting fire from an escort vessel. For saving his ship with the loss of only one crewman, Captain Paulsen was awarded the Lloyd's War Medal for Bravery at Sea; he received an OBE at a later date.

On 25 July 1942, the SS *Broompark*, now with a new captain – John Leask Sinclair – was attacked east of Newfoundland at 3:52am when on Convoy ON-113. The SS British Merit had been damaged and a few moments later *Broompark* was torpedoed by U-552 ('The Running Devil') commanded by the legendary U-boat ace, *Fregattenkapitan* Erich Topp. Four of the crew were killed (including Sinclair), but there were forty-five survivors. The ship was then taken in tow but sank on 28 July some 50 miles southwest of St Johns, Newfoundland.

Despite his devotion and strict attention to duty, Captain Olaf Paulsen suffered the fate all shipmasters dread – the stranding of a ship while under their command – a great blow to his pride. So much so, that as he was now, in 1938, over 60 years-old, he decided to retire. He then purchased a grey Austin saloon car, learnt how to drive and became a salesman. But war intervened again and there was a shortage of shipmasters. Paulsen came out of retirement and was given command of a new steam-powered merchant ship: SS *Broompark*.

But what Paulsen really loved most of all, was to regale people with stories of his ship and recite poetry he had written in relation to various incidents:

> 'Torpedo struck while captain slept
> And crew in panic fled
> So captain yoost two lifebelts donned
> And jumped back into bed.'

The newly 'obtained' US-supplied machine tools and guns, which Jack and Golding had succeeded in extracting from the naval authorities in Bordeaux, were also loaded on the *Broompark*. Also, since French soldiers had recently abandoned the harbour defences, it was merely necessary to remove the Bren and Lewis guns from their emplacements and carry them onto the ship. It was said, whether true or not, that before leaving Bordeaux Jack found a French warship in the harbour and boarded it brandishing his pistols to commandeer guns and ammunition. Once the weapons and ammunition were safely stowed onboard, Olaf Paulsen made an entry in the ships' log confirming that there were 101 passengers on his ship. In another entry made by Paulsen it noted that he had chosen to ignore a distress call from a ship, 90 miles away, because there were too many people on his ship without life jackets.

After everything had been completed to Jack's satisfaction he poured a glass of champagne for anyone who felt seasick, explaining to them with a twinkle in his eye and a mischievous smile it was the best preventative he knew. Paulsen, being teetotal and the captain, thought it wise not to join in the revelries because where they were sailing he knew he would need a clear head. Finding a spare moment, Jack worked on the rota for the women to do the cooking, not that there was much food, but it would keep people relaxed and quiet. The last thing he wanted was for panic to set in. He also drew up a memorandum in French, *'faites en mer a bord du SS Broompark,'* (made at sea aboard the ...) for Kowarski and von Halban to sign, giving him permission to transport the heavy water out of France without any official formalities. Beryl, always diligent, was on hand to light his cigarette and type his notes.

At the time, Professor Kowarski did not speak a word of English but later he would spend four years in Cambridge, and thanks to a diplomatic blunder, came very close to losing the race for the A-bomb to the Americans. Kowarski, happy in the knowledge that everyone showed complete confidence in Jack, thought in his naïveté that he and his work would have been safe in Paris, and that the Germans would never get south of the Loire. To the professor, Jack seemed to be straight out of a P.G. Wodehouse novel, apart from his appearance. Gone was the dapperness Kowarski had come to expect from those books he had read. The immaculately shaven face had been replaced by a beard of days' duration, yet although Jack's eyes were bloodshot they still retained a glimmer of devilment and intelligence. None of them wore dinner jackets, as they were on a collier and coated in layers of black dust, with seasickness about to become rife: and here he was, this Earl, busy pouring out champagne and telling them it was the perfect remedy. It had all the feelings of a comedy.

A French ballistics expert, once they had reached England, told a group of scientists in London that he thought the Earl extraordinary. 'You won't believe it,' he said. 'But for two days we were all Hollywood pirates. Le Suffolk? He was incredible – a true sea rover. He even had snakes and women and large skull and crossbones tattooed on his arms.'

Hubert Jacques Nicolas, Baron Ansiaux, of the *Banque Nationale de Belgique* was also on the ship, accompanied by his wife and her family. If it had not been for the efforts of a British naval attaché who sought permission for them to board the SS *Broompark*, they would have been left in Bordeaux. The Baron carried with him a briefcase holding 1,000,000 Belgian francs for a stockbroker called Dewaay. He had been informed when he embarked that the ship was on a special mission. Having made sure his family was safe he found out exactly what the mission was. He thought the Earl très chic. Among the many people huddled together on the ship he saw Polish officers, Timbal and van Campenhout, French specialists, several French generals, and a chivalrous British officer who, after seeing the Baron's mother-in-law distraught, offered her his cabin.

Major Golding gave Baron Ansiaux a rifle and three magazines of ammunition along with orders to shoot at the numerous aircraft continuously flying over them. He did this without any success. At the time of departure, the ship had barely got under way when two ships exploded after striking magnetic mines. Apart from mines, the waters were also patrolled by German submarines.

The sun shone and what few clouds there were scurried peacefully by: the boat rolled comfortably and from time to time, to remind them they were at sea, it pitched slightly. One could almost imagine they were on a cruise in the Mediterranean. Around 6.00pm, Major Golding assembled the group leaders, explaining there would be a practice attack drill. Everyone put on their inner tubes or lifebelts then climbed down a very steep ladder into the hold which was dark and coated with a layer of thick coal dust – and there they stayed until the end of drill.

During the trip, a dirty, unkempt Polish army captain tried to learn English from a manual on French and English conversations he had found on the ship. His first words in English were halting, painful and slightly awkward but he persevered while he sat on a pile of thick rope far away from others with his head buried in the book.

Jack strode over to speak to Timbal. A convoy had been attacked by enemy aircraft some 30 miles to the northwest. Consequently, within the next few minutes they could become a target for the same attackers as visibility was excellent. Timbal mentioned that for the people in the hold it would mean certain death if the ship was hit by a bomb. It was the best and only precaution they could take, Jack informed him, after consulting with Major Golding and Captain Paulsen.

The men manned their post. The cannon and the anti-aircraft guns were ready and all eyes scanned the sky. Ten minutes went by in deadly silence. The only sound was the rhythmic creaking of the ship as it slowly rolled and pitched at full steam ahead, straight toward the enemy. The funnel smoked and the British Red Ensign flew proudly at the stern. Captain Paulsen stood bareheaded on his bridge quietly smoking his pipe, scanning the horizon. They waited, and waited, they heard it in the distance – the drone of aero engines and saw, to starboard around a mile distant in the direction of the French coast, several aircraft heading southeast.

The crew must have seen the ship but did not come to investigate. It was too distant to see if they were the enemy. They continued their watch. The coast of Brittany was so close that the aircraft could easily be refuelled and re-armed in time to return and strafe them before nightfall. Perhaps they had sent a radio message to the nearest airfield. Paulsen calmly continued smoking his pipe, his bronzed face lit by the warm glow of the setting sun. The people in the hold were kept there until 8.00pm only to emerge filthy dirty, irritable and starving.

Food was a kind of vegetable stew, it had everything in it but it was very difficult to swallow and tasted of nothing much in particular. Everyone ate it because they were starving, and the champagne made for jovial company. According to his bearings, Baron Anxiaux believed they had sailed west-northwest to move as far away as possible from the French coast and outside the range of action, especially aircraft, but not directly towards the British coast. There were many more ships ahead and astern, all trying desperately to flee. Not long out of the Gironde, one ship ahead of SS *Broompark* struck a mine and sank, another following was torpedoed. Having narrowly been missed and with luck and prayer on their side, the Baron believed they had escaped their fate because the submarine would have had to reload. He noticed the Earl and his secretary Beryl taking particular care of the French specialists and making sure the precious cargo on the rafts was tightly secured. It was the Earl's remarkable organizational skills and demeanour that impressed him the most.

In the direction of northwest they saw the flashing light of a white lighthouse. Was it the light of La Vielle on Pointe du Raz, the light on the Île de Sein, or that of Ar Men guarding an isolated rock? By 9.30pm, the enemy-occupied Breton coast was completely dark. Towards the west the day closed more slowly: the ship silhouetted against the horizon.

At 10.00pm, Timbal went to verify whether the sentry was at his post near the raft; there he met Jack and Major Golding and watched the RAF gunners going to their combat stations. Jack pointed out to Timbal two lights, in the distance astern, signalling in Morse code. Paulsen had ordered identity signals to be flashed but no reply had been received. These were probably enemy surface vessels or even submarines communicating by signals lamp. Perhaps they were agreeing on their method of attack.

Paulsen did not have to consult anyone, for him it was full steam ahead. The ship trembled to the beat of the engines as speed increased to around 13 knots, which was fast for an old merchant ship. The vessels astern continued to signal to each other enabling Paulsen to keep constant track of their position.

On 21 June 1940, Timbal made his daily check on the raft to make sure it was attended but the guard was nowhere to be seen. The next moment he felt the cold steel of a bayonet against his chest. The guard had been standing in a corner seeking protection from the wind. The day once again had turned bright and beautiful. After Brest, the French coast rapidly disappeared. Night fell and the continual zigzag course made it difficult to determine the course they were following – it was northwest.

During the journey, Jack had been seen striding, occasionally limping, across the decks, often followed closely by Beryl and Marguerite taking down dictation. Jack's woollen cap was pulled down deep over his head; he had on the striped turtle-neck sweater of a Breton sailor and a filthy trench coat that flapped about him in the wind. With his pistols jammed in his belt and his black beard being whipped by the sea breeze as the sun sank on the horizon, he was, indeed, the reincarnation of his buccaneering predecessors.

On Saturday 22 June, the passengers woke noticing something quite odd. The ship was no longer moving, there was no pitching or rolling and it was daylight. Timbal woke from sleeping on the deck of the ship's hospital with a sore, stiff back. When he realized the ship was no longer in motion he hurried to the porthole and found that there were green meadows and friendly-looking houses. They were in the middle of Falmouth Bay in Cornwall. He roused his family and tried to clean up a little using a little Evian water left over in one of the bottles. His neck was black with grime and his summer overcoat stained with oil and dirt. He started worrying about the diamonds. What would happen to them if the ship was bombed and sank in the bay? All around them were gathered a few warships of light tonnage, merchant boats and yachts at anchor. Dutch ensigns flew in the breeze, the funnels of two sunken ships stuck out of the water.

Miss Nicolle helped serve a final meal to the passengers, her afternoon spent collecting all the blankets, enamel plates, forks and knives and car inner tubes from the passengers. At 10.00am, a motor launch appeared. Several British naval officers boarded the ship and spoke with Captain Paulsen, Major Golding and Jack. They left 30 minutes later. It had been more than 200 years since a pirate had last brought cargo into Falmouth claiming he had 'saved' it from the French and even longer since one had said that the treasure he obtained was from the Spanish Netherlands. There was no reason for HM Customs & Excise officials to believe this than they would have believed one of the Earl's Tudor ancestors. Jack Howard claimed that part of the cargo was a highly specialized and secret apparatus of which there was no duplicate anywhere in the world. It had been brought into the country on government orders and was of vital interest to the nation.

Jack quickly scrawled a note including two of his favourite words 'to wit', and another that said he was under the impression the document of authority produced by him when goods were imported was sufficient to dispense with all Custom's formalities, and of such special character they were altogether outside the realm of merchandize. A postscript mentioned a further 500 tons of valuable machinery was to be landed and retained in Falmouth until further instructions were received. Another note mentioned the machine tools were to be taken to the premises of the Motor Packing Co. Ltd, Coventry, with a scrawl in the margin saying that part of the consignment should be sent to the Chief Engineer, Locomotive Department, Great Western Railways, Swindon. Later HM Customs were told to 'let the matter drop'.

At 11.00am, a naval launch arrived to collect all the British civilians, among them the wives of British military officers and consular officials from France. At the same time a detachment of British territorial soldiers boarded the ship under the command of an officer who took his duties very seriously. He ordered soldiers to fix bayonets and guard the special cargo. No one was allowed within 10m of the raft.

Having been packed together onboard ship like sardines, sailing in enemy patrolled waters, and having arrived in an English port, the rest of the passengers were, so it seemed, being treated like possible enemies. Timbal could have taken it all with a smile until he saw the officer-in-command throw himself like a rugby player at two passengers who, up until that moment, had apparently not noticed there was a raft onboard. Attracted by the military activity they got too close in an effort to find out what all the commotion was about.

In order to supervise his precious cargo, Paul Timbal asked Major Golding to introduce him to the commanding officer.

'Yes,' he told the British military man, 'those are my diamonds, and no one else but I have the right to them.'

The officer of the Territorial Army did not seem surprised. It took Timbal back to the time when he, in his capacity as a reserve officer of the Belgian artillery, was on duty in military training camps. Everyone told him he had been more exacting than the officers of the regular army. But he felt a certain shyness standing in front of this smartly dressed officer because he was unwashed and unshaven, not at all respectable looking, and dressed in filthy clothes. But at least no one but the British authorities could touch the raft and they could not move it without his consent. He explained this very clearly to Major Golding and Jack in the presence of the officer.

'The diamonds,' he said, 'are going to the Diamond Corporation in London and if that is not possible, I want to speak on the telephone with Sir Ernest Oppenheimer, Mr Chappel, or H.C.H. Bull at the Ministry of Economic Warfare. They also have to be insured for the trip from Falmouth to London.' His words received the outcome he was seeking.

At 12.00pm, another naval launch came alongside the ship and two very polite naval officers from the Admiralty boarded the ship and were introduced to Paul Timbal by Major Golding. Jack and Timbal were requested to accompany them to make arrangements with Port authorities for the landing of the diamonds. His family remained on the ship while Timbal, for the first time in his life, climbed over the side of the ship and down a rope ladder, to the waiting launch. It looked so easy when everyone else did it but it felt very unstable, and the distance from the deck to the sea seemed a very long way down.

Paul Timbal explained to the customs officers that he was transporting diamonds in sealed packages contained in two sealed crates which he could not open. The contents were rough, half-cut and polished diamonds of unknown value. When asked the maximum value, he replied it was approximately £10,000,000. When asked the minimum value, he told them he did not know, perhaps £2,000,000 or even £3,000,000. Only vague indications had been given to him by the depositors so he could not take any responsibility. On the minimum value he was certain but not on the maximum. Timbal was asked for consular invoices of which he had none – for good reason. The customs officials would have to get their instructions through the usual channels from London.

Timbal became irritated at the time it took to sort out the problems. Furthermore, it was Saturday and he probably would not have been able to reach the authorities through the usual channels. He suggested to Jack that he telephoned the Ministry of Economic Warfare because he was worried about leaving the diamonds on the ship any longer than necessary. Once that was done, it was decided to load the raft onto an armed customs' launch which would move away from the other vessels in the bay but would not land. It would stay close to the shore until the necessary instructions were received from London. Timbal reluctantly agreed, hoping that if *Luftwaffe* bombers attacked the ships they would miss a small launch.

Next, Jack and Paul Timbal paid a visit to a local bank where Jack exchanged the French francs belonging to Major Golding and himself and various French scientists on the ship as that was all they had: it was a considerable amount that had the bank frantically phoning their head office in London. While waiting for this to eventuate, Jack requested the manager get in touch with the Ministry of Economic Warfare.

Complete calm remained over the small town. It was an eerie feeling. Everything seemed so normal as though there was not a war on. Hard to comprehend after the dramatic days they had just been through. Jack and Timbal paid a visit to the naval officer-in-command of the Port of Falmouth to discuss the question of landing the passengers. Still no word from the bank regarding the exchange of French bank notes. Around 3.00pm, they were asked if they would like something to eat and were given the ever reviving British tea and biscuits. After the last few months, it was like tasting nectar of the gods.

Suddenly, the air was full of the wailing of air-raid sirens but no one moved, they carried on drinking their tea and talking. From where they sat they could see the entire bay. The customs launch was only a 100m away from the pier. If that sank, Jack reasoned, it would be easy enough to recover the heavy water and diamonds from the water. The SS *Broompark* was at anchor in the distance. But, nothing happened... maybe it was a false alarm, nobody knew. Finally, the authorization they were impatiently waiting for came through from London. The diamonds were to be taken to London under military escort and deposited at the Diamond Corporation who would act as trustees.

During the afternoon, immigration officers boarded the ship. Miss Nicolle spent a few hours in the saloon helping with passports, identity cards and immigration forms. When she emerged she found the rest of the mission had left. Jack and Timbal returned to the ship in the motor launch and climbed the rope ladder to get on board. Timbal followed less ably, and by the time he reached the top he was exhausted. Anxious passengers leant over the ships' rail waiting to hear their fate. Around 5.00pm, customs officials and passport control officers boarded and asked everyone to fill in the usual entry cards; they informed them that each person was to report to the passport officers: all very peacetime, but this time the military was present. Jack handed over a few pounds sterling to Timbal in exchange for the French francs.

The ship was on the move again and moored at the pier where the waiting game began all over again and jangled everybody's nerves. At 9.00pm, another boat arriving from France, packed with Polish soldiers and officers shouting enthusiastically, berthed alongside. Several buses drew up alongside the ship, and finally, at around 10.00pm, they were allowed to disembark. Passengers and crew boarded buses; the doors were closed and guarded by soldiers. A special train was waiting at the railway station. The diamonds and heavy water were locked in the mail van and guarded by soldiers with bayonets fixed under the command of an officer.

CHAPTER FOURTEEN

Diamonds

The day before Jack and his special freight arrived in England, Dr Gough travelled to the Adelphi Hotel to question the issue of accommodation for the expected arrival of the French scientists. The minister, anxious to speak to Lord Suffolk as soon as possible, rang the Admiralty and asked that the First Sea Lord speak with the Directorate of Scientific Research about transport to France. The Under Secretary spoke to the Director of Operations and found a number of merchant ships were already in Bayonne. Armed with the correct information it was decided the best course of action would be to wait for a call from the Earl and obtain a precise description of the French scientists at Bayonne and their location before sending a ship. They were all in agreement that it was completely unnecessary to send a destroyer as specifically requested by Jack.

Those who participated in that journey never forgot it because Jack's personality had changed a death-threatening voyage into a highly-romantic adventure. He had taken every precaution and had put the crew through lengthy drills in case of abandoning ship. They noticed that the Earl had laid aside one of the rafts for his personal possessions, but not one person on that ship knew the contents of the battered suitcases and haversacks which were strewn so carelessly around the captain's cabin. In the end, the entire cargo may have proven to be the most valuable of the war to have reached England.

When the buccaneering Howards of Elizabethan times brought their vessels into port from raids against the Spanish bullion ships, they hauled in the black pirate's flag on their topmast and unfurled the royal ensign. Word spread up and down the coast and thousands lined the shore as chests of silver and gold were carried ashore. Great jubilation and much dancing and merriment ensued. This time, however, no fanfares awaited the 20th Earl of Suffolk when he reached the south coast of Cornwall.

Early on that Saturday morning, when the SS *Broompark* slipped into Falmouth carrying refugees from war-torn France, the Germans were reading the terms of surrender in a railway carriage at Compiègne: the humiliation of France was now complete. Exhausted and filthy dirty, Baron Ansiaux and his stepmother stepped on to the quay looking as though they had been shoveling coal. After managing to find a hotel and enjoying a hot bath, which did not have enough water to get rid of all the grime, the tea and scones went someway to revive them.

Once on the train, with its windows blacked out, Paul Timbal, his wife and children fell into an exhausted asleep. Around midnight the smiling, bustling ladies of the British Red Cross wheeled trollies up to the train laden with hot tea and freshly made cakes; a luxury indeed after eating stale bread. There was even warm milk for the children.

Kowarski took his family to stay with his wife's relations, while von Halban noted the look of surprise on the face of the receptionist at the Mayfair Hotel when he entered. He, like the others, was grimy and weary, wearing clothes covered with oil stains and coal dust. He wondered whether they would be told to leave as there were no rooms available but they were allowed to stay. On arrival, also at the same hotel, the Timbal family experienced the same feeling, but then one of the assistant managers recognized him under his layer of grime. 'Mr Timbal, where are you coming from?' and Mr Timbal replied, 'It's very simple... we have just come from the other side, and we are glad to be here, believe me!' Once shown their room, he rejoiced in soaking in a hot bath. He thought of all those crates and what they had gone through – the roads of Belgium and France, the police station at Compiègne, the *Banque Transatlantique* in Paris, again the French roads, then the *Banque Transatlantique* in Cognac, the French roads yet again, the British Consulate in Bordeaux, onboard SS *Broompark*, and finally the train from Falmouth to London. Next would be the Diamond Corporation, and his assignment would be completed.

Timbal shaved for the first time in days. He had been amused by the surprised look on the clerk's face at reception. They had been unkempt, unwashed and his wife was carried her mink coat rolled up in a bath towel. After a breakfast of eggs and bacon, he called for a taxi and requested the driver to take him to the Diamond Corporation, arriving the same time as military trucks drew up. The soldiers immediately closed the two streets adjacent to the building and stopped all traffic. The unloaded crates were marked 'Banque Diamantaire Anversoise'.

Before leaving Falmouth, Jack sent a telegram to his department informing them of a special train leaving Falmouth at around 11.00pm, and when it arrived in London he would telephone. The telegram was signed: *'Suffolk and Berkshire.'* He also telephoned the ministry to inform them of the nature of the cargo:

600 tons of machine tools and £3,000,000 worth of diamonds (not counting those brought back by Timbal);

Heavy water from the laboratories of Joliot-Curie in France;

The entire secret archives of the Ministry of National Education, together with the Under Secretary of State from the ministry and one other officer;

Two pieces of apparatus of considerable scientific importance;

All the secret documents belonging to himself and Major Golding from Paris;

A new secret machine tool for the manufacture of 20mm Hispano-Suiza cannon;

Another machine tool of a similar nature;

Anti-aircraft weapons, and

Twenty-four high-ranking French scientists and technicians together with two pharmacologists and a ballistics expert.

Suffolk spoke with some urgency to the official at the ministry; he attached considerable importance to sending a special transport to collect the following officers from France, last heard of in Bordeaux, as they were eager to get to England. Hopefully, they had arrived in Bayonne.

Colonel Dupui – an armour-plate specialist;

Colonel Ott – in charge of the experimental establishment at Bourges;

Captain Bichelonne – chief of staff to Mons Dautry;

General Blanchard – head of all gunpowder works in France;
General Mitignon – equivalent to Director General of Design.

When Dr Gough greeted Jack off the train his eyebrows rose in utter disbelief. Jack now sported a thick, dark, unruly beard of a fortnight's growth, and was wearing his 'trademark' broad-brimmed black hat, a ragged trench coat and trousers slicked with oil stains. To Gough, Jack's eyes looked bloodshot from a serious lack of sleep; he had the appearance of a resident from the seedy underworld of Marseilles.

After speaking with Gough, Jack made his way by taxi to the Ministry of Supply with two battered suitcases and some haversacks stuffed with designs for new machine tools, secret blueprints of scientific inventions, and papers of formulas of incalculable value from British officers in Paris and French laboratories. Exiting the taxi, Jack ordered the driver that on no account should he drive off but was to wait for him for as long as it took, and that might be a while. He was running on pure adrenaline.

The sleepy-eyed porter had never before seen such a fearsome sight in the early hours of the morning. Acting purely by instinct the porter pushed an application form across the desk towards Jack and told him to fill it in. Under 'Reason for Interview', the Earl wrote 'Diamonds'. Against 'Full Name', he simply wrote 'Suffolk'. The porter promptly stood more smartly, coughed discreetly then politely told the mad-looking man standing in front of him that he wanted his name, not his address.

Jack barked irritably, 'And Berkshire! I need to see the minister right now.' Jack was in no mood for bureaucracy. His open coat revealed two large pistols in a shoulder holster; he soon got what wanted. Herbert Morrison was out of London at the time so Harold Macmillan, the then Under Secretary at the MoS, was called.

The porter later confided to a reporter from *The Sunday Despatch*: 'Mark you, sir. I thought he was some broken-down actor. And it's worried I was over them suitcases. They might have been full of bombs, you know.' The porter also stated that he had thought at the time the stranger's chances of seeing the minster were nil, but he had done his duty and handed over the form for him to fill in anyway.

Harold Macmillan was at his small flat in London when the telephone rang at around 5.30am. It was the duty officer asking if he could come immediately to the ministry. When Macmillan reached his office he found Dr Gough and other officials waiting. With them was a young man of extremely scruffy appearance, yet he had a certain distinguished air about him. He was waving a cigarette about which he had carefully fitted into a long black holder.

After they had shaken hands, the young man quickly explained his purpose. He had brought with him a large consignment of industrial diamonds, some of which were in the taxi cab outside. He had something else called heavy water and some French scientists. Macmillan did not know at that time what heavy water was and was too confused to inquire due to the early morning wake-up call.

'I've got a party,' the Earl said, 'with more of this stuff waiting on the coast somewhere near Bordeaux.' This 'stuff', as far as Macmillan could determine, consisted of a great number of machine tools and more scientists.

'Here,' said the Earl, 'is a large scale map. I have told these chaps to be hiding at the spot marked.' Jack's finger prodded the mark. 'Send a ship over and get them to flash their lights as I have arranged and everything will be all right.'

This soon passed out of Macmillan's hands. The minister arrived and the First Lord of the Admiralty was consulted, and all discussions were held at the highest level. Macmillan thought the strange man had a combination of charm and eccentricity about him. Later, he got to know him better: it was his first introduction to a truly 'Elizabethan' character

At first, the First Lord reacted negatively to the wild-looking apparition standing before him and his even wilder story, and Jack was having trouble with a deaf spot in his ear to the Admiral's reply of 'No'.

He explained again that the 'stuff' would be found at the spot he was stabbing with his finger at on the map. 'Have your ship flash a signal light when it arrives.'

The map was an official one and contained more detail of the stretch of French coast around Bordeaux than found on any Admiralty chart. When asked where he had obtained it, Jack replied, 'Before I left Paris, I figured that the French government would end up on the coast within 10 miles of the Spanish frontier, so I procured a map in case we needed to evacuate them.'

The Admiral stared at him. There was something about the man's audacity and determination; his plans for the evacuation would not be stopped by any obstacle, and that appealed to the First Lord. Before the Earl left the meeting a destroyer commander was on his way to the Admiralty for instructions. Three days later, the precious cargo guarded by a single man was found exactly on the spot the Earl had given. Jack never spoke about his daring exploits afterwards and when pressed for information, his invariable reply was: 'I've never heard that Drake kept records of where he got his swag.'

Later, Macmillan attended a conference over which Morrison presided and the Earl repeated, in rather a detached manner, his strange story. Such a character as Suffolk seemed utterly remote to Morrison. He could not make him out at all. He was chiefly concerned as to the battle which would soon rage over the machine tools between himself and Lord Beaverbrook. But to meet in real life a mixture between Sir Francis Drake and the Scarlet Pimpernel was something altogether out of this world.

Since the seventeenth century, the Earls of Suffolk had led reckless, exciting lives. They were pirates of the Spanish Main and explorers of unknown continents. Henry VIII had married a Howard; the father of the 1st Earl of Suffolk had been beheaded on the orders of Queen Elizabeth I, and younger brothers had carried the cavalier tradition just as the Howards who went to Virginia and the Carolinas. Jack's birth had provided him with wealth, a great name, and a tremendous heritage.

Having completed his mission he continued his journey in the taxi, something the government had to pay for because he was broke, to his club in Pall Mall where he regaled Lord Clanwilliam, the man who had been Jack's friend and advisor ever since his father had died in Mesopotamia, with the full story. He could tell Jack was in a high state of euphoria, he was edgy, could not sit still, and was smoking like a chimney, like a man just out of action. He had obviously not slept for a week and was heavily armed – he opened his coat and showed his friend his automatic pistols. Jack had spent all of his money in Bordeaux and had to be sent home to Charlton in a MoS staff car.

It would be a long time before the politicians fully understood Suffolk's tale. In secret, men in high places paid tribute to the highly successful efforts made by representatives of the ministry, to the members of the British Consulate and the officers and crew of the SS *Broompark*. A considerable service had been rendered to the Allied cause by the safe arrival of that cargo. But, as the mission was 'Top

Secret', no mention was made of any awards, nor was it recorded that they were brought out of France in a merchant ship.

Herbert Morrison knew the Earl was on a personal mission for him, and for that reason Jack's report to the prominent politician detailed an incident he had experienced:

'When the machine tools were being unloaded from the destroyer a charming gentleman came up to me and said, "I've come from Lord Beaverbrook to take the machine tools to the Ministry of Aircraft Production." I politely explained to the man that he was engaged by the Minister of Supply and not the Minister of Aircraft Production, and accordingly I could not or would not hand over the machine tools. The man replied, "That's OK, everything has been fixed up between the 'Beaver' and Morrison." I told him that I was sorry, but I just could not just hand them over until I have seen the Minister of Supply.'

Consequently, Morrison received the machine tools and Beaverbrook had to admit defeat. Later, Beaverbrook joked with Herbert Morrison, but thought he appeared to be greatly hurt, so he said to him: 'Do you think I'd do a thing like that, Herbert?' Morrison replied, 'I'm bloody sure you would, Max.' Beaverbrook laughed as did Morrison. There appeared to be no ill will between them.

Months later, on 18 September 1940, at the request of the Diamond Corporation, HM Customs & Excise attended their premises at Charterhouse Street, London, and opened the packages of diamonds and found:

Package 30: Contents examined, value £769.14s.6d, addressed to Miss Schnermans care of Order & Freres, Antwerp.

Package 71: Uncut and cut diamonds, value £4,500, addressed to Order & Freres, Antwerp.

Package 82: Four platinum rings, diamond set; one platinum ring set with diamonds and emerald; one platinum ring set with diamonds and sapphires; one pair platinum earrings with diamonds; one pair platinum earring mounts with diamonds; necklace clasps – one gold and platinum with diamonds; one gold set with diamonds, and loose diamonds.

Packages 82 to 92: Cut diamonds, value £15,550. Rough and some partly worked diamonds, value £6,100. Rough diamonds, value £28,571.

Precious stones and cut diamonds and jewellery, value £3,600. Cut diamonds, sapphires, emeralds and pearls, value £13,700.

Parcel R & L Goldmuntz: Eighteen various packets with British, Venezuelan, West African, Cape, Melee dust diamonds, rough value Florins 1,383,405.90, French Frs. 863,146 & £37,197.6s.3d.

Parcel Gutwirth Bros & Coppens & Charles Coppens: Four packets of cut diamonds, partly worked diamonds, and rough diamonds, value £16,250.

Parcel J & H Fischer Freres: Cut diamonds, value Florins 26,524.15.

Parcel I. Lieber & Z Solowieiczyk: Rough diamonds, value Florins 153,293 .17.

Parcel Geb. Biallosterski: Cut diamonds, value Belgian Frs. 71,061.

Parcel Societe Arya Anonym: Cut diamonds, value gold Guilders 177, 617. 57.
Parcel L. Gerder: Rough diamonds, value £15,022.17s. 7d.

Parcel Alice Stern: Cut diamonds, rough diamonds, emeralds, diamond rings, white gold, value £75,000.

Parcel Ernest Order: Rough and partly-manufactured diamonds, value £5,113.14s.10d.

Parcel Elkon & Fils: Cut diamonds, value gold Florins 65,923.57.

Parcel Louis Gurfain & Son: Rough and polished diamonds, value gold Florins 30,501.

Parcel Max Fine & Son Inc: Cut diamonds, value US$ 8,636.

Just before the Second World War no one was sure what to do with the rough diamonds from Zaire, the main producer of industrial grade. People joked about chartering a boat and taking them out to sea and dumping them over the side. The De Beer Company had no in-house knowledge as to the technical potential of such diamonds, and disposed of industrials where they could to a few specialist dealers.

The diamonds' usefulness in wartime inspired a poem called *The Brilliant Armament* during the darkest days of 1941. It was published with a foreword by the Assistant Secretary for raw materials at the Ministry of Supply: 'The stones which the sorters once rejected demonstrate day-by-day in grinding, turning, wire-drawing and countless other engineering operations that adamantine durability and steadfastness which will lead us to Victory.'

CHAPTER FIFTEEN

French Scientists

Once things eventually calmed down, Jack compiled a three page report outlining his dangerous exploits in Europe. In it he thanked Captain Bichelonne and Colonel Raguet of the *Ministère de l'Armement* for their unparalleled efficiency and devoted help in their mission, members of the British Consulate in Bordeaux, especially the minister, Mr Harvey, who had secured them a pass for local bus services and clearance through customs, and the commercial attaché, Mr Irving, who secured their ship. Without them, he wrote, the task would have been arduous and extremely difficult. He also commended the loyal, hardworking assistance of Captain Paulsen, and the officers and crew of SS *Broompark* who made what could have been the most extremely dangerous journey into one of comfort and ease as circumstances allowed.

Jack gave credit to Mr Barton, the director of the International Chamber of Commerce in Paris, who took endless trouble in organizing the food for their trip back, and Mons Berthiez who, when faced with the removal of their dock foreman and dockers, organized a scratch crew from the port, and with the aid of Colonel Liebessart, supervised the very difficult task of loading the machine tools.

Commenting favourably on the efficiency, courtesy and diligence shown to them by Lieutenant Commander Wills, RNVR, of the Falmouth Contraband Control, Jack said he had done everything he could to facilitate the landing and dispatching of their personnel and valuables.

His final comments were left to recognizing the brave efforts of Beryl Morden, Major Ardale Golding and Marguerite Nicolle. They had faced the most uncomfortable, impossible conditions and hours of work that frequently amounted to some twenty hours per day, in grave danger, the ladies had acted with a cool and calm efficiency, and had done all they could to make the operation a success.

The heavy water, now the property of the Ministry of Supply, was the main topic of conversation. Where could it be securely stored? On 4 July, General Sir Maurice Taylor, a senior military adviser, wrote to Lord Wigram, the Deputy Constable of Windsor Castle, letting him know they had rescued from France a small stock of what is probably the most valuable and rare material in the world and one which was most urgently needed, in very small quantities, for what he hoped may prove to be without exaggeration the most important scientific contribution to the war effort. He asked whether Lord Wigram could arrange safe storage in some small chamber in the vaults under the castle.

The heavy water was taken from the Adelphi Hotel and distributed between the Cavendish Laboratory, the library at Windsor Castle, and Wormwood Scrubs Prison (then premises of MI5) under the guard of Brigadier Harker. On 9 July 1940, Owen Morshead, CVO, DSO, Croix de Guerre, the librarian of Windsor Castle, wrote to the MoS informing them he had in his care eight tins (round) and twelve tins (square) containing a special fluid. He also said that the King was aware they were in the castle. The tins would eventually be transferred to the new Ministry of Aircraft Production (MAP).

It was decided by the chief scientists that research would carry on in Canada. That being the case, the following resources were required: 1gm of radium, 3gm of radium mixed with beryllium, 5gm dysprosium (which was available) and approximately six laboratory workers. Scientists deduced from the above that all contemplated reactions would be of the slow neutron type and not explosive in the ordinary sense. It was suggested that the radiation produced would render a very large area uninhabitable. One infra-red receiver, one electrical apparatus (top secret), and secret documents belonging to the Earl, Major Golding, the French scientists and armament experts were also under the care of the MoS.

Two days later, Owen Morshead wrote to Dr Gough acknowledging the importance of what he was holding, and suggested that none of the material in question be released unless he received Gough's signature.

And should Dr Gough ever wish to contact him, he was to telephone the Windsor Castle exchange and ask for him personally. But if Gough wanted to send someone else in his place, then he should furnish 'the bearer' with a signed letter for further security. In case of extreme necessity, Morshead wrote, should he not be available, Gough was to ask for two other very discreet people – Commander D. Colles (Secretary of the Privy Purse) and Mr McIntosh (superintendent of the Office of Works at Windsor Castle). Even though they knew nothing of the heavy water, they did, however, know how to gain access to the Crown Jewels.

The French scientists were housed at the expense of the MoS at the Great Western Hotel in Paddington until Tuesday morning when, hopefully, provisional arrangements would be made for their eventual destination. The list made most impressive reading: :

Col. Paul Liebessart (51) – Member of the *Technical Service des Fabrications d'Armaments*: A specialist in ballistics research (exterior/interior), acoustics, optics, photo-electric cells and related apparatus. Air mines, 'mines fluviales', and anti-tank mines.

Capt. Daniel Cordier (39) & wife – *Directeur du Laboratoire de Physiologie des Gaz de Combat à la Poudrerie Militaire du Bouchet*, Professor of Agrege of Physiology and Therapeutics for the *Ecoles Nationals Veterinaries*, and Secretary General of the Association of Physiologists of the French language: A specialist in gas warfare and physiology of respiration from the point of view of respirators, etc. Madame Cordier has a diploma in physiology.

Georges Warnant & wife – *Ingenieur Commerciale à L'Universite Libre de Bruxelles: Directoire Commerciale Compagnie Ardennaise de Transport à Bruxelles*.

Marcel Mayer (58) & wife – Member of the *Chambre de Commerce de Bruxelles: Président de la Chambre de Fabriquants de Chapeaux*.

Col. Andre Lhomme (44) wife & children – Engineer in Chief, 1st class, Director of the Pubreaux Arsenal (formerly in charge of research), engaged in research of tank guns and anti-tank weapons. Published work on ballistics, guns, etc.

Col. Jacques Martin-Prevel (47) – Engineer in Chief, 2nd class, Head of section dealing with tanks and armoured vehicles at the *Service Technique des Fabrications d'Armament*.

Capt. Georges Darmois (52) & wife – Captain of Artillery, Member of the staff of M. Montel, *Mission Scientifique Franco-Britannique*, Professor at the Sorbonne in statistical section dealing with calculus and probabilities, member of the International Institute of Statistics, Examiner for the Naval College, and Vice President of the *Société Mathematique de France*.

Lt. Jacques Millot (43) – Doctor and Professor of Medicine, Professor of the Sorbonne, Faculty of Science, and appointed Lieutenant Doctor to the *Mission Scientifique Franco-Britannique* at the outbreak of war, also specialist in biology.

Col. Gaston Verbigier De Saint Paul (45) – Engineer in Chief, Head of Section for the manufacture of tanks and automobiles in the *Ministere de l'Armament* (previously *État-Major* in the army), and a Professor at the Tank School.

M. Luce – Head of the mission for improving manufacture at the Arsenal of Putreaux.

M. Laudenbach – Specialist in tank production.

Norbert Galliot, wife & children – Civil Engineer, Inventor of the Muzzle Brake, etc., *Docteur en Droit, Licencie en Letters Philosophic*, pilot in 1914-1918, Chevalier of the Legion d'Honneur, late Director of the Ballot Automobiles (holds several sporting records), and able to bring with him technical records of the Muzzle Brake. Has some English.

Jacques Massenaud (32) wife & children – *Docteur en Sciences*, Paris 1932, manufacturing of explosives, etc., and engaged in important research in connection with arms and munitions, accompanied by his staff (M. Pascal, M. Enderlin, and M. Perlmutter and families).

Professor Joseph Cathala (47) – Doctor of Science (family stayed in France). Assistant at the College de France, Professor of Inorganic Chemistry at the University Laval, Quebec, Professor of Chemistry at the University of Toulouse, and Director of the Laboratory of Electro-Chemistry at the University of Toulouse, specialises in heavy chemicals, electro-metallurgy, especially ferro-silicum.

Dr Michel Faguet (35) – Doctor of Medicine, Laboratory Chief - Central of the Paris Hospitals, Laboratory Chief of Physio-Chemistry Engineer, Doctor of the Faculty of Science, engaged in special secret work, and late assistant of Professors Richet and Urbain; also known to Professor Peters at Oxford. Has family in England.

Dr Robert Le Guyon (41) – Lt. Professor *Agrege de Medicine*, Director of the Laboratory of Hygiene of Paris, late Medicine Chief of the Army

Laboratory, late Chief of Medicine the North Africa sector – specialist in bacteriology, hygiene, dermatology, infectious diseases and tropical diseases; engaged on urgent secret research which he wishes to reveal only to one person – the Prime Minister. Has done research at Harvard and speaks English.

Pierre Baranger (39) – Military engineer in the Reserve. Professor of Chemistry at *l'Ecole Polytechnique*, Director of Research Laboratory for Organic Chemistry and Biochemistry; attached since the war to the Research Department of War and Armament Production. Specializing (ten years) in chemical warfare (asphyxiating gases); engaged in several experiments in connection with protection from poisonous gases and its therapeutic effects which is nearing completion and ready for immediate application. Experiments carried out under direction of Professor Cordier, who has been dealing with the physiological side of the experiments. Monsieur Baranger is accompanied by four of his colleagues.

(Note: this unit, in collaboration with Professor Cordier, is now conversant with almost all questions connected with poisonous gases during the last twenty years. The majority of documents have been given to the English scientific delegates in Paris – General Lindeman and the Earl of Suffolk.)

Jean Marie Mercier (27) – Brigadier Chief, military chemist, engineer chemist (Diploma of State), spent four years with the *Recherche Scientifique* under Professors Urchain and Job, and two years with the *Recherche Scientifique* studying poisonous gas under Professor Baranger.

Paul Thomas (32) – *Licence des Science, Laureat de l'Institute de France*, engineer chemist of the University of Lille, published some twenty articles on his work at the Academy of Science, Paris; working under Professor Baranger, whose team includes Monsieur Cartier – Assistant Chemist, and Monsieur Lacaze – Assistant Chemist.

Henri Longchambon (43) – Director of the *Centre Nationale de la Recherche Scientifique, Section Appliqué: Agrege de Sciences Physique;* Professor of the Faculty of Science of Lyon, Captain of Artillery during last war, and a member of the executive committee of the Institute de la Recherche Scientifique Appliquee a la Defense Nationale under the Presidency of Mons Dautry.

Henri Laugier (52) – Doctor of Medicine, Doctor of Science, and Director of the *Centre National de la Recherche Scientifique, Section Appliquee*, Professor of General Physiology at the Sorbonne (Pure Research), and member of the executive committee for scientific research concerned with National Defence; holds the position of Physician Captain to the army and air force.

Andre Boutillier (37) – Civil Engineer and Licentiate in Science: attached to the *Centre Nationale de la Recherche Scientifique* (CNRS), specializing in electro-technology, thermal machines, and metallurgy.

Mme. Jeanne Lapierre (33) – Secretary to the agricultural engineer at CNRS.

Jules Gueron* (33) – Head Chemist of the laboratory: before the war he was *Chef de Travaux* in the faculty of Science at Strasbourg, and Member of the *Counseil Superieur de la Recherche*, and has worked on physical and mineral chemistry, in particular, electrochemistry.

Yser Van Ermengen-Duwez (25, Belgian) – *Docteur en Medicine Chirugie*: assistant to Professor Rybornt, Université Libre de Bruxelles: engaged in special research.

Jacques Devys (35) (family still in France) – Director of the Kuhlmann Establishment, and Director of the *Société Technique pour l'Application des Carburets*. Has much experience in the manufacture of ethyl fluid, synthetic ammonia, synthetic ethylene alcohol, etc., and speaks English and German.

Etienne Hirsch* (39) (family still in France) – Lieutenant of the Reserve Artillery: Technical Director connected with the establishment Kuhlman, Paris (one of the largest producers of chemicals in France).

Mdm Simone Haurie (33) – Bachelor of Law (*Faculte de Paris*) and Legal Executive of Companies: Madame Haurie was engaged in work by Col. Lhomme ten days before he left Bordeaux, and was furnished with an exit permit by the *Ministère de l'Armament*. Col. Lhomme will vouch and answer for her character (notes supplied by Lord Suffolk and typed by Beryl Morden, 28 June 1940).

Col. Jean Lapeyr wife & children – Commander military engineer (Arms), Head of Services of Mechanical Fabrications and Workshop for the construction of Puteaux, student of the *l'Ècole Polytechnique de Paris*, and has an engineering diploma from the *l'Ècole Superieure d'Electricite de Paris*: speaks English.

Prof. Hans von Halban wife & children (born in Austria, now in France) – Studied physics and took his Ph.D in Zurich in 1934. Worked in the laboratories of Professor Joliot-Curie, and was *Chargé de Recherche, College de France*, Paris: engaged in research on nuclear fission and nuclear reaction in collaboration with Professors Joliot and Kowarski.

Dr Lew Kowarski, wife & children (born in St Petersburg, Russia, French by nationalization, previously Polish) – Degree in Chemical Engineering; Chemical Engineer at *l'Universite de Lyon*, full secondary studies in France (Baccalaureat), and *Docteur-es-Sciences Physiques*. Research work: Laboratory of Physical Chemistry, University of Paris, *Institute du Radium* and Laboratory of Nuclear Chemistry, College de France; author of twenty-four papers, twelve relating to nuclear physics; Research Fellow of the National Centre for Scientific Research at the College de France. Dr Kowarski was to be promoted this summer to a higher position of *Chargé de Recherche*.

M. Berthiez and wife (no details).

*A note on file informs that M. Gueron and M. Hirsch were not of Suffolk's party but would have to be dealt with later.

   (Notes taken and typed by Beryl Morden)

Doctors von Halban and Kowarski met with government officials: Dr Gough, John Douglas Cockcroft – the Assistant Director of Scientific Research, and Baron Zuckerman a member of the Tizard Mission to the USA, who was the advisor to the Allies on bombing strategy and scientific director of the British Bombing Survey Unit (BBSU). Also in attendance was John Desmond Bernal, the British physicist who joined the Ministry of Home Security and was public spokesman for science. Jack had met Zuckerman and Bernal before at a secret meeting in Paris, held at Savoy Hill House, on 24 June 1940.

   Officials were told that both scientists had arrived in England three days earlier and had previously worked together with Professor Joliot-Curie in Paris on applications of uranium for the Ministry of Armaments. They handed over a message written by Professor Joliot-Curie explaining why he would not be leaving France. Before von Halban and Kowarski left Paris, he had instructed them to place all the information obtained in experimental work in the hands of the British government and not take orders from Colonel (later General) de Gaulle as he was not a member of the British authorities, something that greatly irked the leader of the Free French. The two scientists disclosed their discoveries in chain reaction and heavy water, and said they thought

Henry Molyneux Paget Howard, 19th Earl of Suffolk and Berkshire. (*Courtesy of Radley College*)

Marguerite 'Daisy' Hyde Leiter by John Singer Sargent. (*Courtesy of Chloe Howard, USA*)

Studio portrait of 20th Earl of Suffolk and Berkshire. (*Courtesy of National Portrait Gallery*)

The *Mount Stewart*. (*Courtesy of John Oxley Library, State Library of Queensland*)

Newspaper
cutting of Jack
on the *Mount
Stewart*, Australia.
(*Courtesy of
the Honourable
Maurice Howard*)

Jack Howard at prize giving, Scots College, Warwick, Australia. (*Courtesy of the John Oxley Library, State Library of Queensland*)

Jack Howard at the wheel of the *Mount Stewart*. (*Courtesy of the Honourable Maurice Howard and* Daily Mirror *22 February 1934*)

Musical programme front cover featuring Mimi Crawford. (*Courtesy of Alan Craxford*)

Above: Eileen Beryl Morden. (*Courtesy of Terry Oliver*)

Right: Dr Herbert Gough, Jack's 'Master'. (*Courtesy of National Portrait Gallery*)

SS *Broompark* leaving Bordeaux July 1940. The wooden crates containing the heavy water can be seen lashed on deck – fore and aft. (*Courtesy of J & J Denholme Ltd, Glasgow*)

Fred Hards with the famous Bomb Disposal van. (*Courtesy of Lt. Commander Rob Hoole MBA, MCMI, MIExpE, MNI, RN*)

Bomb Disposal van alongside defused bombs in bomb cemetery, London. (*Courtesy of Lt. Commander Rob Hoole, MBA, MCMI, MIExpE, MNI, RN*)

Jack Howard overseeing experiment. (*Courtesy of John Bartleson, CWO4, USN, ret.*)

The Earl of Suffolk's team of Royal Engineers taking a well-earned break. (*Courtesy of Lt. Commander Rob Hoole, MBA, MCMI, MIExpE, MNI, RN*)

Fred Hards and the Earl of Suffolk in Richmond Park with defused bombs. (*Courtesy of Richard Hards*)

Mimi and the Earl of Suffolk before attending King George VI's Coronation. (*Courtesy of the Honourable Maurice Howard*)

The Earl of Suffolk ranting on the phone for more bombs. (*Courtesy of Don Cody*)

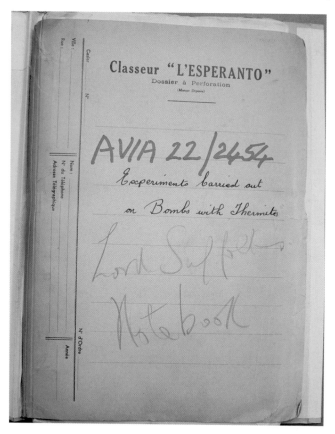

Lord Suffolk's experimental book and signature. (*Courtesy of The National Archives AVIA 22/2454*)

Richmond Park, London, England. Lord Suffolk and RE sapper preparing charges of thermite to burn opened bomb casings. (*Courtesy of John Bartleson, CWO4, USN, ret.*)

Richmond Park, London, England. Earl of Suffolk having target practice. Fred Hards is in the background, others unidentified. (*Courtesy of John Bartleson, CWO4, USN, ret.*)

Above: Fred Hards in background, Jack Howard sitting on a parachute mine (taken by Beryl Morden). (*Courtesy of John Bartleson, CWO4, USN, ret.*)

Right: Painting of Jack Howard in bomb togs by unknown artist. (*Courtesy of the Honourable Maurice Howard*)

Steam powered trepanner. (*Courtesy of Eric Wakeling*)

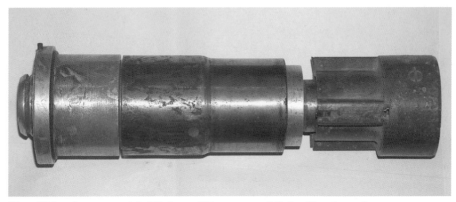

Zus 40 booby trap with 17 fuse. (*Courtesy of John Bartleson*)

Two fuses: top one is a 50, bottom one a 17. (*Courtesy of Steve Venus, UK's expert in German fuses*)

Head of Elaz 50. (*Courtesy of Steve Venus*)

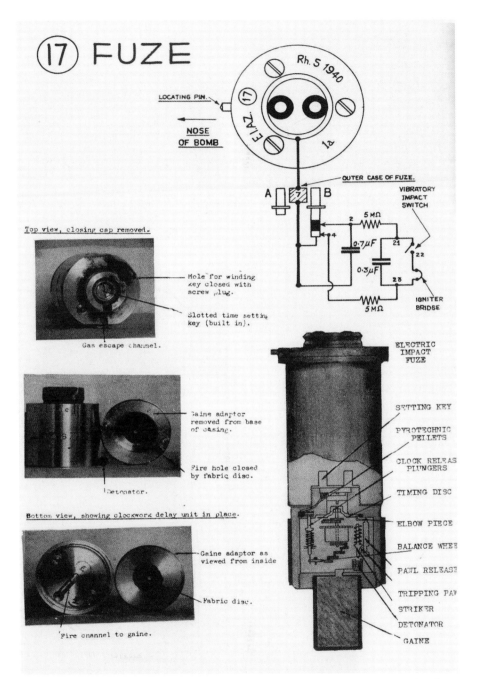

17 fuse (taken from Bomb Disposal Handbook 1940). (*Courtesy of John Bartleson*)

Bomb Disposal van after the blast. (*Courtesy of Lt. Commander Rob Hoole*)

Approximate site of where the Holy Trinity and Jack Howard's team died. (*Courtesy of Chris Ransted*)

Freddy.
(*Courtesy of
Steve Venus*)

Earl Killed by a Bomb

The Earl of Suffolk and Berkshire, thirty-five-year-old scientist who has been killed by a bomb, is seen here with his wife (formerly Mimi Crawford, musical comedy actress), his six-year-old heir and a younger son.

He had been a Guards officer, went round the world as a sailor, worked as a farm labourer in Australia, and at thirty-two gained his B.Sc. with honours at Edinburgh University.

Above: *Daily Mirror*, 14 May 1941. (*Courtesy of Chris Ransted*)

Right: *Sunday Dispatch*, 27 December 1942. (*Courtesy of the Imperial War Museum*)

Sunday Dispatch, DECEMBER 27, 1942   3

BOMB SECRET OF G.C. EARL'S DEATH REVEALED

ONE of the closely guarded secrets of the war—the circumstances in which the 35-years-old Earl of Suffolk met his death, for which he was posthumously awarded the George Cross—is told in the American magazine "The Saturday Evening Post," copies of which, dated December 5, are on sale in this country.

The award was made on July 19, 1941, to:

Charles Henry George Howard, Earl of Suffolk and Berkshire (deceased), Chief Field Research and Experimental Officer, Directorate of Scientific Research, Ministry of Supply.

And the reason given was: Conspicuous bravery in connection with bomb disposal.

It was stated that Lord Suffolk was killed by a bomb which also caused the death of Miss Eileen Beryl Morden, his 28-years-old secretary, and Mr. Frederick William Hards, a van driver, both of whom were posthumously commended.

SECRET RESEARCH WORK

The three formed a team which was engaged in secret experimental research work.

Now, for the first time, the full story is told in the *Saturday Evening Post*. The writer, Mr. William D. Bayles reveals that the earl and eight members of his bombing research organisation were blown to pieces while he was examining a large, old bomb which was thought to be harmless.

"Suffolk's end," says the writer, "was one of those incidents which, had he been permitted to comment upon it, he would have criticised as 'Damn silly.' His organisation had been working hard, and he had planned to surprise them all by taking them to his 10,000-acres estate at Charlton Park for a fortnight's rest.

Earl of Suffolk, lain around for many months.

Tables had also been booked for a final pre-vacation party at Kempinski's.

They spent their last working afternoon cleaning up some odds and ends that had been neglected. One of the odds was a large rejected bomb that had

"Someone had painted the words 'Old Faithful' on its side, and it was regarded as a permanent fixture.

"Suffolk decided to dismantle 'Old Faithful.' No one paid any attention; neither his party nor several soldiers working nearby.

"Windows a quarter of a mile away were shattered, and people in the adjoining towns felt the ground shock. Eight members of Suffolk's organisation were killed.

"In spite of his devil-may-care manner, Suffolk," says Mr. Bayles, "had a premonition of his own end.

PROUD MEMORY

"'Felix,' he used to call to the head waiter at Kempinski's Restaurant as he was leaving the restaurant, 'one of these nights only a little finger or maybe an ear will turn up for dinner.'"

Felix's proudest memory is the morning he served the Suffolks' wedding breakfast when the earl married Mimi Crawford, the actress.

Felix has retired from Kempinski's now, but other members of the staff remember the late earl well.

"Ever since the earl and the countess had their wedding breakfast here, they had been regular clients," a *Sunday Dispatch* reporter was told last night.

"The earl would frequently bring his fellow workers here."

Backroom Courage

Vision Ahead. By Air-Commodore P. Huskinson. Forewords by Lord Beaverbrook, Lord Tedder and General H. H. Arnold. (*Werner-Laurie. 11s. 6d.*)

By E. COLSTON SHEPHERD

AIR - COMMODORE HUSKINSON was blinded when a bomb struck his home in 1941. Up to that time he had been Director of Armament Development in the Ministry of Aircraft Production. Before the surgeons had done with him, he was continuing his work in hospital. Afterwards, still blind, he became President of the Armaments Board, and in that capacity resumed his task of removing obstacles and overcoming opposition so that the R.A.F. might have, in its bombs, guns, rockets and turrets, something reasonably close to what it needed.

In the story as he tells it in "VISION AHEAD," the emphasis is laid on the task. The individual and his personal affairs come modestly into their proper place in the tale. Blindness is acknowledged as a handicap. The ways of overcoming it are mentioned as matters of interest and not of sentiment, just as the author's ways of getting results in the face of obstruction are mentioned or as the driving methods of Lord Beaverbrook are described. This, therefore, is the story of a man's work, much more concerned with things and systems than with people.

It reveals no secrets. We still do not know precisely how the Möhne dam was breached nor how penetration was added to the immensely powerful blast of our big bombs. What the story vigorously shows is how much the thrust of individual endeavour was needed during the war to get anything moving and how grudging was the help of certain departments of State.

Earl of Suffolk and Berkshire, GC, headstone at St John the Baptist Church. (*Courtesy of Chris Ransted*)

THE GIRL IN THE 8.21
And the war job she kept secret

Express Staff Reporter

FAME which she will never know came yesterday to Beryl Morden, once clerk in the office of a motor sales firm in the City, to which she travelled from her home in Leytonstone by the crowded 8.21 every morning.

For when a bomb killed the Earl of Suffolk on Monday it killed her too. She had become his secretary, and high praise was given to her work with him by the Ministry of Supply.

With the beginning of war life became a colourful thing for Beryl. She got engaged to an R.A.F. pilot.

He was sent to Malaya. She took a job at the Ministry of Supply.

Then the 35-year-old Earl of Suffolk, in turn Guards officer, mercantile marine apprentice, farm hand and scientist, was appointed liaison officer for the Ministry between British and French scientific organisations.

SLEPT IN CAR

He needed a secretary who understood engineering terms. Beryl filled the bill.

She volunteered to accompany him when he went to Paris. Adventure came with the Great Collapse.

It was necessary for them to escape with their scientific records. For two days and two nights Beryl slept in a car at Bordeaux.

They saw the ship they were to have caught blown up, eventually crossed to England in a small cargo boat, their records safe.

But all she told her mother when she got home was, "I am tired." She never talked about her work. She was only 28 when the bomb ended her adventures on Monday.

EARL'S SECRETARY KILLED BY BOMB

MISS BERYL MORDEN

Above: Fred Hards in Richmond Park after defusing a bomb. (*Courtesy of Richard Hards, his son*)

Left: Newspaper article. (*Courtesy of The National Archives, AVIA 22/2288A*)

The Long Gallery and Fireplace, Charlton Park. (*Courtesy of the Honourable Maurice Howard, taken from* Charlton Park: A Short History *by Kate Mason, 1996, published privately*)

Below: Charlton Park, *Daily Telegraph*, 1969. (*Courtesy of the Honourable Maurice Howard*)

To the GLORY of GOD. In memory of CHARLES HENRY GEORGE HOWARD 20th Earl of Suffolk & 13th Earl of Berkshire, G.C., B.Sc., who with unselfish devotion faced and met his death in the course of his duties as a Scientific Research Officer, Bomb Disposal Unit. ☙ ☙ May 12th 1941. also holding in remembrance those who went with him This window is placed here by his wife

Stained glass windows in St John the Baptist Church, Charlton, commemorating Jack Howard's heroism. (*Courtesy of Chris Ransted*)

that an atomic bomb would not be explosive in the ordinary sense, but that radiation would definitely cover a very large area.

Norsk Hydro's entire stock of concentrated heavy water was only 180ltr. The doctors related the story of how it arrived at Bordeaux and to the *Banque des Pays et des Bas* who held a controlling interest in Norsk Hydro. The company, through the bank, placed this heavy water at the disposal of the French Ministry of Armaments and understood payment would be made when the war ended. Professor Joliot-Curie, Monsieur Allier, and Monsieur Bichelon had discussed with Hans von Halban the disposal of the heavy water they brought with them, and requested that it be transferred as quickly as possible to Canada. The heavy water had a value of £100,000.

Professor Joliot-Curie had at his disposal 8 tons of uranium oxide in France. It was hoped that some of this would be brought to England. The majority of the stock of uranium oxide was, however, in the possession of the Belgian company, *Union Minière* at Katanga, in the (then) Belgian Congo. There was 500 tons of uranium oxide stored in Belgium, some of which had since gone to the US. The remainder was still in France. The *Union Minière* had followed the experiments of Joliot-Curie with great interest and before the war agreed to provide a sum of 50,000,000 Belgian Francs for them to continue. Dr von Halban indicated he was very anxious to keep in touch with the company since he considered that if contact was not maintained they might well establish relations with other groups.

Both von Halban and Kowarski agreed they were ready to continue their experiments at the Cavendish Laboratory, Cambridge, but knew that the heavy water would eventually be sent to the University of Chicago for safe keeping.

A naval signal received on 22 June 1940 and labelled 'Most Immediate' indicated there were still many French technical experts waiting to be evacuated. It was agreed that first priority should be given to Dayenne, Roland, Jean Panhard, Birkight, Heurtaux, Percal, Brandt, and Kegress. They were to be followed by technicians, Colonel Lhomme, Lieutenant Colonel De St. Paul, Lieutenant Colonel Martin-Prevel, Mdm Haurie, Commander Lapeyre, Monsieur Luce, Captain Laudenback, and Monsieur Berthiez.

The Air Ministry agreed to take care of von Halban and Kowarski and their families and also Dr Van Ermengem-Duwez. Other names of importance were: Captain Professor Leprince, Colonel Raguet, and Professor Neel, also engineer designer Bounard, and Professors Francis Perrin and Auger. While the engineers Lafargue and Sorlt de Levallois, chief engineers Lavirotte and Gabeaud, and Engineer Commander Pounuclet were all anxious to leave France.

HMS *Berkeley* replied the same day informing them they could not make contact with the British Naval Liaison Officer (BNLO) in Bordeaux nor the British Ambassador, so were unable to pass on their message, which meant the Frenchmen would have to stay hidden.

The next day Jack met with Dr Gough and told him that in his opinion every facility should be accorded to the French technical experts. He indicated that the first five of special importance were the chief engineer of Maritime Warfare Dupuy; Engineer Ott; General Blanchard, *Secretaire General des Poudres*; General Martignon, *Secretaire General des Etudes*, and Captain Bichelonne – *Chef de Cabinet et Technique du Ministère de l'Armament*. He also pointed out that one of the professors was an ardent Bolshevic and his wife a member of the Nazi party.

Dr Gough agreed to speak with Captain Bichelonne as soon as possible, as it was he who had made arrangements with the French authorities for them to leave France. A few days later, Major Golding was handed a copy of a 'Very Urgent' report concerning the position of the French experts. Authorization had hastily been given to the Admiralty to send a signal and endeavour to bring back the nominated men. But what would happen to those left in France, wondered Dr Gough? He asked whether Jack, Major Golding or Colonel Liebessart could make definite suggestions about certain groups whose destinations were fairly clear.

Jack's team consisted of five men: Commandant Professor Baranger, Mercier, Thomas, Cartier and Lacaze, who brought with them a great deal of apparatus dedicated to chemical warfare. It was suggested that perhaps Colonel Liebessart with his interests in ballistics, mines and other explosive devices and Dr Galliot with his research on guns, should join the Research Department at the Woolwich Arsenal.

Dr Faguet and Dr Guyon, both Doctors of Bacteriology and engaged in highly secret research commissioned by Paul Renaud, were to be sent to the Medical Research Council (MRC). Monsieur Warnant had been vouched for by the British Embassy, but to date they had no clear knowledge of his classification – perhaps he should be referred to the Belgian Embassy? Professors Longchambon, Laugier, Mons Boutillier and Mdme Lapierre would go to the Department of Scientific Research. Finally, their long drawn out meetings came to a close after they had decided to leave the final arrangements to the Earl of Suffolk.

Commandant Professor Baranger said he needed Package No.1 containing: papers on B.31; mustard gas; vaccination, suintine, ramie; and medicinal products of French colonies. Professor Longchambon wanted Packages Nos. 6, 7, 9 and 10 containing: platinum, two crucibles, two small plates, wire, grill, gold, chloride of gold – 2gm, and cyanide of gold – 1gm, gold leaf, neodymium nitrate – 20gm, barium platinocyanide, two bottles of prasiodynium nitrate, one bottle of thallium carbonate, 3gm of platinum tetra-chloride, also gold and silver wire.

An inventory was carried out by the *Centre National de la Recherché Scientifique Appliquée* (CNRSA), which had been founded in May 1938 and headed by Henri Longchambon on developed applied research in France. When the law on '*L'organization de la Nation en Temps de Guerre*', was adopted on 11 July 1938, the *Ministère de l'Education Nationale* was put in charge of scientific mobilization, and the CNRSA took it on, but only in universities.

It was agreed that all secret patents were to be taken out in France by the CNRSA. Professor de Neel's researchers would concentrate on demagnetization and complete instructions of anti-tank mines, works by the CNRSA, and the dossier with blueprints of Lacroute's anti-aircraft scheme. There was no need to look any further for the dossier on the Planiol project because it was already in their hands.

Professor Cathala took Package 5: the plans of industrial installation for SO_3 manufacture and industrial extraction of SO_2 by roasting gases. Colonel Lhomme had Package 4 containing notes on the study of artillery materials of France, and Dr von Halban acquired Package 6 with documentation concerning heavy water and work on the uranium chain at the Joliot-Curie Laboratories.

On 25 June, the British were told that the French liaison officer had finally contacted Captain Bichelonne who informed him that parties of officers had been prevented by French authorities from leaving the country.

Dr Gough, the Earl, Major Golding, Beryl Morden, Marguerite Nicolle, scientists and technicians at the Air Ministry, Ministry of Home Security, DSIR, also representatives of the Ministry of Supply and the Admiralty met in a downstairs room at the Great Western Hotel, Paddington. Jack, now clean shaven and looking rejuvenated after his visit to Paris, expressed his hope that everyone felt refreshed after their tiring journey.

The aim of the meeting, Dr Gough explained to those present, was to make provisional arrangements in the distribution of their various French friends. Over the weekend he had tried to put together a complete list of the party the Earl had brought over from France but was not satisfied with his efforts as it was incomplete. In his opinion, he said, there would be certain individuals whose appropriate destination in England were quite clearly indicated, either by some previous plan made in France or by the nature of their work. He hoped that their colleagues at the Admiralty or the Air Ministry would sift through the remainder of the people on the list. Furthermore, he asked that Liebessart take responsibility for the party brought over by the Earl. Dr Gough asked whether Major Golding had any plans regarding separating people, and after realizing nothing could be done, they settled on what to do with them – they would send them to Canada.

CHAPTER SIXTEEN

Heavy Water

The path leading to the discovery of heavy hydrogen and heavy water turned out to be extremely complex. A report in the US newspaper *St Louis Post-Dispatch* dated 4 October 1903, mentioned Frederick Soddy, his relocation to London, and the grain of radium to be exhibited there: 'By means of the metal all the arsenals in the world might be destroyed. It could make war impossible by exhausting all the accumulated explosives in the world... It is even possible that an instrument might be invented which at the touch of a key would blow up the whole earth and bring about the end of the world.'

Heavy water, a by-product of ammonia fertilizer production, contained a higher proportion than normal of the isotope deuterium. It was not radioactive and had the physical properties similar to water; very small concentrations of heavy water were non-toxic. Relatively pure heavy water was produced in 1933 and contained as much as 100 percent D_2O; that is water highly enriched with deuterium. It was 10.6 percent denser than ordinary water, a difference difficult to notice in a sample of it (although it was said the water seemed to taste slightly sweeter). It would take very large amounts of heavy water to poison someone.

Deuterium oxide (D_2O) exists in water naturally, though its ratio is normally only about one part in 41,000,000 so it had not been previously observed in significant quantities. To poison a human they would have to drink nothing but pure heavy water for a week for them to begin to feel ill, and ten days to two weeks, depending on water intake, for severe poisoning and death.

One of the few ways scientists demonstrated heavy water's physically different properties without equipment at the time was to freeze a sample and drop it into normal water. Ice made from heavy water sank in normal water, and if the normal water was ice-cold this phenomenon could be observed long enough for a good demonstration, since heavy water ice has a slightly higher melting temperature (3.8°C) than normal ice.

At the time, Europe's major supply of ammonia came from *Norsk Hydro-elektrisk Kvælstofaktieselskab* (Norwegian Hydro-electric Nitrogen Limited founded on 2 December 1905) at Vemork, near Rjukan, in the Telemark region. For eight years the company's scientists had been collecting the liquid for scientific scrutiny, supplying samples to the world's researchers for basic experiments

This substance would play a sinister role in the race for nuclear energy during the Second World War and around 120 people – German soldiers, Allied soldiers and Norwegian citizens – would pay dearly with their lives for the cause. Nazi Germany, when investigating the possibility of building an atomic bomb, found a range of potential paths based on what was later demonstrated to be a technically viable approach. It was found that plutonium-239 made a very effective weapons material.

The main problem, they realized, with nuclear weapon development was securing sufficient weapons-grade material. In order to produce weapons-grade uranium, they had to either extract uranium from natural ore and enrich it, or 'breed' plutonium in a nuclear reactor using unenriched uranium as a fuel, and then chemically separate the plutonium-239 produced. Unlike the Allies who chose to pursue both the enrichment of uranium and production of plutonium in reactors, German scientists elected to focus on plutonium production, as the plant and equipment required to make weapons this way was less expensive.

Although the most common isotope of uranium – uranium-238 – could not be used as the primary fissile material for an atomic bomb (though it could be used as secondary fissile material in hydrogen bombs), it could be used to produce plutonium-239. The fission of uranium-235 produced neutrons, some of which could be absorbed by uranium-238, could create uranium-239. After a few days, uranium-239 decayed, turning it into weapons-usable plutonium-239.

Germany did not realize that the graphite they were using was too impure to sustain a chain reaction so they abandoned it and finally settled on the heavy water-based reactor design that could be used for nuclear fission research and, ultimately, breed plutonium to be used for an atomic bomb.

Five years before the war began Norsk Hydro built their first commercial plant specifically to produce heavy water, with a capacity of 12,193kg per year, at Vemork. The Norsk Hydro plant at Rjukan would figure prominently in the German invasion of Norway in April 1940 for two reasons: the industrial importance of the hydrogen-electrolysis plant itself at Vemork with its the heavy water and high-concentration cells, and the strategic importance of the Vestfjord valley that cut through the central mountain region between east and west Norway. The Allies planned to destroy the heavy water plant to disrupt the Nazi development of nuclear weapons. The German invasion of Norway was very much on the minds of many powerful people co-ordinating work going on in Britain, including the Military Applications of Uranium Detonation (MAUD).

In early summer of 1939, Joliot, Hans von Halban and Lew Kowarski alighted on the idea of using heavy water as a moderator. Halban and Kowarski did some simple modelling of neutron moderation which was enough to suggest D2O as the best candidate.

At the end of October, Joliot and Kowarski deposited a sealed envelope with the Academy of Science with orders that it was not to be opened until 1949. This paper would show that the group had a very firm theoretical grasp of reactor physics, including the Fermi four-factor formula. There was little doubt that, had the war not intervened, the world's first self-sustaining chain reaction would have been achieved in France.

Before the war, a keen alliance developed between Churchill and Roosevelt, which was made even more special when both countries were faced with the issue of atomic energy. Sir William Stephenson, scientist and spymaster, serving as Churchill's personal intelligence representative to the USA, made it his business to provide confidential information to Churchill about how the Nazi government was building up its armed forces and hiding military expenditures of £800,000,000, a clear violation of the terms of the Treaty of Versailles. Churchill used this information to warn Parliament against the appeasement policies of Chamberlain. Stephenson developed an intimate relationship with the Roosevelt, emphasizing the fact that the British, with covert help from the US, were in a crucial race to develop a bomb before the Germans.

Although British officials viewed the possible significance of uranium fission for military application with a high degree of scepticism, some research was initiated at British universities on the theoretical aspects of achieving an explosive reaction, but initial reports were slow and discouraging. So effort was reduced and resources were directed at more promising defence projects at the outbreak of the Second World War. The turning point came in March 1940, when a memorandum by O.R. Frisch, and R.E. Peierls, a German-born Professor of Physics, both working at Birmingham University, predicted that a small mass of pure uranium-235 would support a fast chain reaction. They outlined a method showing how uranium-235 might be assembled in a weapon. This was quickly recognized, and the uranium subcommittee of the committee for the Military Application of Uranium Detonation (MAUD) was set up. MAUD began an experimental research programme at Liverpool, Birmingham, Cambridge and Oxford Universities and at the Imperial Chemical Industries. Just two days before war began, Niels Bohr of Denmark and John Wheeler of Princeton published for the entire world to read a theoretical explanation of the fission process.

The MAUD committee, along with Churchill and the Ministry of Supply's support, arranged for the Earl, Major Golding and their secretaries to 'rescue' the French scientific elite, along with their most top secret commodity. They also settled Hans von Halban and Kowarski in Cambridge at the Cavendish laboratory with the world's total stock of heavy water. The greatest secret of all time had been entrusted into the hands of two refugee scientists who were excused for security reasons from all other wartime work. Britain would not have had a slow neutron project – the basis for the production of plutonium and power – if it had not been for those two men and the outstanding courage of Jack Howard and his team. Britain also recognized that with their limited resources they would need the immense production capacity of USA for the expensive development work.

Joliot-Curie chose to remain in France and thus began a difficult period for him in charge of the cyclotron at the *Collège de France*, as it was the only one available to German scientists in occupied Europe. Although there was another one in occupied Copenhagen, Neils Bohr simply forbade its use by Axis personnel – an act that only Bohr could conceivably get away with. Joliot-Curie vanished from public life and became a leader in the Resistance.

CHAPTER SEVENTEEN

The Holy Trinity

On 3 July 1940, Jack received a visit from a representative of HM Customs & Excise who questioned him on the circumstances of the importation of his cargo. Jack informed him of its importance from a national point of view, and the fact that they had been released without examination on grounds of urgency. He would not divulge the nature of the goods under any condition nor would he permit examination. For revenue purposes then, the representative said, a token value of £5 would be placed on the unspecified analytical re-agents because they were priceless, and no estimate of their value could be made: on the experimental equipment and machinery, a token value of £2,000. They eventually agreed on a figure for the machinery at the interview and both men shook hands to seal the deal.

Later, in the company of Dr Gough, Jack attended a formal dinner held in honour of the French scientists, and it was during this that Gough first heard Jack speak fluent French and easily adopt the various regional dialects of those assembled, coming as they did from different areas of France. The Frenchman sitting next to Gough told him that it pleased him greatly to hear Jack speaking excellent French. Dr Gough could only shake his head in wonder – the Earl was full of surprises.

After the dinner, the Earl left London and returned to his home at Charlton Park, deep in the heart of the Wiltshire countryside, to luxuriate for a while in its restorative powers. He felt at ease to be home with his family, having survived only on adrenaline during his mission to France. Mimi and his sons were totally, and thankfully, blissfully unaware of his escapades over the last few months and would stay that way.

The Paris mission began to wind down, and the MoS finally completed their list of the research centres where the French scientists would be sent. The Research Department at Woolwich was to receive Colonel Liebessart, Dr Massenaud, Mon Pascal, Enderlin, Perlmutter and Galliot. As of 18 July 1940, the Chemical Defence Research Department would take Professor Cordier and Mdm Cordier, Professor Baranager, Brigadier Mercier, Captain Thomas and Mon Lacaze. The Directorate of Scientific Research requested Professor Darmois (who later decided to return to France), Professors Cathala and Longchambon, Mdme Lapierre, Professor Millot, Professor Le Guyon. The Medical Research Council requested Professors Laugier and von Halban. Kowarski decided to join the Ministry of Aircraft Production, and Dr van Ermengem-Duwez joined the Belgian Army. Dr Faguet decided that he wanted to return to France.

On 26 September 1940, a memorandum from Winston Churchill stamped 'Secret' was sent the Minister of Supply, detailing the Prime Minister's growing concern in the matter of Bomb Disposal (BD) which was becoming an urgent problem in the country. Churchill's involvement gave it a high level of importance and any failure to attend to the problem could have serious consequences for the production of aircraft and other vital war material. BD units were to be provided with the most up-to-date type of equipment available, and priority given to the production of any further requirements.

Jack had not realized just how tired he was and slept heavily, happy to be amongst the bosom of his family, overjoyed at getting to know his son Patrick Greville, who was born on 18 August 1940. Jack and Mimi took long autumn walks in the grounds of Charlton Park and, for a while, the place worked its magic and life took on a more halcyon hue. But always burning at the back of his mind was the serious trouble brewing in London; he desperately wanted to be part of it. The excitement of Paris, now but a memory, and the tranquility of his ancestral home were now gradually replaced with a feeling of tedium.

He threw himself into the things he loved most on the rare occasion he was at home: spending time with his sons, riding his horse and talking to the blacksmith, taking the dogs for long walks and chatting to people in the village, checking up on various tenants, buildings and land, and whiling away hours in his laboratory, but somehow they lacked the stimulation he craved. He decided to return to work with only one question on his mind: What shall I do now?

Dr Gough found him various tasks to complete, among them were certain liaison duties with the *Forces Françaises Libre* (Free French Forces), which kept him occupied for three months. At the end of this period he was drafted into important secret development work of a particularly hazardous nature. Sir Leonard Pearce, engineer-in-chief of the London Power Company, telephoned one day to inform them that an unexploded bomb had been found by a very concerned member of public at Deptford West Power Station, and asked whether they should get rid of it. Jack, through his connections, heard about this and immediately set off in search of his friend and mentor. He pushed open the door to Gough's office and said, 'I've heard talk of a UXB found at Deptford, master. Can I go?'

Gough, who could never say 'No' to Jack, took him to look at the bomb, which was how he initially gained an appetite for the new game of removing fuses from unexploded bombs. Due to the urgency England was experiencing Dr Gough quickly formed the first and only experimental Scientific Research Experimental field unit of its kind and placed Jack in charge as chief field research and experimental officer.

'The fuse is all important,' Gough told him. 'If you have it, you've mastered the bomb.'

In less critical times, the ordinary procedure in developing new equipment or apparatus would be to first establish the basic principles by research, then proceed to reasonably safe development by tests using small quantities of explosive, and then by extrapolation to the relatively large scale of an actual bomb (which could contain up to 1,000kg of explosive). Finally, tests would be carried out on bombs under controlled conditions in which the safety of personnel was paramount. The next step was to produce equipment for trials by service users. But such methods were now deemed far too slow for the actual situation. They could not call in the troops for this purpose as scientific manipulation and observations were essential.

This work was to be of the utmost secrecy and Gough was the first to agree that Jack was perfect for the job. His BSc degree and interest in explosives, also his willingness, high intelligence and massive amount of energy, drive and courage were ideally suited for the work. The possessor of a sound logical mind, he was extremely eager to become part of something technically difficult and of vital importance to the nation. Jack's next task took him to London Docks to requisition a vehicle for BD work.

While searching the docks for a likely van he happened across the ideal vehicle. A slightly-built driver smoking a cigarette and wearing a black trilby hat, was nonchalantly leaning against a black-painted Pickfords van registration number FGI 225. Jack, wearing his signature wide-brimmed black hat, strode purposely over in his direction. He stopped and asked the man his name. In a cockney accent, he replied, 'It's Frederick Hards, Fred for short, at your service.' Fred, standing 5ft 10in in his socks, was now being asked another question. Mightily impressed with Jack's commanding presence, Fred heard him inquire whether he wanted to join his unit. At least that's what he thought he said. Fred's face lit up, this employment opportunity would exempt him from military service and, as it was a gift from the gods, he stubbed out his cigarette and promptly agreed and shook Jack's hand.

Frederick William Hards, born in Lewisham on 15 June 1905, had left school at 14 years-old to earn a living and help support his parents, Jack and Elizabeth Florence Hards, and his siblings. Fred was now 35 years-old and still driving for Pickfords Removals of Hays Wharf, London. He and his parents and his four brothers and two sisters had always been very close, and, if asked, he had to say his greatest passion in life, all he really ever wanted, was to play football. So whenever he got a spare moment he was the first one to suggest a game. Fred, not hugely religious, had been christened into the Church of England.

He was almost 21 years-old when he proposed to his sweetheart Elizabeth Hutchings, they married on Boxing Day, 1926 in Penge. They found a house to live in on Clarina Road, Penge, and it was not all that long before he became a proud parent of two daughters June and Olive, and son Richard who was 2½ years-old. Fred was fiercely protective of his family, and they came first in his life.

Fred's wife did not believe it him when he told her he was going to work for the 20th Earl of Suffolk in bomb disposal. He was always joking around with her so she thought nothing of it. But she changed her mind the day her husband walked through the door with a tall imposing figure behind him. She became very flustered as Fred introduced her to the Earl. To put her at ease, Jack turned to Fred and told him he would love a cup of tea.

Fred's wife was not always kept aware of Bomb Disposal (BD) matters and what Fred did when he was not at home. He had told her that he had met the Earl at Hays Wharf and that he had commandeered his van. The Earl had said to him, 'I'll have that one', pointing to the van. Fred, now 35 years-old, was due to be called-up any moment but the Earl told him not to worry about it because he was now working for him. Once Jack found out the type of man Fred was – always laughing and joking – they became inseparable and called him 'Fredders'. When circumstances dictated, they drove madly through Beckenham at 70mph in the van with 'Unexploded Bombs' emblazoned on the side. Wherever they went they had a police escort: when they drove at night, in the blackout, they had only two hooded headlights for illumination. His wife knew that Fred loved his work and was not frightened by what he did.

Being a frequent visitor to Fred's home, Jack always had, in his pocket, pieces of bomb which he would place on the table so that he and Fred could examine them. Another time, Fred invited him to come and watch his beloved game with him at Crystal Palace where Jack, dressed in his unusual attire, cheered heartily with the rest of crowd when Fred's team scored a goal. When Jack talked of Australia with a faraway look in his eye, Fred realized he loved that country. One day Jack asked him if he and his family would consider living there and working for him after the war was over, and Fred readily agreed. Working for Jack, hot sun instead of in constant rain and winter snow, won hands down every time.

Throughout the remainder of Jack's short life, Fred was his chauffeur, a competent mechanic, a handyman, and devoted confidante: a man ready and willing to assist the Earl during his bomb disposal days. They became inseparable, and Fred thought nothing of wrapping his muscular arms around a 250kg bomb and lugging as if it were a mild form of recreation.

Jack also commandeered Beryl Morden once more as his secretary. Both she and Fred freely volunteered their services even after having the job and its hazardous nature explained to them. They were being asked to do something that was absolutely outside the scope of anything the MoS, as their employer, could expect under the original and normal terms of employment.

Long before Beryl knew the Earl and before her days in France working alongside him, she used to catch the 8.21am train every morning to London where she worked for a motor company; it was not stimulating work but it was a job and the wages were adequate. After arriving back from her mission in France, the only words she said to her mother were, 'I am tired,' and slept a solid twenty-four hours. Then, just as before, she caught her early morning train to London the next day to report once more for work.

She never talked about her work to anyone, not even her family. Beryl, like Fred, was more than happy to accompany the Earl on his crusade against Britain's enemy, taking shorthand notes and typing up his dictated notes even in the most trying and terrifying of circumstances. The notes she took down would eventually help form the basis of the bomb disposal manual for others who were involved in that area of work. Jack, even though he needed Beryl to be within hearing distance so that he could explain the procedure he was about to undertake, would order Beryl out of harm's reach and keep her notes safe when he was about to defuse a bomb. Having cleared everyone away from the danger area he would proceed to operate alone, deliberately exposing himself daily to danger.

Once when Jack and his brother Greville shared a few moments together, he told him he was a fatalist but he never brooded; 'If my name is on the bomb,' he said, 'that's it.'

At the end of a difficult job he would bundle his seven-strong team of soldiers and civilians into the van and head for the best meal money could buy at the Ritz or, his favourite, Kempinskis: his 'honoured' guests wearing battledress and stained overalls. Jack, Beryl and Fred quickly became known as 'The Holy Trinity' and were often seen driving around London in their black van. They were famous for their prowess in successfully defusing thirty-four unexploded bombs with modest, smiling efficiency. The Holy Trinity's work was kept Top Secret and was so sensitive that even the Countess of Suffolk never knew the true nature of her husband's work.

Other members of Jack's unit were Royal Engineers from 719 General Construction Company attached to No.2 Bomb Disposal Company, and proud owners of those precious qualities – guts and guile: Lieutenant

Richard Godsmark, Corporal Francis Baxter (from Matlock), Driver Patrick Travers (from Paisley in Scotland), and Sappers George Routhan (in official documents Routham is sometimes referred to as Routham, from Brighton), Reginald Dutson, Carlo Laposta (from Birmingham [billeted in Surbiton, Surrey]), Jack Hardy, Bertie Gillet (from Stratford-on-Avon), and William (Bill) Fullwell (in official documents is sometimes referred to as Fullvel) who all worked in very close proximity to bombs and continuously put their lives at risk.

Jack kitted out the frequently seen BD black van at his own expense and used it as a mobile laboratory. He and his unit experimented with various methods for rendering bombs safe, which involved burning out explosives, using plastic explosives or acid to open up bomb cases, bodily trepanning of complete fuse pockets and, most alarmingly, shooting fuses in order to disable them. Their work often took them all over the country with all three of the services, but most of the actual experimentation often took place in London bomb 'cemeteries': large open spaces like Richmond Park, Hackney Marshes, and Erith (also known as Belvedere) Marshes. The Earl's methods of working on bombs were very simple and very direct.

'You cannot play puss-puss with a bomb,' he often told them. 'You've got to be tough with it; otherwise the devil will trick you.'

One mid-October day in 1940, recently promoted Second Lieutenant Herbert Hunt met with Jack when working with fellow Royal Engineer Captain Michael 'Max' Blaney, who had been detailed to accompany Jack and provide him access to bomb sites. Captain Max Blaney later died on Friday 13 December 1940 overseeing the removing of a UXB from a vast crater in Romford Road, East London. It had two detonating fuses: a clockwork time fuse with an 80-hour limit, and a motion sensitive fuse with a life of 60 hours.

Up until that moment, Jack spent most of his days in his laboratory researching various ways in which to disarm fuses – the only trouble being there were not enough. His mounting frustration was the result of having to wait for bombs or fuses to be brought to him. Finally, as waiting was not an option and time was of an essence, he went out into the field to claim them for himself.

Lieutenant Hunt tried without success to hide a smile when he saw what Jack was wearing: a local defence volunteer's armlet, probably a cover for his secretive work and more than likely 'borrowed' and worn on Jack's own initiative. He also had his two pets – 'Oscar' and 'Genevieve' – as personal weapons. Hunt likened the Earl's defusing apparatus to that of a Heath Robinson-designed contraption, but whatever Jack did with this, it brought results. By then he had developed a method of destroying bombs by burning, rather than exploding them, or sawing the cases in half to remove the explosives. In his laboratory, away from bomb sites, he continued his experiments on fuses and anti-handling devices in the most unusual manner.

England was in dire straits. During the first attacks on London in September, 5,730 people were killed and 200,000 houses were damaged, mostly beyond repair. On 15 October 1940, some 430 people were killed in a bombing raid; major railway stations had been badly damaged, the City of London's water mains were smashed, as was the major Fleet sewer. By mid-October, 250,000 people had been made homeless by the Blitz.

In October 1940, a letter marked 'Secret' from the Ministry of Aircraft Production (MAP), Millbank, London, SW1, arrived on Dr Gough's desk. They were considering assuming financial responsibility for the heavy water throughout the duration of their research at Cambridge and, as Gough was no doubt aware, Hans von Halban was being kept extremely busy and would soon require part of the heavy water to check its purity before handing it over to US scientists. That being the case, they deemed it necessary to release some of the stock and transfer its safe keeping to them. So would Dr Gough be so kind as to tell them where it was being stored?

In his reply to MAP, Gough informed them that the greater part of heavy water brought from France was now in Windsor Castle, while a smaller portion of it remained at Wormwood Scrubs. Mr Moreshead, at Windsor Castle, was in charge of the consignment of twelve square tins of highly-concentrated water and eight round tins of less concentrated water and had been directed to release it only at his request. To this effect, Gough enclosed a letter enabling their representative to obtain release of this precious commodity. Three square tins of highly-concentrated water and three round tins of less concentrated water were held at Wormwood Scrubs prison, and that consignment could only be released through Brigadier Harker, DMC, Ministry of Supply, at Gough's request.

Dr von Halban's research in Paris had consisted of trying to capture a cross-section of deuterium for neutrons. This experiment was checked and found to be extremely low, and it appeared that a certain chain reaction with uranium was possible. An experiment to test this had been planned but so far had not been carried out. While in Paris he had also investigated the possibility of chain reaction with fast neurons, this, however, turned out to be impossible due to the large cross-section for inelastic collisions.

During experiments, von Halban devised a method to overcome resonance capture using cubes of graphite or heavy water embedded in the uranium, thus allowing the neutrons down below the resonance band when inside the cubes. His research showed that by using this method the amount of twenty-five minute activity had been substantially reduced. Han von Halban requested the MoS take out secret patents corresponding to those already issued in France.

Chapter Eighteen

Jitterbug

Scientists were inclined, at first, to see Jack as a thrill-seeking dilettante but they soon changed their minds and began to recognize him as one of the best among them. They came to realize that the Earl possessed a rare combination of steely nerves and a scientific mind, and his unquenchable enthusiasm spurred the usually slow-plodding experts in the Directorate of Scientific Research to out-and-out scientific sprints.

'He had us all slapping bombs around as if they were ostrich eggs,' a research physicist recalled. 'We made progress that we'd never have made without him.'

Jack's ritual never varied. First, he would fit a scented Dubarry cigarette into one of his two holders and light it. Only then would he examine the bomb from all sides and angles, tap it, listen to it, and address it in colourful language. There was never any doubt that Jack regarded each bomb as a tricky personal adversary against whom he was matching his skill and courage. His watching co-workers became fascinated by the flow of unprintable language that poured from his lips. After the first examination of the bomb was completed, he would dictate to Beryl his plan of attack, a precaution so that if he failed others would know at least what not to do. After that, he removed his cigarette holder from his mouth and the spare from his pocket and handed them over to the nearest member of the unit, saying: 'Hold these a minute. They might get broken.' That was the signal for the group to move back to a safe distance and for Beryl, holding onto her notes for safekeeping, to move out of blast range.

A British actor walking in Richmond Park by chance witnessed the Earl during one of his BD operations.

'He was tinkering with the nose of a simply colossal bomb and filling the air with a barrage of profanity that it was an inspiration to listen to. Every few minutes, he would carry a piece of the bomb to the van some distance away and hand it to one of his companions then rush back shouting instructions to his secretary over his shoulder as he went. After an hour or so of this, with the profanity becoming louder and more elaborate every minute, Suffolk got up and walked slowly towards us carrying a small bit of mechanism from the bomb. He seemed utterly exhausted, his face wet with perspiration. "Cor blimey, lads," he said, " 'e was a bastard 'e was.'"

The underground bomb-storage vaults held endless fascination for Jack. He could be found at any hour of the day or night browsing through them, slapping the shiny sides and nose cones of the lethal weapons. Often he would stop and examine an occasional one that caught his eye. Night or day held no meaning to him. The only timepiece that tempted him was the clockwork mechanism of a bomb fuse.

Jack was not reckless even if he was flamboyant. The work he had taken on was of a delicate nature but he reduced the peril to a minimum by taking every known precaution to protect himself and his unit. He was on first name, personal terms with the experts in the Directorate of Scientific Research regardless of rank or title. While in company he had often shouted across the room to a colleague:

'Craigie, old boy! Remember that little trick we talked over last week? Well, it was a right fucking failure. Sorry, old boy,' then continue to explain in colourful language why the trick had failed, while a dignified red-faced Dr Craig mumbled and stuttered confused introductions to people standing around him, explaining that the Earl of Suffolk worked on bombs.

The Directorate of Scientific Research was at a loss to explain the survival of Jack after one of his failures; he calmly reported a bomb had gone off during an experiment. It was impossible to pry out of him how he had managed to survive.

'Jack had a kind of sixth sense as far as bombs were concerned,' said a scientist who worked with him. 'And he was seldom wrong.'

The Earl's team was a tight knit unit, and he never tired of regaling people with their exploits. His team basked in the glow of his affection, at times exceeding themselves in daredevilry just to give him another story to narrate. Once, he turned to one of his men and asked him to stir up the fire in his office. Suddenly there was a brilliant burst of flame followed by a cloud of smoke that filled the room.

The man, coughing somewhat and flapping away the smoke, asked Jack what had happened. 'I couldn't get the bloomin' fire to burn, could I? So I just bunged on some TNT that was lying around 'andy.'

The Earl loved telling that story whenever he could find someone to listen. His team was at a loss as to what to make of their boss. They had heard rumours that he lived in a palace and had marched in the coronation procession wearing an ermine-trimmed cape and coronet with his wife Mimi. But he could speak Cockney to perfection and enjoyed spending evenings with them in their rundown little flats in London's East End or small suburban homes. Quite often Jack curled up on their sofa or on the floor with a blanket and a cushion rather than face the drive back to his flat in the blackout. Jack loved his men and spent hours devising surprises for them.

One wintery, cheerless afternoon they happened to be driving along the bleak country roads of Wiltshire when he suddenly said, 'Lads, what would you say to a nice cup of hot tea and some scones?'

The lads were all for it, eager to rid themselves of the damp miserable feeling that had plagued them all day, but knew there was not a cat in hell's chance of it happening any time soon.

Jack suddenly slapped the dashboard and shouted, 'Here, stop the van. Pull in here, lads.' Once they came to a halt he jumped out of the van, pulled out one of his pistols from its shoulder holster and the unmistakable sounds of two gunshots pierced the air – the lads thought he had gone completely barmy. Almost immediately a large Bentley limousine slowly appeared over the hill and stopped nearby. The chauffeur and butler, their faces devoid of expression, calmly got out and set about preparing an elaborate English high tea complete with a fold-up table and chairs, starched tablecloth, china cups and saucers and silver tableware. His companions never realized they were within a few hundred yards of the Suffolk estate and that the chauffeur and butler had been carefully prepped on what to do at the sound of his gunshots. After that, his men believed Jack could achieve anything.

Jack loved to celebrate the completion of a task, and when he celebrated he did so with the same zest that characterized the way he lived his life. After loading his group into the van, along with a bomb or two for company, they would head off in the direction of Kempinskis Restaurant, just off Piccadilly Circus. Being a regular diner, there was always a table reserved laid out waiting for him. The restaurant did not seem to mind what time of the day or night he made an appearance or the state of his clothes. Usually they arrived just after they had finished working on a bomb wearing filthy overalls and muddy boots, chattering excitedly about their last job. The more fashionably attired patrons were invariably shocked when the unwashed motley crew arrived. Someone in the room would let it be known that the Earl of Suffolk had just arrived, whereupon inbred snobbery turned their disapproval into one of curiosity.

Jack's place was at the head of the table. George, the resident pianist, would play his signature tune – a ribald student song – with Jack beating out the accompanying rhythm with two dessert spoons. He was in his element and enjoyed sharing his wealth with those he thought were most deserving. He always ordered his usual meal, one that he loved, chicken chasseur with rice and asparagus tips, and insisted on ordering all the delicacies on the menu for the group. He would then roar with laughter at their grimaces after they tasted caviar and *pâté de foie gras* for the first time.

Felix, the Polish headwaiter, served the best his wine cellar had to offer for the Earl and managed, on one occasion, to provide him with a rare bottle of Framboise, a raspberry-flavoured crème liqueur. Felix commented to another waiter that some men would mix it with soda and say it was almost as good as cherry fizz, 'but le Suffolk, he like it, and I do it special for him.'

As time marched on, the party progressed and much had been drunk; out came pieces of bombs from their pockets which were then passed around the table. Once, out of sheer devilry, Jack invited restaurant guests to come outside and admire a large newly obtained bomb lying in the rear of the van. Some of the ladies became very nervous until he reassured them the bomb was harmless, as vital parts of the fuse had been removed and were at that moment in the safety of his pocket.

He said, 'Isn't it a beauty?' slapping the side of the casing and pointing out the finer points of the fuse to the nervous diners.

But despite the Earl's devil-may-care attitude, he did have a premonition of his own end.

'Felix,' he once said to the head waiter when leaving the restaurant. 'One of these nights only a little finger or maybe an ear will turn up for dinner. Be good to it because it will be all that's left of me.' One of Felix's proudest memories was when he had served him his wedding breakfast.

Jack loved to dance and executed an outlandish sort of jitterbug that was far too complex to describe except that it required the entire dance floor and wore his partner down in no time. Always intent on making sure that he and his friends wrung out every ounce of enjoyment they could from every minute of every hour, Jack was oblivious to the attention he was attracting. When the restaurant closed at night he, armed with a few bottles of wine tinkling against bomb parts in his pockets, frequently led his noisy entourage up Regent Street to the Coconut Grove Night Club. On celebration nights, Jack had no doubts that his skill at playing the drums was very good, although his piano playing was reserved for more dignified occasions – if someone asked him to play a song he would ask them to hum a few lines then pound the piano with total disregard for vocals or melody until people complained loudly and held their ears.

'It's marvelous how I can play any tune I hear,' he would shout to his onlookers as sweat glistened on his forehead.

Being a social animal, his wit and manner gave him a remarkable sense of freedom. Clothes were the least of Jack's worries: he would wear whatever was at hand at the time as long as it was comfortable and warm, as he could not tolerate very cold weather. His clothes were often the talk of the town and flamboyant to the point of eccentricity. His working clothes usually consisted of corduroy riding breeches and boots, a fleece-lined flying helmet, tweed hunting jacket, garishly checked trousers and other colourful items; but when social occasions demanded, he could be seen dressed in an elegant tuxedo and a bow tie. His long sideburns and moustache gave him the appearance of an old time 'Mississippi River Jim Dandy'. Always accompanying him were his two constant companions – 'Oscar' and 'Genevieve'.

On one occasion, Jack's brother Greville arranged to meet him at White's, one of the most exclusive and oldest clubs in London: traditionally the membership was from the higher ranks of the aristocracy and the upper echelons of government. The Earl, along with his long cigarette holder clasped firmly between his teeth, arrived wearing a shabby double-breasted overcoat with Home Guard flashes on the shoulders, a dark blue silk shirt and a white tie with orange and yellow spots. His favourite black hat was crammed on top of a balaclava, his flannel trousers tucked into black gaiters. On his feet he wore zip-up felt slippers which served an important purpose when approaching a bomb.

As they were leaving the club, Greville heard the hall porter explaining to an outraged clubman, 'It's alright, sir, its Lord Suffolk in his bomb tackling togs.' Jack could conform – almost – on occasion. Greville saw his brother leave his London flat for Westminster Abbey to attend the coronation of King George VI, looking handsome and splendid in his ceremonial robes, every inch the Earl of Suffolk and Berkshire. No one ever suspected he had a flask of brandy and a ham sandwich tucked away under his coronet.

Once, while waiting for someone in the lounge of the Piccadilly Hotel, dressed in his usual attired bomb disposal clothes, he overheard a woman guest ask a porter in a surprised tone, 'Who is that man?'

Suffolk rose and bowed gravely to the woman, doffed his hat, and said in his best Southern drawl, 'I'm the hotel dick [detective], ma'am. Has anyone been molesting you?'

The woman quickly shifted her glance from the Earl to her feet, muttering something under her breath that he could not understand and turned to leave. As she was going out the door she stopped and to ask the desk clerk for confirmation. He said, 'Yes, Madam, that's the Earl of Suffolk.'

The woman left tutting and shaking her head, uncertain if she had just been mocked or accidentally met with a bunch of lunatics.

The Earl took a room at the Royal Automobile Club just off Piccadilly, one of London's finest private members' clubs. His mansion and estate at Charlton Park had been converted into a hospital and convalescent home for soldiers so there was no use going home when he was looking for peace and solitude away from defusing bombs and raids by *Luftwaffe* bombers. Besides, it was too far to drive as he could be called away at any moment.

When bombing raids on London began, he often walked the streets alone, fascinated by the ear-splitting roar of explosions. The following morning after an all-night raid he had appeared clear-eyed and refreshed, joshing with the research workers at the MoS who could barely keep their eyes open.

'There's nothing quite so frightful as a quiet night,' he shouted cheerily while the rest of them were silently praying for a chance to get some sleep.

One day he parked a lorry with 'Bomb Disposal' painted on each side in front of his club. 'I'm taking between twenty and thirty delayed action bombs to the Green Belt Park to deal with them,' he told the members. 'Like me to give you a demonstration? I'll bring the biggest bomb into the hall here and dispose of it without cracking a single pane of glass. What do you say?' Sadly for Jack, his offer was firmly refused.

When Jack caught an infrequent moment of solitude, he would relax in his favourite chair in the club and stare out of the window into the mass that was London with a glass of Glenmorangie, his favourite single-malt whisky, in one hand and his long cigarette holder in the other. Life was not so bad and it could be worse. But in those rare moments when the world around him became quiet and still, when there was nothing to distract him, his fears edged closer towards the forefront of his mind, niggling away at hidden insecurities. He would never admit it to anyone, but he feared his health, something he had no control over. He wondered if it would let him down in his striving to rid England of its enemy and in looking after his family. He did not know the answer to that but it caused him anxiety nonetheless; it was his cross alone to bear. The rheumatic fever, caught when he was a young boy, had left him with permanent symptoms: swollen joints, sometimes stomach pain, always feeling cold and the possibility of some heart damage.

Then, of course, there was the Howard name to uphold and all that it encompassed. Charlton Park was a sanctuary to him but also a financial noose around his neck – the upkeep of the house was phenomenal – gone were the glory days of the Howards. Now they were at war and that required money. He came from a collapsing aristocracy which was and had been supported by American money, and the relationship he had with his mother was not what one would call friendly.

He hardly got to see Mimi and his children; he tried not to think about that too much as he missed them dearly. And then there were the people who wanted to get to know him or needed things from him because he was a Howard and connected in high places. Some thought him a 'toff'. Jack smiled at that: give him the working class any day – they were alive, there was never any pretence and one always knew where one stood.

He knew. He had an inkling that one experiences, a tiny voice that whispered in his ear that he would try and brush away like some irksome fly. He heard it every time he approached a bomb. His heart would pound and his palms would sweat as he tried to push that voice to the darkest recesses of his mind. But he knew, he knew that was the way he would die but he could not change anything. Things were what they were: it was his destiny, the same as his father's.

Jack drew comfort from his close associates who spoke to him in Cockney rhyming slang, or whenever he discussed the French front with someone he knew well, while consuming a bottle or two of brandy in a Soho restaurant, and everyone had taken to the shelters as bomb blasts filled the air and pieces of plaster fell down around their ears onto the table and floor. He stoutly maintained he was not a communist and regularly paid his fees to the Conservative Club, but do not, under any circumstances he told anyone who was listening, make any mistake, he was no Conservative either. A lifelong friend thought Jack a rebel against everything in his own past and against everything the society he was born into stood for.

He was the greatest socialist that ever existed though nothing made him madder than being told so. He loved sharing what he had and gravitated towards groups of people he could do the most for. One of his pet hates was the stuffiness of court society and the inane snobbery of the so-called aristocracy.

Harold Macmillan kept his thoughts to himself on the Earl. He knew Jack was devoted to the problem of bomb disposal and knew he worked hard, learning how to isolate fuses and then open and empty a bomb. Macmillan never shared his concerns with the man himself because the work was extreme difficulty and dangerous: hazardous because of the many unknown types of fuses involved and partly because many bombs were in dangerous positions.

Before the Earl took on this job, bomb disposal was generally regarded as a pastime for public-spirited suicides. But Jack would not have it. He thought that it would be safer for all if a few experts took exceptional risks in finding out how to deal with a live bomb. Only in this way could fatal accidents, such as those that frequently occurred when volunteers attempted to remove bombs from crashed aircraft, be avoided and the element of chance reduced. Macmillan found the man had a natural bent for devising highly original but effective methods of procedure.

To lend proportion to his new job, Jack opened an office in The Strand. A visiting Oxford scientist stood in dazed wonderment when he entered Jack's room. He found the Earl of Suffolk dressed in the most extraordinary outfit consisting of riding boots, corduroy trousers, a striped sweater and a white flying helmet. He was pacing up and down with a large pistol in his hand, raging in a frightful manner at the War Office for not giving him more bombs to examine.

CHAPTER NINETEEN

Bomb Disposal

The London Blitz came in phases. The first phase fell between 9 September 1940 and May 1941. During the autumn of 1940, the capital was raided on seventy-six consecutive nights with only one exception. The second phase began with the bombing of Coventry on 30 November 1940.

Winston Churchill kept many notes of the new and damaging form of attack being used against London. Long stretches of railway line, important junctions, the approaches to vital factories, airfields, main thoroughfares were blocked and denied to the people of London. Bombs had to be dug out and taken away and exploded or rendered harmless in place. This task was of the utmost peril when means and methods had to be learned by experience.

Churchill's interest in the delayed-action fuse had been with him since 1918 when the Germans used it on a large scale to deny Allied forces the use of the railways they had planned to use to advance into Germany. He thought it a most effective item in warfare because of the prolonged uncertainty it created. A special organization was set up to deal with the matter under General King who Churchill interviewed at Chequers. King eventually passed the position on to General Taylor.

Hearing about a special type of auger [boring tool] manufactured in the USA that was capable of cutting, in less than an hour, a hole of such size and depth that usually took two or three days to dig manually, Churchill strongly advised that a number of these tools be ordered for bomb disposable squads as time was of the essence. They were expensive but he had a duty to provide the men with the best technical equipment available.

On 15 November 1940, the Luftwaffe returned again to London with a vengeance, hitting almost every borough, using a new bomb (nicknamed 'Satan' by the Germans) that brought dread to BD personnel – it was massive – 1,800kg of high explosive, with a delayed-action fuse. During that month around 3,000 unexploded bombs were waiting to be defused.

On 29 December, some 10,000 incendiaries dropped on the City of London caused over 1,400 fires, including six that were classified as conflagrations, one of which covered half a square mile. St Paul's Cathedral was surrounded by fires, the Guildhall was damaged with only its walls left standing, and eight churches designed by Sir Christopher Wren were destroyed, as was Paternoster Row, a major telephone exchange, the Central Telegraph Office, and guild company halls. Five main-line railway stations, nine hospitals, sixteen Underground stations were also damaged.

By the end of June 1940, it was apparent that the twenty-five BD sections already formed would not be able to cope with the expected deluge of bombs. Another 109 new BD sections were authorized; volunteers were called for but only a few came forward. Most of the young officers came from the Royal Engineers officer cadet training unit, some of them receiving an immediate commission because of their technical or professional qualifications. All ranks were told they could, after six months service in bomb disposal, elect to transfer to another branch of the Royal Engineers. This offer was made because it was thought the strain would be too much on the men: few took up the offer because of the camaraderie they felt when facing intense danger together, and also the knowledge that they were saving lives, brought its own rewards.

In every city, town and district, special companies were being formed and volunteers came forward for the deadly game. From then on, throughout the war years, men and women in bomb disposal were placed on permanent duty. Some survived, others did not. Many managed twenty, thirty or even forty disposals before they met with the 'grim reaper'. They were taught to treat bombs like a woman – with gentleness and respect – and were asked if they could run a 100yds in a split second. There were no guidelines, no training courses and no manual to go by – what they learnt, and what Jack learned, they learnt by watching others and by sheer luck. There was a lack of technical equipment: all they had were hammers and chisels, lifting tackle, a few road-repair tools and some explosive for detonation. Unfortunately the chain of command proved unworkable.

Even though the regimental and administrative part of the Royal Engineers was controlled at War Office level by the Director of Anti-Aircraft (AA) and the Coastal Defence who worked in close liaison with officials of the Ministry of Home Security, they occasionally received their orders from civilian authorities. At the same time BD sections were formed, another valuable step forward was taken. The Unexploded Bomb Committee (UXBC), appointed by the Minster of Supply, considered disposal problems as they arose and advised sections and the MoS in methods and equipment.

Due to their wide variety of experience, men who volunteered for bomb disposal were not to be wasted, so a system of tests and examinations were instigated and conducted by the Royal Engineers. Answers to the questions disclosed to the examiners the extent of a man's capacities and often produced an illuminating feel to the character of the student or his instructor. They looked for careful judgment, depth of concentration, self-confidence and control, a certain calmness and leadership: whether they were a team player or whether they were happy working on their own. The question – What do you consider the ideal qualifications of character for a member of a Bomb Disposal Unit? – evoked a variety of responses:

'The first and foremost qualification is caution. If a BDS man is a 100 percent careful he is 100 percent safe – if he is 99 percent careful he is a danger to the squad.'

'A member of the BDS should be strong, unmarried and be able to run fast.'

'A member of the squad should not be indispensable to the factory. He should be of excellent character and be prepared for the afterlife.'

Unexploded bomb (UXB) detachments paraded wherever Winston Churchill visited. Their faces varied from those of the ordinary men, their eyes glinted with intensity and they appeared calm and confident. Churchill thought them different to ordinary men. Distinguished in their uniform, women loved them while men eyed them with awe and admiration. Without their uniforms they looked half-starved and weak, such was the stress caused by the work. The nerves of men in Jack's team, and others all over the country, gradually wore them down over time.

They laughed, drank together and sometimes argued. Sometimes they annoyed each other and flared with irrational temper. They were the most patient of men and the most impatient; the most temperate and the most intemperate; the most certain of mind and the most exhausted. When they slept, it was the sleep of the dead. When they died, there was nothing to pick up. A grave but no body.

And when they took the walk, the long walk, to the bomb, they went alone. They trusted nothing, suspected everything and were most careful when they were tired. They were alone; the courage that was demanded of them was courage of ice. Emotion would kill them, passion would kill them, and hatred would kill them.

It was their skill against the ingenuity of German science. The Germans did not present their genius to them on a platter; the answers to the problems the Germans had set were hidden, guarded, and even defended. Science guarded science. Ingenuity defended ingenuity. The way in to the mechanism of a mine or bomb was not an open door. It was very personal. The courage demanded of them was constant and calm. They could not tremble or fumble because this might trigger the weapon. They could not hesitate or take the wrong process or blame. (*Softly Tread the Brave* by Ivan Southall)

Where their courage came from and what kept it going no one knew. It contravened every basic instinct of self-preservation, demanding without limit self-confidence, self-reliance, self-discipline and self-sacrifice. It compelled them to become the most introverted of men for the most extroverted of reasons. Where was that courage to be found? There was no answer, because there was no knowing.

During July 1940, casualties were high and the number of UXBs waiting to be dealt with rose alarmingly. Roads were closed, industrial production disrupted, and undamaged homes left empty. By September 1940, the number of live UXBs recorded was 3,759. Specialist RE units were hastily diverted to BD. Men had little time to learn and had to cope with bombs mostly without training. Bomb disposal was learned from bitter experience that the clockwork mechanism, set for long delay, had a habit of stopping either because of a weak spring or a minute fault in the assembly. A slight jolt, tilt or vibration caused by a passing vehicle could be enough to re-start the mechanism.

On 28 November 1940, the Inspector of Fortifications sent a letter to Dr Gough, the subject being the use of Thermite for burning explosives out of bombs. The writer had been to see Lord Suffolk's most recent and successful demonstration on the previous Thursday, and was very anxious to obtain supplies of Thermite as soon as possible so they could issue instructions to all BDUs. He mentioned the washing out process and was sure Gough agreed with him that the process was now sufficiently developed enough to be used, and suggested that Lord Suffolk get in touch with Colonel Bateman with a view to drafting the necessary instructions. The writer estimated they would require sufficient to deal with an average of thirty bombs a day for the next three months.

John Stuart Mould from HMS *Vernon* received his first introduction to the Earl of Suffolk's name when he was told there was another mine at Meopham, near Rochester. Nervous and more than a little excited, he and McClinton jumped the ditch and pushed through a break in the hedge. The ground was firm, everything looked perfect. Mould found the mine identical to one he had rendered safe, the same odd smell, the same dark-grey casing, the same stencilled letters, the same tangle of cords and parachute. It looked enormous.

'Is not there anything else we can do?' asked Mould.

McClinton replied, 'We could do a lot of things, Mouldy, but we would only kill ourselves, and that would not help anyone, not even us. If you look round, there's not much damage it can do. You've always got to consider that, of course, before you burn. It's a good thing, really. It'll show you another part of the job. A practical demonstration is worth a book full of notes.'

McClinton brought up the tools and produced an earthenware flowerpot, a bag of aluminium powder and a short length of fuse. Beside the mine he began carefully building a platform using bricks and stones.

'Make sure it's secure, Mouldy…if the bricks topple and fall against the mine it can make a frightful mess of things, particularly you. It's always a bit tricky, old chap, getting the wretched flower pot to sit right. You've got to get the hole in the bottom over the casing of the mine. Have you a penny?' McClinton got the flower pot balanced.

'Looks pretty shaky to me,' said Mould. 'Do you mind if I duck off to see my aunty?'

'Now the penny goes over the hole in the bottom of the pot: like so. Then the aluminium powder goes in the pot, so. And the fuse – its ordinary magnesium ribbon – you poke it into the powder, so.'

'Now what?' said Mould.

'Pick up your tools, strike a match, and run like hell.'

Mould peered round the side of the haystack. The aluminium powder had ignited and a pinpoint of brilliant light seemed to hang, suspended, over the mine.

'It's the old principle of Thermite welding, Mouldy. Terrific heat: it'll melt the penny in a moment and start dripping through the casing. You might remember I placed it as far from the fuse as I could get it. It doesn't take long to melt through the casing – it's only aluminium – and once it's through, the explosive will burn. It might burn for five minutes or fifty minutes and then she'll go up. The longer she burns the better. The more explosive burnt, the less violent the eventual blast.'

'TNT or anything like it – the stuff in the Jerry mines is not strictly TNT – won't explode unless it's detonated. There has to be an explosion to make it explode. And that mine won't go up until the fire gets to the detonator or unsettles the bomb fuse. That's the problem. You cannot predict time lag.'

Suddenly, it seemed, the flame was through the casing and it flared with the brilliance of a rising sun, a brilliant orange flame, almost too brilliant, initially, to look at. In seconds, the height and the breadth of the flame was almost terrifying.

Clouds of dense white smoke mushroomed above the flame and a firepool spread around the mine. Mould could actually feel the heat. It felt evil and looked evil and smelt evil. Mould shivered. The haystack now seemed far too fragile. A solid wall of bricks or concrete might have felt more secure, although in fact would have been highly dangerous. His boisterous confidence of the last hour or so was running away from him. The glare from the burning explosive was horrifying.

'He's a useful friend, the Earl; quite a character. You'll have to meet him some time. Mixed up in some extraordinary business at the time of Dunkirk. Frightfully hush-hush. Real cloak-and-dagger stuff. How's that mine look?'

'He's a chemist, the Earl. strictly amateur, of course. Works with his chauffeur and his secretary. Chauffeur helps him, secretary takes notes. They're a fantastic sight, particularly that girl standing beside the bomb, recording everything the Earl says. They call themselves The Holy Trinity. They rush hither and thither delousing [sic] bombs all over the place. Just for the love of it. The Earl cooked up this burning business with Brock of Brock's Fireworks. Every child knows Brock's Fireworks. This burning business has been known as Brock's Folly.' (From *Softly Tread the Brave* by Ivan Southall)

'Well they do blow up sometimes, old chap, with a pretty awful bang. Better keep your head in or it'll be off.'

CHAPTER TWENTY

Brock's Folly

Beryl had just finished typing up her notes on the Earl's experiments. His report dated 17 November 1940 read:

Experiment No.70 – carried out at Richmond Park using a 1,000kg bomb with the tail plate and fuse removed. The bomb was half full of caked TNT. The point of attack was 2in above the nose weld. The Thermite was ignited by means of a Blackford burster. Thermite was ignited at 2.51pm and at 2.52pm there was a crack like a rifle shot followed by a minor detonation. At 3.05pm, thick clouds of grey TNT smoke appeared and at 3.11pm, there were dense columns of black TNT smoke. At 3.16pm smoke was decreasing and lighter in colour, and by 3.25pm there was hardly any smoke visible. By 3.45pm, smoke once more was increasing in volume and darkening in colour. By 3.52pm thick clouds of smoke and strong orange flame and at 4.05pm no flame was visible but there were fairly thick clouds of smoke still appearing. By 4.10pm smoke was hardly visible.

Visited the bomb at 4.20pm where it was found the case had split into three pieces, the nose weld having completely separated from the body and the body having split twice longitudinally. No alteration could be observed in the contour of the crater.

Experiment No. 87 – carried out at Strawberry Hill Golf Club in Twickenham on 11 December 1940 on a 250kg bomb with Type 17 fuse. A dome-shaped base was secured to the body of the bomb by 'grub screws'. Seven ounces of PE [plastic explosive] was placed within 2in of the fuse and ending opposite the base of the fuse pocket. It was lit electrically with Primacord.

Result – complete detonation of the bomb. A point of interest being the fumes of the bomb had no smell of TNT whatsoever but an exceedingly strong smell of the characteristic nitro-glycerine fumes, such as might be smelt from an explosion of gelignite or an allied explosive. Note: It might be valuable to have the dome-ended 'grub screwed' bombs opened for examination of the explosive.

Experiments Nos. 88 & 89 – carried out at Richmond Park on 11 December 1940, with a 50kg bomb without fuse. A tin cone, whose strip is always the diameter of its base, was placed 5in abaft of the fuse pocket. It was fired by an electric detonation but no Primacord was used: Amount of Amanol - 4ozs.

Result – a singularly violent detonation: In my opinion, rather more violent than the normal explosion of a 50kg bomb. Definite shock was noticed.

Experiment No. 89 – the same method was used on a 50kg bomb but with less than half of the explosive.

Result: the bomb case was broken open and TNT was strewn about the hole but no detonation.

The Earl carried out the following experiments at Richmond Park on 21 January 1941:

Experiment No. 76 – A fused 50kg bomb was used: 1¼ozs of PE was placed in the centre of the bomb. Result: case split open nicely.

Experiment No. 77 – A fused 50kg bomb was used. 1¼ozs of PE was placed in the centre of the bomb. Result: case split, partial detonation of the bomb.

Experiment No. 78 – A fused 50kg bomb was used. 1¼ozs of PE was placed in the centre of the bomb. Result: case split open nicely.

Experiment No. 79 – A fused 250kg bomb was used. 4¾ozs of PE was placed round the neck of the tail plate. Result: complete detonation.

Experiment No. 80 – A 50kg bomb mock-up fuse was used. 1oz of PE was placed in the centre of the bomb. Result: case spilt open nicely.

Experiment No. 81 – A 50kg bomb with mock-up fuse was used. 1oz of PE was placed in the centre of the bomb. Result: case split open nicely.

Experiments Nos. 82 to 94 – Exactly the same as Nos. 80 and 81: with same results.

Experiment No. 95 – A 50kg bomb with mock-up fuse was used. 1oz of PE was placed in the centre of the bomb. Result: dent made in bomb case.

Suffolk dictated his findings on Thermite and other methods of dealing with unexploded bombs to Beryl, mentioning the Thermite method brought to his attention by the Director Scientific Research (DSR) who asked him to carry out a series of investigations on this method. After preliminary work at the Brocks Fireworks Factory at Hemel Hempstead he ascertained that Thermite would in fact penetrate steel over $^3/_8$in thick. He then proceeded to visit Richmond Park where he commenced a determined attack upon various unfused bombs.

Jack encountered a number of powder-filled bombs. Acting on the suggestion of the DSR he developed the technique of washing out explosives, through a hole in the tail of the bomb, by means of a water jet powered by a trailer pump. At this juncture, he also attempted to wash out the solid explosive, but was unable to report any success since he did not have the correct nozzle or that the pump did not have sufficient pressure.

The next technique Jack tried to elaborate on was that of smashing the bomb casing by applying PE. Finally, due to an experiment and information culled from the station officer at Ruislip Fire Station, he began experimenting with the washing out of the solid charge by using a special nozzle. Although at the time this method and the PE method required far more experimental work, he was convinced that both showed promise and would continue with his experiments.

The Earl's men, after arriving at a bombsite, invariably found Jack already there; he had become a regular visitor to sites all over south-east England, showing a keen interest in what was going on. His attire and demeanour still very much the same: his signature plus fours or tailored trousers and duffle coat tied around the middle with a belt, a piece of thin rope or old tie, and his long cigarette holder. A former sapper, Cecil Brinton, had his first conversation with the Earl after a very lucky fuse extraction.

Brinton had been in the Coulsdon area and had been digging up a bomb. They had to shore-up the hole because the ground was unstable, unlike the clay they were used to. When he climbed down to the bomb he found that it had two fuses: a Type 17 and a Type 50. He did not know anything about them at the time and just took them out and climbed back to the surface. The Earl was there waiting to congratulate him on his work, and Brinton handed over the two fuses. The Earl looked at them and asked him if he knew what they were. Brinton said, 'Yes, they are the fuses I've just taken out of the bomb.' The Earl said, 'Well, lad, you'll see one is longer than the other. The longest one has a clockwork mechanism on the end.'

That was the first time Brinton had been told there could be a delayed action fuse. Previous to that he had taken a number of bombs to the Earl in Regent's Park but he had never spoken to him. After that, every time he took him a bomb the Earl recognized him and they became quite friendly. He learnt more from him about bomb disposal than before. The Earl taught him practically everything there was to know at the time. Whether that was useful or not, he did not know. Up until then he would just go and take the fuses out, whereas in the future he would think twice.

Cecil Brinton was one of those men in bomb disposal who had not been told about the provision of transferring out after six months. Unsurprisingly, none of the men in bomb disposal, when asked, would have left even if they had known there was a choice – even when, as was more often the case, there was no officer to actually defuse a bomb and the job fell to a sapper.

Brinton's officer-in-charge of the section was killed around that time and it fell to him to take over. He was totally unaware of the danger he faced. He did not know there were Type 15, 17 or 50 fuses. He knew later, but at the time he had no idea. He presumed the officer had known. It was many weeks before they had a replacement officer and their section was up to strength again. He was removing fuses, but had no idea of what could happen. He must have had a guardian angel on his shoulder. There was one bomb he went to with only a key because the stethoscope had disappeared and the two-pin plug had been discarded because they thought it had been booby-trapped. So he went down, undid the fuse and took it out. People got themselves killed doing that.

Ernest Acton was an officer among the top military personnel attending a demonstration of a bomb defusing technique ('Brock's Folly') in Richmond Park that involved chemically burning a hole in the bomb case and burning out the explosive. He, like everybody else, had heard many stories about the Earl and the people he had selected, and that he had done a lot of good work. The Earl was respected by people like himself (the Section Officer). Lieutenant Godsmark came to see him and told him the Earl of Suffolk had got hold of a new idea of tackling the infernal bombs so that they did not have to defuse them, because on some of them you could not remove the fuse. The Earl had this idea you could burn it out. Ernest said it sounded interesting and Lieutenant Godsmark recommended they go along the next morning to the common and watch the demonstration. The next day, Godsmark arrived, wearing his service dress complete with 'Sam Brown' and pistol. They arrived at the common and well, he had never seen so many red tabs. There were many people there: senior and staff officers, examining a trench. It was only a small trench and, in the bottom of it, the Earl of Suffolk had his bomb. The filter cap on the end was off, at an angle of about 60°. On top of it the Earl had placed an earthenware crucible on a little frame.

Jack said, 'I am now going to light this and it will set the whole thing going. It will drip onto the bomb, make a hole in it and the explosive will burn. When it's burnt out, all we will be left with is a fuse pocket and that's easy to deal with. We can take it away, no problem,' and grinned. Ernest thought that was a bit funny seeing as it would still leave the picric acid pellets in the fuse.

Anyway, the Earl lit it and they all stood around trying to look knowledgeable. It burnt through and the explosive filling began to burn. Smoke billowed out of the back of the bomb and after a while it began to look like a rocket and started roaring. All of a sudden, as if someone had told them to, everyone turned and ran and at some point they threw themselves to the ground, just before the bomb stopped roaring! It was incredible, just like it had been planned. Everybody got up, nonchalantly dusted themselves off, and walked away in total silence.

While this was going on, Lord Suffolk, wearing a white flying helmet and fur gloves, was sitting on a shooting stick watching all the fun. A BD squad who had been using a home-made method of burning-out defused bombs with paraffin-soaked rags for months gave the Earl's scheme a cool reception. No one seemed impressed by the new method. The view was that some of the scientists were so scientific, that if they wanted to open a bottle of beer they would cut a hole in the side first instead of removing the stopper. Not everyone cared for Jack; he was not disciplined nor was he one of the army boys.

Noel Cashford, MBE, served in the Royal Navy's Mine and Bomb Disposal Unit and had in his time made safe over 200 devices, fifty-seven in a mere three days. His senior officers thought Jack Howard a bit of a nuisance, an eccentric busybody and more than a bit weird, which was obviously due to his unconventional ways of working, his unusual character and disregard for rules, though he did have rules – his own, and more than often they worked.

Alexandra Mary Gregory was a personal secretary to Sir Percival Robinson, Permanent Secretary at the Ministry of Works, which also included Bomb Disposal. Her office was situated in Whitehall, London, overlooking St. James's Park and next door to the office of Sir Philip Sassoon, Commissioner of Works. Part of her duty was to source and organize relief for bombed cities, and prepare progress reports on the supply convoys and trains that took materials to cities for rebuilding, places like Coventry, Plymouth, Liverpool, and Southampton. Her reports were distributed via Sir Jock Colville (Churchill's personal private secretary [PPS]) who would then pass them onto Churchill. She was frequently in contact with the great and the good and the some not so good. She thought Lord Beaverbrook one of the rudest, silliest men she had ever met.

She did, however, develop a liking for the Earl. She thought him very dashing, very handsome and utterly heroic. The Earl had frequent meetings with Sassoon. Before a meeting could begin he would enter her office and ask her if he could leave his son in her care. Maurice, the little boy, was left to play happily in the bottom drawer of her desk while he waited for his father to emerge. Once, Alexandra picked up the Earl's sumptuous coat, with its sable lining, brushing it against her face as she hung it on a hat stand; so soft. One of her more extrovert colleagues found her trying the coat on and from then on she was constantly teased by Sassoon.

Chapter Twenty One

Flecks of Red Blanket

Defusing bombs was made all the more difficult over winter for Jack and his team. If left undisturbed, the frozen earth during those months often prolonged the life of the battery of bombs fitted with motion sensitive fuses. The weather was usually dreadful, with torrential rain and thick heavy mud everywhere. The men battled on in snow, sleet, ice and exceedingly low temperatures. Even though they tried to blow warmth into their hands it was often a losing battle: hands, fingers, feet and toes became painfully numb. Thawing ice and snow turned fields into quagmires but they had to keep going and be cheerful. Bombs lay everywhere: in houses, back gardens, in the streets, railways, schools, industrial areas; often in the bleakest, most desolate of places.

The long walk: that fear provoking lone walk to the bomb once everyone was well and truly out of harm's way. Jack experienced it thirty-five times during his life; thirty-five times when he consciously shut off his emotions, to enable him to do his job. He, and others of his type, who worked in bomb disposal, made that surrealistic walk to where the bomb lay portentously waiting, urging him to make that one mistake. Just one mistake was all it took. It really was a long walk, or so it seemed. Palms sweated, skin itched from perspiration that ran down into clothes and body crevices, just asking to be scratched, even though it was cold outside. But composure, above all, had to be maintained; after all, everybody thought or hoped to God he knew what he was doing. Jack always attempted to think three or four steps ahead or at least tried to. He relied on his knowledge, his nerves and his tools, not technology. Before setting off, he made doubly sure he had with him his leather case or canvas haversack containing wooden or special tools manufactured from non-ferrous metals, because he never knew if the bomb was magnetic.

At the beginning of bombing raids, no one had an idea as to what type of bomb they would find, so they used what tools they had to hand, even a hammer and chisel. They soon found out that with one smack of the hammer they could end up in the next world. Gradually, tool kits became better designed to handle various types of fuse, and contained a variety of spanners, keep-rings (threaded keep-rings that retained the fuses and clock mechanisms in their flanges, allowing them to be unscrewed with the right tool), a Crabtree Mk1 for a Type 15 fuse, used to unscrew the locking ring, plus a number of screwdrivers, hammers and special gadgets developed over time after encountering various types of bombs and mines.

The bomb could also be acoustic, in which case Jack was in trouble because he would have to work in silence. He never had a clue what fate awaited him. Maybe it was a fuse he had never seen before. He may have even felt a slight tremble in his hands. Perhaps he whistled a tuneless song through clenched teeth to give him courage. On those occasions, time stood still but on the other hand it raced faster than his rapidly beating heart. Pulse rate, blood pressure, glucose and lipids all became significantly raised; everything seemingly unbelievably clear as crystal, yet his brain could not retain a single thing. Riding high on adrenaline, he was either barking mad or a serious extrovert.

His team was safe and just as anxious as he was; they puffed on their cigarettes, joked amongst themselves, and blew on their hands or stamped their feet to keep the cold at bay or just because they needed something to do. Civilians relied on men like Jack, they pinned their hopes on his experience not to blow them and their precious possessions to smithereens.

One such man who often took the long walk and had heard rumours about the Earl was Captain John Hannaford of the Royal Engineers. He and his men were being addressed by the head of bomb disposal: 'We've just heard from the medical boffins that if you're sitting astride a bomb and it goes up, you won't feel a thing because the reaction of the body's nervous system is not as quick as the explosion.' As if those few words of comfort would set their minds at rest.

Hannaford and his men heard on various occasions talk about the Earl's role in the war effort. He never met the man, but knew several who had and the view at the time was that they wished him luck but would rather keep their distance. To Great Britain, the Earl's story was a godsend to the government-led wartime press and heavily biased towards morale-boosting propaganda, all a part of warfare. The country was on the brink of defeat and morale was alarmingly at low ebb. News was coming in from their forces wherever they were fighting and it was consistently doom laden. Churchill, above all others, deeply believed in the power of propaganda, so it can be assumed that he encouraged the story.

As a nation, Great Britain still retained a medieval attitude towards the aristocracy, so put together the Earl of Suffolk and Berkshire and Bomb Disposal and Churchill had a winner. However, what had to be said was that they knew him to be a brave and well intentioned individual, serving his nation in a time of dire crises and he believed that what he was attempting was right. The press homed in on it and the value as propaganda was immeasurable. In war, sanity is lost and the sacrifice of life meant absolutely nothing.

The Royal Engineers Bomb Disposal Unit consisted of a lieutenant, a staff sergeant, also a sergeant, corporal, a lance corporal and some thirty other ranks. On the lower left sleeve of their uniforms was the striking bomb badge, a symbol of excitement and courage. The officer did the actual defusing, but relied heavily on the expertise of his chosen team to dig to the required depth and operate the specialist equipment. Sections were well provided with numerous skills required to deal with ever-changing challenges.

By nature, John Hannaford was a cautious man not prone to taking risks and his pre-defusing thoughts went as follows: 'I possibly will not survive this but if it happens it will be blissfully quick.' But accidents occurred and comrades with him were killed. He suffered deep shock on two occasions and it was a terrifying experience. But despite the shock, he was expected to and did carry on the next day. He could not understand it but he feared going out in the blackout. He had worked in London, Cardiff, Liverpool, Swansea and – perhaps worst of all – clearing minefields (British) laid on some beaches in Pembrokeshire. Clearing up their own mines was truly awful as there were many casualties. To be killed by an enemy bomb was one thing, but to lose your life on a peaceful beach to a British-laid mine seemed the ultimate obscenity of war.

Their technical information arrived from HQ in London and was brilliant; details of new or modified German fuses were transmitted to them within hours via teleprinter. They also had 'Priority Phones', which were rare indeed. After initial training with an 'experienced' officer – who had been practising for perhaps a couple of months – Hannaford was sent to Ripon, North Yorkshire, on a three week intensive training course. The course was memorable because of a mix-up; another team exploded a practice bomb and, but for a good thick hedge his career would have ended then and there. There was the BD manual, by which he worked; it saved the life of his sergeant who he stopped from invoking the half hour rule. The explosion would have killed him, and John never forgot his thanks.

To elaborate more, in London and specifically for BD, a high-powered scientific team met on a daily basis to consider all aspects of German fuse technology, the methods to make them safe, and the design and production of the complex equipment required by BD personnel. The men valued them enormously. In the face of this, it did seem odd that the Earl was allowed to independently experiment with his own strange ideas. Perhaps to the nation he was a glamorous hero and as Churchill probably would have said: 'Worth two brigades in the field.'

Lieutenant Stuart Archer of 105 Bomb Disposal Section, Royal Engineers, said that he was there to do a job and it was no use saying: 'I don't like the sound of that.' One just got on and did it, there was no choice.

There was talk going around, there was always talk, of a sapper who was a nervous wreck, and committed suicide by putting his head in a gas oven. Some men drank to forget. Their motto: Join the army and see the world. Join bomb disposal and see the next one.

Jack returned from Bury St Edmunds with the first ever 250kg anti-personnel bomb to be recovered. On 7 October 1940, he was told a large bomb had landed on a house in Charlbury Grove. It seemed to have penetrated deep underground and Jack was eager to get his hands on the fuse. It was the first time Sergeant Brian Moss met Lieutenant Howard. Sergeant Moss was asked to supply two men for a special project so he sent Gillett and Dutson, and also a tall Glaswegian driver who had been billeted with Moss in Gillingham. Apparently, all three had joined Suffolk's team.

Moss had worked on bombs before. As was often the case, he and his men often spent days and days digging down only to find nothing. Then there would be a moment of horror when their pickaxe clanged against a bomb casing. Their first thought would be – had it started the clock ticking? After getting over the initial shock and getting down on his knees to use a trowel to carefully uncover a bomb to expose its end, they found it was generally a 250kg. After kneeling beside it, whispering to it, man to man, Brian Moss tried to persuade himself it only had a Type 15 fuse, because, God willing, it very often was.

That day both Moss and Jack thought it very likely the bomb had a delay fuse, since the others in the same stick had not gone off until several hours later. Little did they know that Sergeant Moss was going to spend nearly a month on the bomb.

Sergeant Moss, the first UXB person on site, was quickly shown to the house by a special constable who quickly left the site. Civilians had already been cleared from the street. The front door stood forebodingly open, the tiled floor on the porch was damaged, but he could not determine whether this was the point of entry. His team arrived and he set them to look around the property. The hallway had a fireplace, in front of which the carpets and floorboards were displaced. Taking his time, he explored the rest of the house. As he climbed the highest flight of stairs he saw a large round hole in the roof. He found another hole in a bedroom floor and traced the trajectory downwards. The bomb had gone straight down into the cellar.

The men set doggedly to work, ripping up floorboards in the hall. Many bottles in the cellar had to be moved to one side; some were drunk by the men after they finished for the day. The team under Moss consisted of six men, he kept three men working while the others rested by the truck 100yds away up the road, swopping duty every hour. It was necessary to keep the second team nearby since their job would be to help if the bomb detonated under them.

They dug down about 10ft below the cellar floor and found the fins. Moss took out a shaft about 6ft square. The wall between the living room and the hall was directly above the centre of the shaft. It was astonishing that one could excavate under the footings of a brick wall without having the whole thing collapsing on top of them. They had no timber or the time to fix it in position to support their excavation.

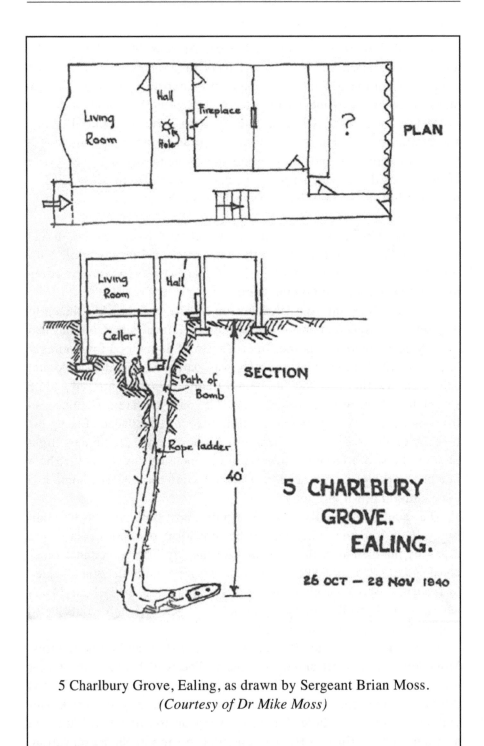

5 Charlbury Grove, Ealing, as drawn by Sergeant Brian Moss.
(Courtesy of Dr Mike Moss)

Several days later, when it was obvious that it was going to be a long job, they started shoring up the footings with borrowed timbers.

Their shaft followed the bomb's path downward like the journey to the centre of the earth. By the end of the first week they had dug 20ft down and were still sitting above unknown kilograms of explosive that might, at any second, send their fragmented bodies into the unknown. They reached the base of the shaft by a rope ladder slung from the joists of the living room floor. Bucket and rope were used to bring up the excavated clay. Two rooms of the house had already been filled with this so they began filling the hall and then the front garden.

It was completely dark 20ft down below the floor of the cellar. No power existed so they used an enormous acetylene-powered lamp at the bottom of the shaft. They were fearful of asphyxiation and tried pumping air down by hand before discovering that there was a great uplift of hot, foul gases. They extended a length of suction pipe from the front garden to the bottom of the hole which supplied fresh air to the digger.

Moss studied the dark brown London clay at length. It contained tiny sparkling chips of mica and was hard, excellent for their un-shored hole, which eventually become twice as deep. Mounds of clay were piled everywhere.

The shaft continued to go deeper. They were now 30ft down and still digging. At lunchtimes, they were invited into a house at the western end of Charlbury Grove, owned by Christmas Humphreys. (In 1950, Humphreys was the Crown Prosecutor in the trial of Timothy Evans who was convicted of murdering his baby at 10 Rillington Place and subsequently hanged [Evans was later granted a posthumous pardon]. Sometime later, Humphreys prosecuted John Reginald Christie [coincidentally living at the same address], who was convicted and hanged for serial murder, and he was the Crown Prosecutor for the trial of Ruth Ellis in 1955.)

They ate lunch in the garden shed and Moss was permitted the use of the workshop where he unscrewed protective sheaths from fuses and disassembled difficult fuses. There he made his own contribution to science. The 1kg B1-El incendiary bomb was being dropped over London at the time from a suitcase-like container that opened as it fell from the aircraft.

Studying the B1-El, one stuck out. On the end opposite to the fins was a letter 'A' in red. He wondered whether the 'A' stood for 'Achtung'.

He examined the fins which appeared normal but something made him gently lever them off. The small rivets gave way and off came the fins. There, hidden, screwed into the back cap, was an ordinary sheath filled with highly-sensitive penthrite wax. On landing, the bomb began to burn then the penthrite would become hot and explode, spraying people nearby with molten magnesium. Moss made his discovery known to HQ but he never heard any more about it.

At 40ft down, Shepherd shouted, 'It's turned!'

Moss raced down and sure enough the tunnel drilled by the bomb had turned horizontally and was now heading towards the back of the house. Digging horizontally into a hole that had somehow shrunk into a 3ft 6in diameter section was not easy, so he obtained an earth auger with which to drill.

On 27 November, they located the bomb. Sergeant Moss got out his stethoscope and ordered everyone to be quiet, and prepared himself to listen. After the 40ft vertical plunge through London clay, it had travelled another 14ft horizontally. It was a 500kg bomb – they quickly found a Type 17 fuse. After investigating it thoroughly along the side of the bomb he found a second fuse – another Type 17. The stethoscope told him that both clocks had stopped. This type of clock was prone to stopping about two seconds from 'Doomsday'. They fitted a clock stopper, a heavy electromagnet which stopped all known mechanisms. So far, they had been lucky. Chances were slim enough that both clocks had stopped, and it seemed even less likely neither would fail to restart as they worked on the bomb.

A specialist team arrived and trepanned the bomb case and injected steam. This in turn melted the TNT and blew it out of the bomb like sticky toffee. All this was happening at the bottom of Sergeant Moss' crazy un-timbered shaft.

The following day Sergeant Moss was waiting outside in the road when several officers arrived escorting a lone figure. It was the Earl of Suffolk dressed in strange attire puffing on a cigarette holder. He had come to defuse the bomb. As Moss helped him down the rope ladder, he noticed flecks of red blanket or wool in the Earl's long hair at the back of his neck, (it probably came from sleeping on a couch while covered with a red blanket).

Even mine disposal officers who sought perfection and speed and timed each other on stop watches in order to better each other, got the chance to meet Jack. They had travelled to Richmond Park, unsure of what to expect because they had heard so many odd things about him, to meet the Earl of Suffolk, the legendary character everyone was talking about. A prohibited area was fenced off in the park and within it the Earl conducted his experiments. Jack daily played with death in his own private battle of wits against Germany and made each move in the dangerous game himself, refusing to detail his work to others.

The Earl was a fascinating fellow. They could not mistake him. He was working in the open air beside a bomb, lost in concentration, unaware of their presence or of anyone else's. Shaggy, unshaven and untidy, his shoes and clothes were discoloured with the muddy yellow stain of explosives, his fur hat was that of a Hudson Bay trapper. While he worked he spoke in commentary while his secretary, standing nearby, noted down every word. His helper was his chauffeur and the three of them worked as a team, as a remarkable unit. To watch this self-styled 'Holy Trinity' was to sense their unusual dedication; to be with them for a while was a moving experience.

Bert Woolhouse, aged 25 years-old, from bomb disposal, stood near an Anderson shelter in Connor Road, Dagenham, that had received a direct hit. He had just been made Staff Sergeant. He was waiting for Lieutenant William Ash to arrive when a black Austin Seven motorcar came to a screeching halt beside him. Out got a big man wearing an Anthony Eden-style black felt hat and a long black coat. He was smoking a cigarette in a very long cigarette holder.

The commanding figure said to Woolhouse, 'I am the Earl of Suffolk, old chap. I've been sent by Bomb Disposal Headquarters to look at the bomb to see whether it's a 17 and a 50.'

But the Earl never got to examine the fuses because the bomb exploded five days later. Men had been working on it when it happened. Luck must have been with him that day because Woolhouse survived.

Over time, large cities in Britain became used to hearing the crump of exploding bombs and to the 20ft deep craters and the gaping holes in rows of terraced houses. 'Danger UXB' signs were now as familiar to everyone as red double-decker buses. But the one thing they never got used to was the sight of dead bodies. The sight of mutilated bodies was all too common to Bomb Disposal men. Coffins of BD men were sealed, not to be opened, and were most probably filled with sand.

Jack took no interference from anyone and was unmoved by rank or personalities. When he spoke, his word was law. A number of Australian officers often went to watch because the Earl had developed a new method of destroying a mine or bomb that refused to yield to normal treatment. Along with Brock, he devised a system of burning mines; his second method, known as trepanning, was an ingenious attempt to prevent the disasters that sometimes occurred when a burning mine or bomb detonated early.

The method had been developed recently but the equipment had yet to be produced. Air raids had left hundreds of unexploded mines and bombs at widely dispersed places to be dealt with by a few overworked, overwrought men. Out in the fields or the towns or the cities men used what tools they had and what methods they knew. There was neither time nor opportunity to master new techniques. There was not even time, during that initial rush, to master the primitive techniques they did use, so they learnt by experience or died.

Jack, indirectly, developed a trepanning process from his unceasing war against the devil's instrument, the ZUS-40 anti-handling device. This almost unbeatable booby-trap device was fitted under the bomb fuse, and triggered mechanically when the fuse was removed. To defeat this Jack mounted a rotary cutting tool over the fuse to cut a circular hole through the casing of the weapon. Once this was cut to the required depth, it was possible to remove the piece of casing with the fuse and the ZUS-40 as one unit. It was an extremely daring and dangerous operation. From this the next extraordinary step evolved, though initially it was again directed against the ZUS-40. Instead of removing it, Jack decided to remove the main charge.

The simplicity of the idea was genius. He took his cutting tool away from the bomb fuse and mounted it lower down. He cut a hole in the outer casing some 5in diameter, removed the disc of metal to expose the solid mass of Hexanite (a German explosive made from 60 percent TNT and 40 percent HND [hexanitrodiphenylamine]). He then inserted a high-pressure steam jet that progressively melted the entire charge, allowing it to run out of the same hole. Once it became a stinking yellow mess, the fuse could be withdrawn by remote control and the simultaneous explosion of the ZUS-40 made relatively harmless.

Jack's achievement was excitingly important. It meant the mines and bombs that officers had been unable to render safe were no longer a hazard to life and property. The same steaming-out or trepanning process could be applied to both. It meant that explosive weapons of new types, provided they were not acoustic, could be safely handled. The charge could be removed first and the firing mechanisms examined later. The process was very slow and tedious and the necessary equipment too bulky to be used on every mine or bomb, but it was there for the special occasions when normal methods failed or when unpredictable booby traps were believed to be present.

This was the method Jack demonstrated to them and they realized some of their problems had been solved. But the problem of the acoustic mine remained unsolved – any sound was sufficient to detonate one – a raised voice, a passing car, a nearby aircraft, even an accidental touch against the mine's casing. How did one defuse a mine that one could not touch? Jack did not have a clue.

In December 1940, the MoS received a report regarding fuses, the removal of the explosive contents of bombs, and finally the destruction of the bombs. Magnetic clock stoppers had been issued to a number of Bomb Disposal units for stopping a clockwork time fuse, and the production of an improved model which kept the clock stopped had begun but was held up due to the bombing of a factory. The search for apparatus to isolate fuses would continue; in particular, the clockwork fuse and anti-handling fuse, which was fitted in conjunction with time fuses.

Around half of the BD units had been provided with fuse extractors that were more powerful and of a simpler type, and which had been successfully trialled: some of them were on order for pre-production trials. With regards to removing the explosive content of bombs, thirty-seven trepanning and steaming out plants had finally been delivered, of which twenty-five were in use in the UK. The training of personnel to work the apparatus was keeping pace with the output: by now thirty-six operators and twenty-three military mechanics had completed the course.

An alternative method of burning through the bomb casing with Thermite and quenching the burning explosives then washing out the explosive with a water pump had been successfully developed for bombs with powdered-explosive fillings. To permit the destruction of a bomb in situ, and thus the need to reduce the force of the explosion, part of the explosive could burnt off with Thermite causing the bomb to eventually detonate.

In early December, Jack found himself on the Barnet by-pass defusing a 500kg bomb with a Type 17 and a Type 50 fuse combination. They were recovered intact, including the ZUS-40 under the still ticking Type 17.

Various kinds of bombs were dropped on Britain during the Blitz. Incendiary bombs – a bomb that was 9in long and made from a magnesium alloy – were ignited by a small fuse, burning for ten minutes at very high temperature. High-explosive bombs ranged from the most common bombs: 50kg and 250kg, the SC100, 1,000kg bomb (known as 'Herman' because it looked like the rotund shape of Göring) – to the massive 'Max' weighing an impressive 2,500kg.

Churchill sat at his desk with his glasses perched on the end of his nose, studying a report he had just received dated 3 January 1941. A frown appeared on his forehead as he read about the number of unexploded bombs still to be dealt with. From 12 September to 21 December 1940 the enemy had dropped 11,682 unexploded bombs, of which 1,050 had detonated spontaneously, leaving a total of 13,356 to be dealt with by BD units. Results were impressive, but they had not been achieved without considerable loss of life. Casualties to date were 124 killed and 75 wounded out of a total of 6,546 officers and men employed on bomb disposal. German time-fused bombs were set to explode at anytime, anywhere between 2½ hours and 80 hours after they fell. With this in mind, work on digging down to buried bombs would not begin until four days after the bomb had landed.

Examples of every known enemy bomb had been found, including the 1,800kg ('Satan'), 1,400kg ('Fritz') and 1,000kg ('Hermann' and 'Esau'). A pamphlet on the recognition of and safety measures to be used with unexploded bombs for the use of all the Services had now been compiled, and a *Manual of Bomb Disposal* was nearing completion and was to be published by the end of the month.

CHAPTER TWENTY TWO

Jack's Pride

Whenever a report of an unexploded bomb thought to incorporate a delayed-action or anti-handling device came in it was quickly brought to Jack's attention, especially if it seemed tricky. Also he was not above using his considerable influence in obtaining it with a priority claim to investigate. Among various techniques and procedures used by him was one highly characteristic of his methods. This technique inhibited a delayed-action fuse by firing a bullet through the fuse head. The shock of the bullet's passage was intended to impact on the electrical components and by deforming the clock-body arrest. Jack called in a celebrated gunsmith to help with the research.

A specially modified rifle with a muzzle attachment was manufactured so that a .303in bullet could be fired into the face of the fuse from various angles. Dummy brass clocks were used in the experiments; it showed that the mechanism could be fragmented this way. But they soon realized the bullet could hit something sensitive like the fuse cap or protective sheath and it was finally abandoned. The following year the Germans introduced a new type of clockwork fuse in which the percussion cap, not the clock, was uppermost. Through all this, Beryl and Fred were Jack's constant companions.

Jack was full of pride for his team and never too proud to let everybody share in his enthusiasm. On 14 January 1941, he wrote a letter to Major General Taylor at the MoS concerning one of his men, Corporal Frank D. Baxter. He was pleased to be able bring this NCO to Taylor's attention, and extolled the man's abilities. Baxter, he wrote, had behaved most excellently while under Jack's orders. Baxter kept good discipline in his men, and at the same time was obviously extremely well liked by them. Jack was indeed proud to inform the General that Baxter showed much intelligence and initiative in his work and, because of that, he felt that he would make an excellent sergeant, and it was his pleasure to recommend him for such a rank.

Next day, Jack dictated another report to the Major General regarding another of his team members, Lieutenant Richard Godsmark, detailing the man's conduct and his eminently satisfactory manner in his work. He thought Godsmark most diligent, exceedingly intelligent, who showed no signs of timidity, and observed a very proper degree of caution for himself and his men. Jack pointed out that Godsmark exhibited a rare ability for getting the best out of his men while maintaining discipline, which kept them in a contented frame of mind thereby enormously increasing their efficiency as a unit. The lieutenant had won the admiration and affection of those who had dealt with him in his duties, and so Jack was delighted to inform Taylor that he held the highest opinion of him as an officer and as a man.

On a sadder, more personal note, the next letter Beryl typed was to Colonel King at the MoS concerning the letters Jack had written about Lieutenant Godsmark and Corporal Baxter. The Earl had learnt that very evening from Colonel Bateman that it was almost certain he was to eventually lose his squad. Quite apart from their efficiency, he had formed the friendliest of relations with them and held a high degree of personal regard for them. He felt that if, on their return to the Royal Engineers, Colonel King could see his way to send some form of recommendation he would be doing him a great favour.

The Earl's letter writing was prolific during this time because another letter to Major General Taylor on 15 January 1941 mentioned the following men: Driver Peter Travers, Sapper J. Routhan, Sapper R. Dutson, Sapper C. Laposta, Sapper J. W. Hardy, Sapper B. J. Gillett and Sapper William (Bill) Fulwell. These men, while being at Jack's disposal, had proved themselves to be the most excellent and intelligent of workers, showing a real love and enthusiasm for their work, always eager to learn and very quick on the uptake. Moreover, insofar as their personal characters were concerned, Jack could not wish for a more pleasant, finer squad of men to work with and he very much regretted the exigencies of the Service to remove them from his unit. He now took delight in taking this opportunity of commending them in the highest manner to Taylor's notice. He signed the letter: Your obedient servant, *The Rt Hon. The Earl of Suffolk & Berkshire, BSc, FRSE, M.Inst.W[welders], Principal Scientific Officer, Directorate of Scientific Research*, with his Elizabethan-scrawl signature. To show their appreciation and loyalty, his men presented him with a silver cigarette case engraved with their names.

Comfortable with the common, working man, Jack never dreamt of asking anyone to do anything he would not do himself. People often asked him for favours and more often than not he would reciprocate by smiling that charming smile and oblige. On the other hand, he never took kindly to someone challenging him – it was far more likely he was the one doing the challenging. His status symbols – 'Oscar' and 'Genevieve', his cigarette holders, his eccentric clothing – were a large part of his persona. His team, by trusting and obeying him without question found that they, too, attained good results and were always rewarded for a job well done.

Above all, Jack was fair, believing when men achieved something their spirits soared, and success was the bridge between. Once the men were satisfied, their leader then had it in him to build for victory. They no longer questioned his will but gladly committed their lives to his keeping.

Every forward-looking mind believes his own profession is the most hidebound, but radical changes are only accepted at the hands of genius, or slowly and grudgingly by the sheer pressure of events, and the Second World War certainly laid high demands at their feet. The rules of the game had been dramatically broken. Jack treated his team as though they were part of the cement that strengthened the eroding structures and beliefs of the times. He owned a rare ability of being able to physically put himself outside his aristocratic society, though he could never truly escape his own culture. The class system he was born into brought with it its own rules and certain roles to play, and initiation was very subtle. He rebelled often and sometimes opposed it but he could never truly act independently of it. As a young boy growing up he had not always complied and frequently set his own ground rules.

The Earl was every bit his ancestors. It was in his blood and in his family and peers, and in the walls of his home at Charlton Park where he grew from a happy, eager boy to the youth who set sail for adventures new. It was in the Old Masters on the walls and artefacts, the scent of polish on furniture that had been handed down through the years, the aroma of food wafting up from the kitchen, in the leather and wood furnishings, also the curtains and carpets, and the lingering smell of the family dogs. Property was power, and power led Jack to positions in the political, educational and cultural spheres. He revelled in his family, his work and his team, his friends and social gatherings and causing a stir. His future was bright and his background as diverse as you could get.

Germany and Hitler held a quiet fascination for him; he often talked about the country and its people, and gave thought to the problem Britain was facing. He felt alive when given a chance to work on bombs because it suited him. He owned the power and the will to drive others, but often did not have the physical resources for the part in which he played. His body frequently became tired and the strain immense. Could that be why he pushed himself so hard? Was it because he never knew how long he had left? Or could it be that he wanted to make the best of who he was and do what he could for as long as it took.

CHAPTER TWENTY THREE

Freddy, Fuses and Bombs

Research was alive and kicking in Bomb Disposal and new processes were being experimented with all the time. Burning a hole in a bomb with Thermite not only burned through the bomb casing but set fire to the filling, causing it to burn freely until it reached the fuse then it detonated. If BD teams were able to defuse the bomb first, the entire explosive content could be burnt without a detonator and subsequently sluiced out under water pressure.

Thermite, invented in 1893 and patented in 1895 by German chemist Hans Goldschmidt, was a pyrotechnic composition of aluminium powder and a metal oxide that produced an aluminothermic reaction. It was sometimes called the 'Goldschmidt reaction', the 'Goldschmidt process' or the 'Thermite reaction'; it was not explosive but could create bursts of extremely high temperatures (c.25,000°C) that focused on a very small area for a short period of time. It released a dangerous ultra-violet light that could not be viewed directly and was extremely hazardous, and once initiated it was very difficult to smother a reaction. Small streams of molten iron released in the reaction could travel considerable distances and melt through metal containers igniting their contents. This process appeared to be applicable to all bomb fillings except solid TNT and the Germans were now using that less and less. This method of dealing with bombs would, one hoped, replace that of trepanning and steaming out.

Trials were pressed forward in the use of Thermite for burning bombs in situ. At the worst, detonation occurred after around one third

---

185

of the explosive content of the bomb had burnt away. This method was expected to become the standard practice of bomb destruction. Experiments were also being done with oxyacetylene. Freezing the bomb with liquid oxygen or CO_2 was a complete failure.

Research solely concentrated on establishing a technique and the production of apparatus to reduce to a minimum the conditions of danger. Methods of dealing with bombs were summarized as hand digging and following the path of the bomb. Excavating plant was often obtained as rapidly as possible, but was not suitable in London due to obstructions caused by water and gas pipes and the underground railway.

Apart from following the path of entry (a slow process as the bomb nearly always 'jinked' sideways), water jets and compressed-air probes were being rapidly developed, as were earth augers (twelve sets had been purchased from the US). Electric and magnetic indicators, in the final stages of development, showed the exact location of the bomb from the bottom of a probe hole.

Fuse isolators of various types were rapidly developed, and a magnetic clockwork fuse stopper was in production as well as types that injected a fluid to jam the clock. Stethoscopes were used at a distance and in safety conditions to indicate whether the clock fuse was ticking or not. Trepanning and sterilizing sets were on the production line and groups were being trained in their use at the National Physical Laboratory (NPL).

Germany and their Allies were using Thermite in incendiary bombs that mostly consisted of dozens of thin Thermite-filled canisters (bomblets) ignited by a magnesium fuse. They had the capacity to destroy entire cities due to the raging fires that resulted, and were chiefly utilized during night-time air raids as bomb sights were not used in the dark, thus creating the need to use munitions which could destroy targets without the need for precision targeting. Older cities primarily containing wooden buildings were especially susceptible.

Bombs were not sophisticated technology; they were sinister instruments of destruction and cold to the touch. They lay where they fell, forcing BD men to come out and defuse them, and could obliterate them in one blinding flash. Working on a bomb down a dark, usually muddy, cold, claustrophobic hole, BD men existed in a subterranean world. Life expectancy was around ten weeks for an officer, and death was never very far away. Bombs caused far more effect if they did not explode on impact. Some could detonate two hours after impact, some a day or even a month later, no one knew.

Jack and his experimental research team discovered three main possibilities regarding bombs: they could be time fused, magnetic (metal response) or trembler (movement response). Photo-electric seemed fundamentally improbable. The German ECR (Electrical Condenser Resistance) fuse was first manufactured by Rheinmetall in the 1930s. Trials were carried out in Russia on the use of mechanical and electrical bomb fuses: some 250 mechanical and 250 electrical bomb fuses were tested, and the electrical fuses were found far superior.

A bomb was designed so that there was the least possible chance of it being found unexploded and examined. Moreover, all evidence suggested that the weapons only exploded when they were approached or touched. On the other hand, it was not easy to see how a simple trembler fuse could be made to stand up to being dropped from an aircraft. The two charging pins at the top of a German bomb fuse were clamped onto a telescopic charging head in the aircraft. Inside the bomb casing, below the charging pins, was a switch block containing sensitive contacts (like metal balls inside a steel tube). When they touched the sides they short-circuited. Next was the capacitor: a device for storing the electricity known as the 'charge'. After the bomb hit the ground, the sensitive trembler switches shorted out and discharged the capacitor which ignited a small match head (in the case of the Type 17 [a long-delay clockwork] fuse was Thermite).

The match head then melted a wax pellet containing a steel pin and once the wax melted, the pin dropped through the clockwork mechanism and started the clock running. This would occur anywhere from two to eighty hours after the clock began to function, then a flash pellet (match head) fired a flame into the steel container filled with a sensitive explosive penthrite wax. This exploded, setting off the picric acid rings (another explosive) around the gaine which in turn fired off the main charge.

Exactly the same applied to the Type 50 fuse except charging time took longer, giving the bomb a chance to come to rest on the ground and the extra sensitive switches time to settle down before becoming armed. After that, any jolt short circuited the switch and set off the bomb. The Germans were fond of using a Type 50 anti-disturbance fuse in conjunction with the Type 17 fuse in any bomb 50kg or upwards. This

Type 50 fuse had to be dealt with first by using a liquid discharger. Once the discharger, which injected a mixture of benzene and salt into the fuse, was put in place to breakdown the charge in the firing condensers, BD men stood back for thirty minutes to let it do its work. No one moved a bomb fitted with a Type 50 until it was rendered harmless.

Day after day, Jack isolated these fuses, opened and emptied bombs, and was liable to be switched to any location at any given moment, and sent any interesting samples to headquarters for examination.

'Where are you going?' his friend Lord Clanwilliam once asked him. 'To Richmond Park to deal with unexploded bombs,' Suffolk replied with increasing excitement in his voice, while waving about his cigarette holder. 'There are twenty or thirty to be dealt with.'

His friend saw him again later in that evening and told him how glad he was to see him back alive. Suffolk looked as though he had just come back from a day's shooting. Jack knew his work was a closely-guarded secret, even more than radar, and he revelled in it. He endeavoured to return to Charlton Park as often as he possibly could but never divulged anything to his wife about his work; he did, however, regale her with the antics of his team, which included his devoted driver who had never let him out of his sight and his secretary who prepared his reports and cheerfully accepted all the risks.

There had been a time when not all his sappers trusted him. In earlier days when working on something where welding was necessary, Suffolk, with his customary long cigarette holder in use, tried to explain to the men how he wanted a hole cut. The men looked at each other. One turned towards the other with an aside. 'What does the Earl of Suffolk blinkin' know about it anyway?'

'Give me your goggles,' Suffolk demanded, taking them from the man. 'Keep this going for me,' he said, handing him his cigarette holder then cut a perfect hole.

'That's how I want it done,' he told the amazed sapper who could hardly have known that 'the bloomin' Earl' was also a fully-qualified member of the Institute of Welding. Once they realized, he rapidly won the confidence of the sapper experts who were involved in his adventures.

'He'd go through concrete to get what he thought to be the best result,' one of his team said with admiration in his voice. 'If it's good enough for Lord Suffolk, it's good enough for us,' was the reply once a particularly dangerous piece of work was in progress and leave was given to move to a safe distance. When a factory making fuses for one of the Earl's experiments was bombed, the Earl's brother Greville watched him pick up a machine weighing nearly 200lb and carry it to safety over a collapsing floor.

The first fuses were all Type 15s, and it was soon discovered they could be immobilized simply by depressing the plungers in the top of the fuse a few times. That allowed the electrical charge in the firing condenser to leak back to earth, thus making it safe. The bombs the Germans had at that time were categorized under three headings:

SC: *Sprengbombe Cylindrisch* – a thin walled, general-purpose high-explosive bomb (containing some 55 percent explosive to 45 percent steel. Used in the bombing of British towns and industrial sites)

SD: *Sprengbombe Dickwandig* – a thick-walled fragmentation bomb (the ratio was only 35 percent explosive and 65 percent metal)

PC: *Panzer Cylindrisch* – heavy armour-piercing bombs (mainly used against shipping and specific heavily-shielded targets)

Holes in the ground between 8in and 12in indicated a 50kg bomb, holes between 14in and 18in signified a 250kg bomb, and holes over 18in concealed a 500kg bomb or larger – when a bomb of 1,000kg or larger fell, a crater could be as big as 10ft in diameter and 4ft deep.

The depth bombs penetrated the ground, according to the BD manual, depended upon the altitude from which it was dropped, the weight of the bomb, what it hit before reaching the ground, and the nature of the soil. The size of the crater left when a buried bomb exploded varied with the depth of penetration and the nature of the soil:

50kg bomb	10 to 15ft diameter
250kg bomb	18 to 25ft diameter
500kg bomb	25 to 30ft diameter

For Jack and other bomb disposal men it was requisite to fill in a questionnaire when one sighted a bomb. Paperwork in abundance! It required the exact location, date and hour of falling, whether it fell on open ground, hard surface or building, and whether there were any parts of the bomb exposed. Also, the diameter of the hole, estimated depth, whether a crater has been formed, if windows over 20ft away had been broken, whether splinters or splinter marks had been found and if there were any signs of blackening. Reasons for believing the bomb had not exploded were also required. Once the bomb had been attended to and deactivated the questionnaire was signed off, stating whether or not it had been dealt with and the time and date and signature of the person filling in the form.

Germany even had the gall to patent their electrical fuse in a British patent office. This transverse fuse was approved for all German bombs. The early Type 15 could be defeated by the small Crabtree Mk 1, a two-pin device made by Crabtree & Co with the help of Dr Merriman costing three shillings (a total of 5,800 made). It was pressed down for a few minutes on top of the fuse then clipped into place by a knob on the side. The depressed plungers caused it to short circuit and discharge the electric charge, making the fuse harmless. The Crabtree discharger had a ring fitted in the top to which a piece of string could be tied, allowing a BD officer to extract the fuse from a safe distance.

When the Type 25 fuse was introduced, the two pins were removed from the discharger and then used to extract the fuse. Another piece of equipment was the Universal fuse key: a steel bar about 12ins long with two adjustable lugs that could be fitted into the two slots of a locking ring. They discovered the locking rings were standard so no adjustment was needed. Subsequently, a much better fuse key was designed with fixed lugs. Once the Germans found that the British were defusing bombs with some ease they made matters more difficult – they added the anti-handling device: the ZUS-40 (*Zundersperre* 40) with a housing cast from Zamac alloy.

This small device was fitted under most Luftwaffe bomb fuses, and was often added to the twin-fused 250 and 500kg bombs which were specifically designed to kill bomb disposal personnel. The ZUS-40 contained two mercury tilt switches that could detect vertical and horizontal movement. These fuses became fully armed within approximately thirty seconds after hitting the ground or if moved in any way. Some German bombs had two separate fuse pockets fitted, with different fuse types screwed into each one. One bomb could incorporate two separate anti-handling devices working independently of each other. Utterly nerve-racking for the BD personnel when encountering a ticking fuse that could trigger at any given moment.

When a delayed-action bomb was dropped on a target, the massive jolt after it struck the ground freed a ball-bearing inside the

ZUS-40, arming a spring-loaded firing pin. So long as the main bomb fuse remained inside its housing, the cocked firing pin in the ZUS-40 was prevented from springing forward.

But Jack would not be deterred by this. This booby trap gripped the inside end of the bomb fuse and fired the main charge mechanically when the fuse was pulled out, so he devised a method by which he cut a hole through the casing of the bomb, which enabled him to remove the whole core containing the ZUS-40 in one complete unit. Before long, he had developed another method by carefully removing the main charge by means of inserting a high-pressure steam jet. This was an extremely important discovery and saved many lives, and even though it was slow and tedious it meant that every type of bomb and mine could be handled with increased safety providing, of course, it was not acoustic.

There was really no way to see if a ZUS-40 had been fitted to a fuse until the advent of Field Photography (X-Ray). When BD officers found a Type 17 clockwork long-delay fuse (which often could not be heard ticking) that had a separate clockwork mechanism screwed into the bottom of the fuse and a No.50 anti-disturbance fuse, it was most important to make sure that this was neutralized first, otherwise turning on the clock stopper jolted the sensitive fuse and set off the bomb.

Removing the time-delay fuse more than 2cm from its pocket (without having neutralized the anti-handling device underneath) automatically released the cocked firing pin inside the ZUS-40, which then sprang forward to strike a large percussion cap, causing detonation of the bomb and the death of anyone in the vicinity.

The clock, which had two plungers, was screwed into the base of the Type 17 externally and often covered with waterproof black rubber sleeve. The Type 17A fuse was a clockwork-type fuse with the same maximum delay as the original Type 17, but was capable of being set with a minimum delay period of zero instead of 2½ hours. Another difference was the clockwork action built into the fuse in the reverse position to that which it occupied in the Type 17. The marking 17A indicated a new fuse so the recovery of an intact specimen was essential. Thus, the only conclusion to be drawn amongst the Earl and BD men – NEVER TRUST A CLOCK!

Fuses were now no longer removed with any degree of confidence. One response to this was 'Freddy' a device designed by Eric Moxey and Merriman, which was clamped onto the fuse head and set in motion. The men could then retire to a safe distance and let Freddy pull out the fuse. After use the device had to be taken to the National Physical Laboratory (NPL) in Teddington to have the 'Sparkletts' CO_2 cartridge replaced.

Providing German aircraft flew a straight course and did not turn, a 'stick' of bombs was dropped one after the other, giving a straight line of bomb craters caused by each detonation. This straight line pattern was reasonably accurate. If Jack or his men walked along the path of craters and saw one missing where one should be, there was a good chance that one or more bombs had hit the ground and failed to detonate. If that was the case, the bomb left a hole of entry, leaving the tail fins on the surface or somewhere along the entry hole. The size of the fins identified the size of the bomb, and depending on soil conditions it could be estimated how deep the bomb may have penetrated.

Having said that, bombs sometimes penetrated deep then detonated, leaving no evidence of an explosion. Great care was taken when this happened or Jack and other BD men faced a quick death caused by poisonous gases remaining in the underground cavity. Because bombs in England were known to penetrate as deep as 30ft (sometimes more), it took several hours or even days to arrive at the bomb. Sappers had to first shore-up the hole with timbers for safety. An ELAZ-17 clockwork fuse could detonate at any moment, making it a distinct danger for the sappers because side shafts often had to be dug to one side of the main shaft due to the bomb making a turn in its path.

Positive identification was made using the size of the bomb and the type of fuse by reading the markings on the fuse head – Germans never mismarked their fuses. The fuse was determined by the RSP (Rendering Safe Procedure), which dictated the necessary safety precautions to be observed. In the early days of the war BD men had no references to go by and worked by trial and error.

Typical equipment and procedures Jack used to render a bomb safe included a locating ring which he would use first; its small pin fitted into the corresponding hole in the bomb's fuse pocket. After that came a locking ring which was screwed up tight to stop the fuse from falling out. For a clockwork fuse, a magnetic clock stopper, weighing around 81.5kg (180lb) was used to stop it running.

Freezing out was achieved by using liquid oxygen to lower a fuse battery's potential below firing amperage for electric primers and mechanical switching dischargers to bleed off firing condensers in early impact fuses. Specially made spanner and wrenches had been developed to remove the fuse locking rings. Tape and line were tied to the fuse head to remove it from its pocket while standing at a safe distance.

After a fuse was rendered safe enough to move, the bomb could then be hoisted out and transported to a safe disposal site, a bomb cemetery, to be detonated. Some fuses were deemed so dangerous that the bomb could not be removed; in such cases, a steam-driven mechanical cutter (trepanner) was employed to remotely cut a 4in diameter hole in the bomb case which allowed them to steam the high explosive out of the casing. Liquid TNT had been poured into the bomb casing during manufacture, thus, hot steam could be used to melt it and let it flow out of the hole. When it solidified again, the explosive was gathered up and taken away to be burned or detonated. The bomb, still in the shaft and empty of high explosives, could now be sandbagged, and the fuse detonated with no damage to the surrounding area.

Newspaper articles boasted about the prowess of British bomb disposal personnel, so the Germans retaliated by installing the famous ZUS-40 under the ELAZ-17. Again, newspaper articles boasted of British engineers' success in defeating the Germans. Accordingly, the Germans began adding a second fuse pocket in the 250kg and larger bombs. They also placed an anti-disturbance Type 25B (known as the Type 'Y' to BD units) in to protect the Type 17 fuse until it had time to detonate the bomb. Once the British newspapers realized the Germans were taking note, they stopped issuing information. And so, this 'competition' continued until the end of the war.

Different types of fuses:

IMPACT FUSES
Impact fuse, (*Aufschlagzuender*): AZ
Electrical impact fuse: ELAZ

TIME DELAY
Time delay, (*Zeitzuender*): Zt

LONG DELAY
Long-delay fuse, (*Langzeitzuender*) LZZ

The Germans always marked and stamped their fuses around the shoulder. Interpretation of these fuses as follows:

Anti-disturbance fuses: (50) (60) (70) B

Mechanical/dual purpose fuses: (41)

Used in incendiary bombs: (12)

Mechanical fuses: (63) (73)

Special fuses: (24) (34)

Electrical impact fuses for general use: (5) (15) (25) (35) (55)

Electrical impact fuse for special use: (26)

Delay fuses: (17) (67)

Electrical impact fuses with slight delay for use against maritime targets: (28), (38)

Aerial burst fuses: (9) (59) (79)

Between 1937 and 1940, some 1,600,000 Type 15 fuses were manufactured. The Type 25 that replaced the Type 15 fuse was produced in nine variations, and approximately 2,200,000 were made. The fuse warned that it armed in three seconds. It was found that the Type 25 fuse was quite expensive to manufacture so the Type 55 fuse was produced instead and made between 1940 and 1942; a quantity of 840,000 were produced.

Another contender to add misery and chaos to the masses was the 'Butterfly Bomb' or 2kg *Sprengbombe Dickwandig* (SD2), anti-personnel bomblet, first dropped on Ipswich in 1940 by the *Luftwaffe*. The British government deliberately suppressed news of the damage and disruption they bought with them so as to not to encourage the Germans to keep using them. They were so named because of its thin cylindrical metal outer shell which hinged open when the bomb deployed, giving it the superficial appearance of a large butterfly. It was very distinctive and easy to recognize. They were not dropped individually but used as the payload of various cluster bombs.

The bomblets were an 8cm cylinder, slightly smaller in diameter before its vanes deployed and could be fitted with a type 41 fuse – triggered detonation immediately on impact with the ground, a Type 67 fuse – clockwork time delay, adjustable between five and thirty minutes after impact, or a Type 70 fuse – anti-handling device, triggering detonation if the bomb was moved after initial impact. The Type 41 and 70 could detonate if it received even the slightest tap. The Type 67 could take up to thirty minutes to detonate if it did not jam. The bomb contained 225gm of TNT and was generally lethal to anyone within a radius of 25m, and could injure people as far away as 150m.

Defusing Butterfly Bombs that failed to detonate or were equipped with the anti-handling fuse was not considered practical. The only way to deal with these nasty things was to destroy them on site. Most were painted a green or a dull yellow colour to camouflage with grain crops at harvest time in order to kill the workers, unsuspecting people and even curious children. Cities and towns became massive booby traps when thousands were dropped.

They were a curiosity at first. An inquisitive adult, or a child out collecting shrapnel or playing in the garden, would come across one and pick it up and it would explode, killing them on the spot. A fireman said he had found them on roofs, on beds, hanging from bushes, trees, in lofts, or woods, on telephone wires and gutters, even hanging by one wing though a ceiling. The only way for the bomb disposal squads to deal with them was to blow them up with a charge just where they landed. They caused whole towns to be isolated for days, everything came to a standstill. Britain ordered a news blackout on everything to do with these weapons in order to give the Germans the impression they had made no impact. This worked and the Germans never used them again.

Commander Sir Aylmer Firebrace said that a German prisoner-of-war told bomb disposal people that the Germans dropped containers of butterfly bombs on a racecourse in order to give their bomb disposal squads the experience of coping with them. The result was a number of German casualties.

THIS

I think that all your years led up to this,

and all your lives.

I think it was for this that,

worlds ago,

You came to greatness.

Your every man, of all your times,

was born and lived and died.

To have his part in the

great march of things.

That led to this.

Helen Mackay
(London, One November, 1915-1916)

CHAPTER TWENTY FOUR

Old Faithful

In 1941, Winston Churchill, the first British Prime Minister to address a joint meeting of the US Congress, spoke about the progress of the war in Europe. Germany had taken to bombing the south-coast cities of Plymouth and Portsmouth with fire and high explosives, causing fires and mayhem throughout.

On 10 May 1941, a raid by 550 bombers dropped more than 700 tons of bombs and thousands of incendiaries, probably the worst raid ever in the Blitz. Casualties were high with some 1,500 people killed and over 1,800 seriously injured. The chamber of the House of Commons (Parliament) was destroyed; and the House of Lords, Westminster Abbey, Westminster Hall, St. James' Palace and Lambeth Palace were among the many buildings damaged. Almost all major main-line railway stations were damaged as well as fourteen hospitals, the British Museum and the law courts of the Old Bailey.

After this first onslaught on the East End, from mid-September the Luftwaffe attacked the rest of London; it was during this period that the famous bombing of Buckingham Palace occurred when Queen Elizabeth (later the Queen Mother) made her remark about being able to look the East End in the eye. People became so used to the raids they just carried on as normal. Cinemas continued to show films during raids and the audience remained watching them.

By May 1941, some 43,000 people had been killed across Britain, and one 1,400,000 were made homeless. Coventry, Plymouth, Manchester, also Glasgow, Liverpool, and Southampton suffered the same fate as London. May was the last of the major raids on London during this period.

Although bomb disposal had faith in Jack's methods there were some that harboured many doubts over the way he went about his work. An officer accused him of carelessness when a 500kg bomb wrecked half a house while he was trying to neutralize its fuse with gelignite. Jack told them they were meddling in matters they did not have a clue about, and a few weeks later a detachment of the East Surrey Regiment stationed in Richmond Park made complaints about several violent explosions set off by him that had, without any warning, sprayed red-hot metal close to the guard room and Officers' Mess. One man, to his complete surprise, saw the Earl dressed in airman's boots and a Stetson, strolling around company HQ.

Jack was exhausted and cold to the bone, something he did not readily admit, and could not remember when he last experienced a decent night's sleep. His eyes were red and felt gritty all the time, the muscles in his neck, shoulders and back ached through sheer concentration, and the Germans were not letting up. His life and his team's, up until this point, was bound in the mire of searching for certain fuses, visiting various dumps, collecting likely bombs and taking them to a safe place for examination.

He spent the weekend of 8, 9 and part of 10 May at Charlton Park, away from the wretchedness of London, relaxing with his family in his comfortable familiar surroundings; no better salve to his physical, mental and emotional health. The weather, settled and sunny though a little cool, was an added bonus. Mimi and Jack shared joyous, precious moments together after being separated. Even though she was not kept informed as to what her husband was doing in London and the southeast, she knew it to be dangerous work and she worried for him because Jack would give no quarter, no matter how his health affected him. It seemed to Mimi he was on a mission and he would see it through to the bitter end. It was a joy to watch him taking delight in playing with his three sons, his third son Patrick Greville was now around 7 months-old, teething and babbling away in baby language. Her husband rejoiced in those few days and surrendered himself up to the attention showered upon him. How he had missed them.

His next job was just like all the others. There was no reason to think otherwise. Old Faithful had been lying around for months over winter.

The 250kg bomb with two separate fuses – a Type 17 and a Type 50 - was just like many of the others they had worked on. In a few hours' time he and his team would be going to Charlton Park for two weeks rest. Jack had promised them a rest, and that is what they would get. They were, if being honest, more than a little curious about the Earl's lifestyle and his home. They had heard snippets of talk about his stately home called Charlton Park and its grounds, and the Earl's famous wife, her picture having been shown everywhere, even on buses and billboards. The air was quite still that Monday: they heard blackbirds singing and the sparrows chirruping, and the mumbling sound of traffic and life going on in the distance. Now and then the voices of children playing punctuated the air. The bomb had been thoroughly checked over by the Earl the day before, on 11 May 1941, and the lads were confident.

Sergeant Cole was at the scene because Captain Privett had requested he be there and also because Staff Sergeant Atkins offered to drive him to their detachment at Bromley after he had delivered the Mk II electronic stethoscope and Mk II electronic clock stopper the Earl had requested.

Atkins met the Earl at the bomb site at Belvedere Marshes then drove both them and the equipment to the bomb, a distance of about 400yds, and the men began working. Beryl was busy taking down the Earl's notes in shorthand from a nearby lorry, Fred was kneeling by his friend's side handing him the tools he required while Jack sat astride the bomb. Everything was as it should be, when, without any warning, the bomb exploded in a thunderous, blistering, red hot blast of noise and light.

Lance Corporal Brownrigg and Sergeant Cole were sitting in a vehicle some 400yds away when it happened; they were completely deafened by the sound, after which shock took over, their minds not fully comprehending the enormity of what had just taken place. Their ears rang with the resounding reverberation of the blast. It took a few moments for them to return to reality. They finally picked themselves up and rushed over to scan the devastating scene of death, and just stood rooted to the spot, gazing at the scene in horror. Grey, black billowing smoke, twisted steel, debris, a massive hole in the ground and bodies greeted them.

The Earl's lorry was upright and ablaze, the engine block perforated by fragments, only the frame was still intact as were the wheels. Equipment was scattered on the ground and the oxygen cylinder had burst. The doors and name board of the van had been wrenched off and flung 60ft into the air by the blast. Part of the front of the Guy truck had also been blown away, the other lorry just beginning to burn. A number of people were obviously severely injured.

Panic stricken, Sergeant Cole ran among the tragic debris but was unable to find the Earl, Staff Sergeant Atkins, Driver Sharratt, Sapper Jack Hardy, and Fred Hards (who had been with the Earl for seven months). They had all been working close to the bomb they had been so sure it was not lethal. All precautions had been taken. All that remained was a 5ft diameter shallow crater some 18in deep because the bomb had been laying on the ground, the blast having gone out and up. Lance Corporal Brownrigg tried his best to help the casualties until the ambulance arrived then proceeded to put out the flames on the second largest lorry.

They found Beryl in an extremely serious condition. Fred Hards had managed to drag himself a few yards and died calling for Suffolk. One man thought to be Sapper Reg Dutson died within a few minutes of Cole's arrival. Cole assisted the best he could and helped take the casualties to Erith Cottage Hospital. Brownrigg travelled in another ambulance with a number of others who were injured. Beryl, who had been in the service of the Earl for eleven months, sadly succumbed to her injuries and died in the ambulance. Bertie Gillet died of his wounds in hospital in the early hours of the following morning. Of the others, Routhan received wounds to his left arm and side and had a puncture wound in his face. Bill Fulwell's right arm was shattered, Nicholls' injuries were to his throat and face, Travers had wounds deep in his buttocks, and Baxter was in desperate need of an operation for serious abdominal injuries.

Sapper Liposta was in a complete state of shock but still managed to relay to his commanding officer details about what had just taken place. Lance Corporal Brownrigg went and assisted the doctor at the hospital with identifying the bodies then a stretcher party vehicle drove him back to HQ. He sat at his desk and put his head in his shaking hands and wept. He could not take in the enormity of what he had just witnessed. It was hellishly awful. The Earl, along with Beryl and Fred and the team, were gone. He would never speak to them, see them nor laugh with them again. He squared his shoulders, wiped his tears, took a couple of deep breaths and began writing his report while it was still fresh in his mind. What happened would stay with him forever. Some of the casualties of the blast had only been ascertained by counting the living, it being impossible to put what was left into a specific number of bodies.

Captain Bainbridge learned about the catastrophe and arrived at the hospital after the casualties had been brought in. He spoke with Liposta who, in his shocked state, barely managed to inform him of what had taken place before the bomb went up.

Dr Gough was walking into his office around 6.30pm when the telephone rang. It was Dr Paris giving him the appalling news that the bomb the Earl had been working on at Erith Marshes had exploded, killing him and most of his team. It had exploded at 3.20pm. His good friend who, only hours previous, had leant over an office boy's desk and smiled at him in the Borax factory, the man he had travelled to see to ease his mind that all was well at the bomb site, had just become another statistic of war. Dr Gough was devastated. Everything had been fine when he left Jack. He did not want to think the worse thought of all – he would never, ever, get to see his friend again. He found his chair and slumped in it and stared out of the window with unseeing eyes. The enormous loss would eventually sink in. A light had gone out in his soul.

In a dazed state he arranged for Dr Paris to go straight to the site to obtain all possible information and to keep in touch with him by telephone. As soon as that was done Dr Gough ordered a car to be made available for his use at any time during the night. Owing to the breakdown of telephone communications in south-east London, his repeated efforts to obtain additional information were useless so he was forced to wait for a message from Dr Paris.

At about 11.00pm that night, Dr Paris telephoned and told him of the position. Realizing nothing further could be done until morning when urgent action must be taken which included calls on relatives of deceased, Gough arranged for a car and Major Sumner (ADSR) to meet him at 7.30am the next morning. They were to drive to London to meet with Paris as soon as possible.

At 1.30am, Gough managed to contact Sir William Brown by telephone and brought him up to date. It was agreed Gough would drive to Charlton Park to break the awful news to Lady Suffolk and make any necessary arrangements. He got little sleep that night.

At 7.30am, Major Sumner arrived with the car and drove him to London where he spoke with Dr Paris and Dr Roffey. It was arranged they would visit the relatives of Beryl Morden and Fred Hards, and that Captain Drane would revisit the site; 25 BD Coy to deal with the scene of the accident and talk to witnesses. Gough suggested a posthumous award of the George Cross which Captain Drane warmly supported. He then travelled on to the village police station at Charlton to find that no police communication had yet been sent to Charlton Park. Having traced his telegram, that had only just been transmitted, Gough sighed deeply. He found it had been received by Lady Suffolk at 11.30am that morning. God help us, he thought.

Driving to Charlton Park was not a journey he wished to make. His slowness in getting out of the car, the careful placing of a shined shoe on the gravel, the unspoken words, the sympathy and sorrow that filled his eyes, portrayed everything. Words were not required. He spoke with Mimi alone. Her hand fluttered to her mouth and her thoughts flashed to her now fatherless children. Michael was only six; far too young for the task ahead of him; much younger than Jack had been when his father died. Her heart beat fast in her chest and a feeling of numbness and shock filled her body, just as it must have done when her mother-in-law received news of her husband's death in Mesopotamia. She could not bear the thought that she would never see her husband again. That he would never walk into Charlton, his home, with that beloved cheeky grin on his face, his cigarette placed permanently into his cigarette holder and black hat crammed on his head. The children would laugh no more when their father got on his knees and played with them. Jack's whole being had always lit up the room – but no more.

What would become of her and the boys now that her larger than life husband was gone? Charlton Park was now a military hospital and the family was living in only three of the rooms; the War Office had yet to pay them any rent. Her husband's mother, Daisy, had stopped his allowance some time ago because she said he was working for the government. That maybe so, Mimi thought, but they still had yet to pay him.

Breaking the news to her was extremely painful for Dr Gough, as one might imagine. He could honestly say he loved Suffolk; a remarkable person, the reincarnation of all his great ancestors. In fact, he was a sort of modern day buccaneer – fearless, charming and gay – and what he set out to do he did with great thoroughness and aplomb.

Dr Gough felt utterly drained. Poor Lady Suffolk – nothing he said could stem her heartache. The children, thankfully, were not in the room. He later joined Lady Suffolk's mother and Major Sumner and inadequately, he thought, expressed the sympathy of the Minister and Secretary and spoke of the excellent services rendered by Lord Suffolk. But they were just platitudes. Nothing one said at a time like this really made much difference. A good man was gone. He sighed deeply then drafted a cable to Lord Suffolk's mother in the USA.

Gough agreed to take the following steps: to sort out all Lord Suffolk's personal papers, books and other belongings at Great Westminster House and have them sent on to Charlton Park. Also he would communicate with the family's solicitors, and arrange for Lieutenant Hon. Greville R. Howard, RNVR, to be informed via the Admiralty. His tasks were numerous. Dealing with any press enquiries arising from the secret nature of Lord Suffolk's official duties would take time. He made a note not to forget to recover any personal tools of Lord Suffolk that remained undamaged and forward them to Charlton Park.

The question of a funeral was delicately raised and information indicated that 'no remains' had been found. This aspect he tried very gently to convey. Before leaving Charlton Park he spoke with Mr Moore, the estate manager, and asked him to let him know if any matters came to light which were unnecessary or undesirable for Lady Suffolk. Thoroughly shattered, Dr Gough finally returned to London about 8.00pm. He tried over the next few months to get Lady Suffolk a war widow's pension but it met with unsympathetic ears. They found it hard to believe that someone living in a stately home could be in desperate need.

Henry Bishop, now in his nineties, had worked for the Borax factory for over forty-five years; at the time of the explosion he had been working on the cranes on the wharf in the immediate vicinity of the marshes, only five minutes from his home. He had climbed up the jib of his crane but all he could see was dense, black billowing smoke. The first signs that something was amiss to the men working in the factory was when a large crowbar from the bomb site came crashing through the roof, narrowly missing machinist George French. Later, George gave the crowbar to Henry's father as a souvenir, who in turn gave it to Henry. At the time, Henry heard a rumour that Jack had been sitting astride the bomb when it exploded.

Bishop's uncle, Charlie Cooper, was walking down Norman Road, Lower Belvedere, on his way home from work when the bomb went off. As he reached the site he saw three army trucks on fire. He ran over to one of the vehicles in case anyone might be alive, and found a horrifically injured woman. Gently, he lifted her out of the wrecked vehicle, but he knew from her condition that she was unlikely to survive.

One of the drivers delivering the equipment had a very lucky escape. In urgent need of a pee as they entered the marsh, he jumped down from the lorry and ran to a bush to relieve himself; an action that saved his life. Henry's brother-in-law, Bob Wilkins, an officer in the Royal Artillery, was in the Royal Herbert Military Hospital, Woolwich, recuperating from a wound when they brought in another patient – the soldier who got out of the lorry for a pee before the blast. What a tale he had to tell.

Ken Tinker, the office boy at the Borax factory, was in the middle of completing a routine task when he heard the massive explosion. It rocked and shook the building. He and the others raced outside and saw a plume of black smoke rising over the dump and three army vehicles blazing. Debris rained down on the factory's corrugated roof: amongst it was a 6ft crowbar and a lot of marsh mud. One of their drivers who happened to be crossing the marsh at the time witnessed the Earl and one other person sitting on the bomb just before it exploded. Ken suddenly felt a deep sadness well up inside him. The image of the Earl dressed in a duffle coat, walking into the office to use the telephone appeared in his mind: he was such a kind, gentle giant of a man.

The incident remained vivid in Ken Tinker's memory while many other events of the war faded into the dim past. He lived on throughout the Battle of Britain as a mere messenger lad on a bicycle answering the call to replace damaged telephone services throughout the long nights or making tea for his others in the frontline of London's defences.

Ken believed himself to be one of the very privileged few to talk with the Earl before he died. Crossing back over the marsh that night, Ken peddled slowly through the twilight and dimly saw the wreckage of the vehicle that had brought the Earl into his life for one brief instant before he was gone forever. Next morning, he hurried past the site where an army team was searching amid the bombs now scattered by the blast, and no doubt examining other bombs for signs of revived activity.

Once the area was made safe, the team began the task of collecting bombs that littered the ground, dragging them with the lorry and placing them in small piles before blowing them up. Bombs lying on the surface of the ground were no problem. It was the ones that had rolled into the

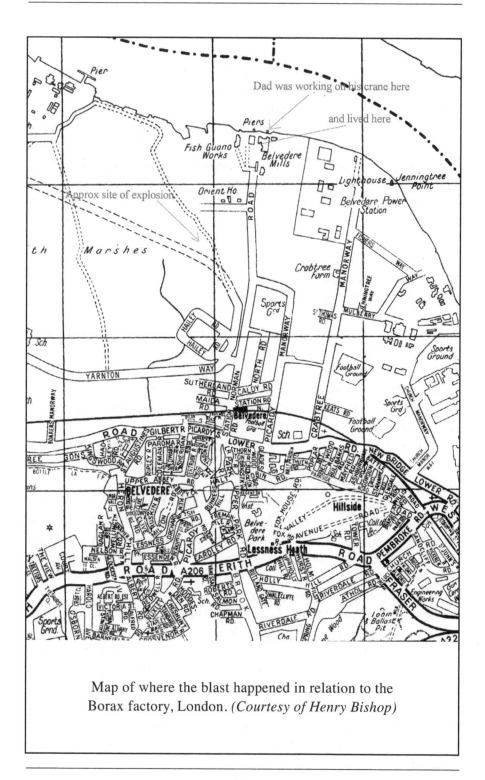

Map of where the blast happened in relation to the
Borax factory, London. *(Courtesy of Henry Bishop)*

water-filled craters that were causing trouble. The men had to undress, climb into the craters and put a rope around the bombs so that the lorry could pull them out, all the time acutely aware that some of the fuses were intact and of the same type that killed the Earl and his team.

On that particular day, 12 May 1941, no different to any other day in the war, businessman Arthur Stanley Steward, who because of his poor eyesight worked as an ARP volunteer ambulance driver, and his female assistant were sent to Erith Marshes to collect the remains of those killed. They drove them to the mortuary at Joyce Green Hospital in Dartford. Afterwards, Arthur took the ambulance home and washed it out to clear away the sickly smell of death. His 8-year-old son, John, listened in fascinated horror as his father told him and his mother of the terrible events. Although they had never met the victims it was still an awful shock because they had heard of the Earl's, and The Holy Trinity's, daring deeds.

George Routhan was one of the lucky ones. He was with the squad when the bomb exploded, and they had just arrived at Erith Marshes to work on it. All were wearing their best battledress ready for going on to Charlton Park. He had walked away from the bomb after having rubbed the casing to see the fuse number – a Type 17, to light a small paraffin-fuelled device.

George had squatted beside a man called Reg Dutson from Birmingham to light it, and said, 'I don't know about Charlton Park. It looks as though we'll be here till seven o'clock.'

It was at that precise moment the bomb had exploded. When George regained consciousness, Beryl Morden was lying next to him. He could see she was fatally injured. Another soldier was standing by the truck, staring at his arm which was lying on the ground at his feet. There were only four survivors.

The blast shattered windows some 400yds away; across the river the windows at the Ford Motors factory were blown out, and people in the adjoining town felt the ground rumble and move beneath their feet.

Jack had always done things his own way and his last farewell to all was in the manner in which he had lived his whole life. He always had a choice to do what he loved or walk away but walking away was never an option. Beryl Morden and Fred Hards were civilians and they too were free to walk away but they chose to volunteer for the most hazardous of all duties, which they carried out most ably. The course of the war had rendered it imperative to set up the experimental unit in what were exceptional circumstances.

All that was found among the wreckage which belonged to Jack was the present given to him by his men – the engraved silver cigarette case. His 410 gauge repeater-action shotgun and pistols were also found in the van but were so badly damaged as to be unserviceable and were disposed of for scrap. The Earl of Suffolk and Berkshire's few remains, recovered from the crater by the rescue team, were placed in a small, 6in x 6in x 8in, wooden casket and buried in the graveyard of the old chapel at Charlton Park.

'The Holy Trinity' were to be the only civilian casualties working on bomb disposal during the Second World War.

These, in the days when heaven was falling,

The hour when earth's foundations fled,

Followed their mercenary calling

And took their wages and are dead.

Their shoulders held the sky suspended;

They stood, and earth's foundations stay;

What God abandoned, these defended,

And saved the sum of things for pay.

A.E. Housman
Epitaph on an Army of Mercenaries, 1914

EPITAPH

**Charles Henry George Howard
20th Earl of Suffolk,
13th Earl of Berkshire,
BSc (Hons.), FRSE, FRSSA, GC.**

Charles Henry George Howard, the 20th Earl of Suffolk, 13th Earl of Berkshire, also known as 'Mad Jack' or 'Jack', joined the comradeship of his ancestors – the illustrious House of Howard. To its coat of arms he added the highest honour England could pay her civilian heroes. This most extraordinary young man was only 11 years-old when his father died on active service in Mesopotamia. He became head of one of the oldest families in England whose line had not changed in hundreds of years. He was also owner of Charlton Park, Malmesbury, one of the largest estates in England. His ancestor, Lord Howard of Effingham, a buccaneer and Lord High Admiral who led Queen Elizabeth's navy against the Spanish Armada, would have doffed his feathered cap at him in appreciation; the seventeenth century poet, John Dryden, who married the sister of a Howard, would have adorned his name in verse.

Jack was a true Howard in every sense of the word, rather like a Drake or a Raleigh who braved scurvy, high seas and fierce battles in pursuit of adventure. He had caught his love of adventure from his mother, who thought nothing of adventuring in exotic countries, flying aircraft and driving fast cars but he was at his best in the Australian outback, free from the confines of all he stood for, where he could be himself.

He was indifferent to the most limiting restrictions and hated being tied down and robbed of his freedom. The one thing no one could ever accuse him of was being bland. He became temperamental if bureaucratic nincompoops got in his way. Rank did not impress him. He treated generals and privates with the same courtesy. He was a master of satire and a practical joker with a caustic wit. People, deceived by the tall, stooping figure with the long black cigarette holder, thought him a titled eccentric playing with danger, but they soon changed their minds.

The one thing Jack never did enough of was take care of his health which was never robust at the best of times but, when the situation demanded it he drew on a hidden reserve and strength. There was nothing he loved more than a good rousing Cockney song in the bar of a local pub. The Cockney workers in the blacked-out pubs across London paid a different kind of tribute to the Earl's memory:

'Suffolk,' they said when you talked about him. 'Yes, we know Jack Suffolk. 'E could 'old 'is booze, 'e could. And at darts 'e was a blinkin' wonder.'

No formal recognition was ever given to the Earl for the part he played to relieve France of the heavy water which was of 'incalculable scientific importance'. His experiments led to the development of a cutting tool used to remove the ZUS-40 anti-handling device that had plagued bomb disposal officers during 1940 and beyond. Captain Charles Currey, RN, a naval bomb expert, was heard to say that Suffolk's brilliant idea was of the greatest possible value, saving many lives and much destruction.

Professor Neil Campbell uttered the Poet Laureate's lines when he heard the Earl had died: '... The beauty of a splendid man abides.' Greville Howard, when pressed, divulged that his brother never talked much about the assignment Morrison had given him. It was only when the war ended he had been able to piece together from British and French sources something of his adventures in that disastrous spring of 1940.

The Rt Hon. Herbert Morrison, CH, MP, wrote in his foreword to Major A.B. Hartley's book *Unexploded Bomb – The True Story*, that he was glad tribute had been paid to Lord Suffolk. In *The Blast of War 1939-1945*, Harold Macmillan wrote that the 20th Earl of Suffolk was a direct descendant of one of the greatest Elizabethan families, and that many of the qualities of reckless, exciting Howards seemed to have been passed to him from those times, but then perhaps he also gained something from the blood of his mother's family. The progeny of an English aristocrat and an American millionaire's family turned out very well with Churchill; and so it was with Suffolk. He may have owed as much to his grandfather, Levi Zeigler Leiter, the Chicago wheat baron of the 1890s, as Churchill did to Leonard Jerome.

Macmillan had the good fortune in his life to meet many gallant officers and brave men, but he had never known such a remarkable combination in a single man of courage, expert knowledge and charm.

Mimi had nothing but good to say about her husband, 'he had a gay and infectious personality with a terrific sense of humour combined with great seriousness of mind ... and a wonderful father and devoted husband, and a joy to live with.'

The History of Radley College 1847-1947, page 369, mentions that, 'an Old Radleian gained the George Cross, paying for it with his life, ... probably one of the most striking characters that Radley ever produced, certainly the only one who has been the subject of a film, *The Incredible Earl of Suffolk*.' (The film was never made). On page 374 of the book, it states, 'the Radleian of today is, as he has generally been, pleasant and tractable; he has always been tolerant, but his tolerance is now more firmly established and based on sounder values. He is taller, heavier and more physically fit than he used to be, and he has acquired three immunities which have not been always his: he can work hard and not be victimized; find interest in things of the mind without being called 'high-brow'; show a feeling for religion and attract no adverse comment. He has not been trained for the barren ideal of a leadership that knows not where to lead. He belongs to a community that is unique ... Opportunity waits on him...'

Many former students of Radley College lost their lives in the Second World War. A visible memorial erected at the college is inscribed with the names of the fallen opposite the names of those who fell in the Great War. Some 1,800 were in the Services of whom 220 laid down their lives.

A note, undated but initialed, reads:

'As we are in secret session I am able to tell the House (of Commons) of a piece of work by two officers of the ministry who were in Paris as Liaison Officers with the Ministry of Armaments. These officers, with the co-operation of certain patriotic Frenchmen and the British Embassy, succeeded in obtaining a ship and arming it against attack from the air. This ship was loaded with, among other things, machine tools and large quantities of valuable and secret stores, some of them of almost incalculable scientific importance. There were also embarked on this ship, owing to the effort that was made, a considerable party of key personnel consisting of eminent scientists and armament experts. In spite of an attempt to bomb it, this ship arrived safely in England. Arrangements are being made for the personnel to continue their work in the service of the Allied cause and the stores have been safely disposed of. Although I cannot do so publicly, I should like to pay tribute to the highly successful effort of the representatives of the ministry and also to the member of the British embassy and to the officers and crew of the ship. A considerable service has been rendered by the safe arrival of this shipload.'

An English expert who travelled to Paris to secure certain vital French patents for the British government factories described, on his return to England, Suffolk's system of overcoming native French stubbornness and trade resistance. The Earl held conferences with the French patent holders in his hotel suite, and when the negotiators arrived they found a bottle of Napoleon brandy and a glass standing on the table in front of each chair. The first hour was devoted to toasts and a long speech made by Suffolk in voluble English. Business discussions then began, but were interrupted most frequently for more toasts and embraces of amity. These negotiations continued for three days and each day new bottles of brandy were opened at the beginning of each session. At last, French resistance collapsed and an agreement was signed. Suffolk then planned a real party but no one attended because, he discovered afterwards to his utter amazement, his colleagues had taken to their beds suffering from exhaustion.

Jack's remains were claimed for burial by Mr Leslie Williams of 11 Old Jewry, London, EC2. His official burial was later held at St John the Baptist, Charlton, on 21 May at 3.00pm. His remains were cremated at Golders Green Crematorium in north London, and his ashes interred in the churchyard of St John the Baptist.

At a meeting held by the Advisory Council on Scientific Research and Technical Development, the Research Bomb Committee tribute was paid to Lord Suffolk's memory by standing in silence for a few moments. Dr Gough apologized for his inability to take the chair due to the additional burdens that had suddenly been thrust upon him as a result of the accident and the heartfelt emotions he felt at that time.

On Tuesday, 20 May 1941, another tribute was paid in the House of Lords: 'The noble Earl, Lord Suffolk, who was not very well known to your lordships, met his death in an air-raid. He was a man in early middle life, of varied experience and great promise, having done scientific work of distinction and lately having accepted a post of importance in connection with his special subject under the government. I am sure your lordships would wish me, on your behalf, to express our sympathy with the Countess of Suffolk and the bereaved family.'

The Earl of Clanwilliam said in his emotional speech: 'My Lords, may I add one word about Lord Suffolk? I feel rather sad today because if it had not been for me Lord Suffolk might perhaps have been with us still.

'When war broke out, Lord Suffolk, who had already suffered from rheumatic fever, was unable to join the infantry, and through one of the members of His Majesty's Government, I was able to get him into the Ministry of Supply. There he did extraordinarily well. As the noble Viscount Lord Samuel has already told your lordships, he had a great career before him in the scientific world. He had spent years at Edinburgh learning chemistry and it was for this reason that he was taken into the Ministry of Supply. There he was thought so well of that the government sent him to Paris as liaison officer between the French Government.

'When the Germans went into Norway, the Allies used some particular chemical, the only supply of which was in Norway, and they got it to Paris. When the debacle took place in France, Lord Suffolk, on his own initiative and with great enterprise, seized this supply of chemical and took it to Bordeaux; he had next to get it to England. He went onboard a French battleship and demanded an escort and a machine gun and got them. He put them into a lorry and took this precious consignment of chemicals – and brought it to England together with a large supply of diamonds. 'After that, Lord Suffolk was employed by the Ministry of Supply and he took on the most dangerous work of destroying unexploded bombs. One morning I met him and said where are you going? "I am going," he replied, "to Richmond Park." I asked him what he was going to do there and he answered, "I am going to deal with unexploded bombs." I asked him if there were many there and he said, "Yes, twenty or thirty." I saw him in the evening... This brave man thought nothing of dealing with unexploded bombs. I would like to add this tribute to him because I think he was not well known in your Lordships' House. We shall never see him here again and I think this tribute ought to be included in your Lordships' records. As Lord Samuel said, he was the head of a great family of very ancient lineage. His father died for his country in Mesopotamia in the last war and he has died for his country today. While the heads of our great families continue to show this great example we need have no fear for England.'

Churchill wrote in *The Second World War*, Volume Two: *Their Finest Hour*, there was one squad he remembered which may be taken as symbolic of many others, consisting of three people, the Earl of Suffolk, his lady private secretary and his chauffeur. They called themselves The Holy Trinity... the 35th claimed its forfeit. Up went the Earl of Suffolk in his Holy Trinity. But we may be sure that, as for 'Mr Valiant-for-Truth' (John Bunyan, *The Pilgrim's Progress*), all the trumpets sounded for them on the other side.

On 21 May 1941, an article entitled *A Friend's Tribute* written by Mr H.J. Gough in a national English newspaper stated: 'By the recent death, due to enemy action, of Charles Henry George Howard, 20th Earl of Suffolk, 13th Earl of Berkshire, this country has lost the services of a very gallant gentleman, possessing an unusually wide and varied knowledge and experience of men, affairs and things, allied with a fearless and forceful personality tempered with great charm of manner and infinite courtesy and tact. A deep, almost fierce devotion to duty; with work to be done all obstacles and restrictions, human or material, which threatened the allotted objective, were firmly overcome or circumvented, yet in such a manner that no sense of grievance remained except in the petty-minded. Yet in lighter moments, there appeared an entirely different being, displaying an almost boyish delight in simple matters and objects; blessed with a vivid dramatic sense, his remarks would often be expressed in extravagant terms.

'There flashes to my recollection an impromptu café supper party very late at night – or was it early morning? – when after a long and exhausting day's work, Lord Suffolk was on his best form. An erudite Sorbonne professor was treated, in rapid, fluent French – which Suffolk spoke like a native – to a dissertation on pharmacology, lapsing into some Parisian gossip which the professor certainly appeared to thoroughly enjoy. Then, arising from the remark of an army officer, a feat of conjuring produced from hidden shoulder holsters a pair of automatic pistols, lovingly referred to as 'Oscar' and 'Geneveve', whose merits were expounded with boyish delight. At a later stage the company were entertained with a masterly and dramatic rendering of a dialogue between a Cockney using rhyming slang and a Chicago gangster conversing in his local idiom: a very extensive knowledge of these 'argots' was another unexpected possession of this most versatile man. This brilliant, complex character would alternate between the sublime and the ridiculous so rapidly that the newcomer would receive a kaleidoscopic impression that was always bewildering and sometimes misinterpreted. But in the wide circle of those who knew him well he invariably evoked feelings of liking, regard and esteem, while in the hearing of the relatively few admitted to his intimate friendship he created that deep affection and love which men rarely extend to men, and never confess to.

'How was such a rare character to be created? Was he a direct throwback to some remote ancestor of his lineage? What a companion spirit to a Drake or a Morgan he would have made – for the true buccaneering quality and instinct were latent and actually brought out nearly a year ago in a brilliantly daring episode which must, for security reasons, remain untold during the war. Or were the foundations laid during his earlier years, consisting of the rich experience gained in many parts of the world, as a sailor, or as a farmer or as a student at university. What is important is the fact that from the outbreak of war – when Lord Suffolk offered his services in any capacity to assist the national effort – until his death, special duties occurred which gave him the utmost scope for his unique combination of personality, courage and experience. It is generally known that until the collapse of France, Lord Suffolk was entrusted with the important post of liaison officer in Paris, between the Ministry of Supply and the Ministry of Armaments. Suffice to say that his mission was brilliantly handled and crowned with conspicuous success; his own ministry in particular and the country in general owe him a deep debt of gratitude for that work and its results. Following his return to this county, he volunteered for altogether different and very special duties, again of prime importance and of a secret nature. Of a most exacting and hazardous nature, they were most faithfully discharged: once again, and perhaps even to a greater degree than formerly, did Lord Suffolk earn the gratitude of his country.'

On 13 July 1941, King George VI graciously showed his gratitude and appreciation to Jack by awarding him, a posthumous George Cross medal, the highest gallantry award for civilians, for his work in bomb disposal.

With support from the present Earl and his brother, the Hon. Maurice Howard, the Civil Defence Association tried from February 2008 to October 2010, to 'extract' the Civil Defence Medal from the Cabinet Office; which is responsible for the awarding of all medals. A Defence Medal was applied for – and failed. The latest rejection was on the grounds of 'it was all too long ago', and 'an award once made cannot be changed.' It was a lost cause.

A 60-year-old Cockney known only as 'Pop' had his story published in *The New York Times* on 19 July 1941. Pop, who had followed the Earl of Suffolk on many a successful job, told of how the crew worked, but publication of his story was not permissible due to strict censorship.

'It was not often you saw a man with a three hundred-year-old title out diggin' for bombs,' he said, 'but the young Earl went right after 'em.' 'He had a pretty secretary,' Pop said. 'She waited in the car at what they thought was a safe distance.'

'The Earl would string a telephone line from the car to the bombs and dictate. He'd keep on smoking until he was almost up to the bomb and then would hand it to somebody and say, "Hold this a minute" and then tackle the bomb.'

The death of Beryl Morden shocked the town where she had lived and the people she had grown close to and loved over the years. She was remembered as such a bright, intelligent woman and an extremely brave soul who gave her life for her country. She had been deeply committed and loyal to the Earl and to the devotion he gave to his work; she knew her job had to be done and she did it to the very best of her ability.

Donald Hind, an undertaker, of West Street, Erith, Kent, made the necessary arrangements regarding her funeral. This took place at Erith Cemetery at 3.30pm on 19 May 1941. She was buried with other war dead in Section I. The local council provided the grave as she came from a poor family.

The esteem in which Beryl was held was shown by the large number of mourners that included members of the Auxiliary Fire Service, wardens, ambulance personnel, the British Red Cross, members from the first-aid posts, Miss Nicholls, Mr Baxter, the ARP Controller, incident officers and the head of the Civil Defence Services. Dr Gough was also present, along with Mr J. Gray, the Senior Experimental Officer, and many others.

Beryl's surname was spelt incorrectly on her gravestone – someone had written 'Norden' instead of 'Morden'. However, Erith council undertook to correct the error and also clean the headstone and others nearby. Beryl was commended by the Ministry of Supply in a letter:

'Dear Mrs Morden,

The Scientific Advisory Council met yesterday for the first time since the accident to your daughter, and they asked me to express their deepest sympathy with you in your bereavement. Several members of

Tel. No.—Gerrard 6933.

Any further communication on this subject should be addressed to :—
The Secretary.
Ministry of Supply,
London, W.C.2.
and the following number quoted.

MINISTRY OF SUPPLY,
THE ADELPHI,
LONDON, W.C.2.

TO WHOM IT MAY CONCERN: Miss E.B. Morden
is, in my opinion, a very suitable secretary and
stenographer to fill any position.

I have found her able, very willing and of a
pleasant disposition.   She takes shorthand extremely
well and her typing is impeccable.

Miss Morden carries my good wishes with her
in any future employment.

EARL OF SUFFOLK & BERKSHIRE.

Earl's reference for Beryl.
(Courtesy of National Archives AVIA 22/2288A)

By the KING'S Order the name of
Miss Eileen Beryl Morden,
Shorthand Typist,
Experimental Unit, Ministry of Supply.
was published in the London Gazette on
18 July, 1941.
as commended for brave conduct in
Civil Defence.
I am charged to record His Majesty's
high appreciation of the service rendered.

Winston S. Churchill

Prime Minister and First Lord
of the Treasury

Beryl Morden's Commendation.
(Courtesy of Eileen 'Frankie' Clarke, Beryl's niece)

the guild had the opportunity of seeing for themselves the nature of the work on which your daughter was engaged, and they realized how much her unsparing assistance and her disregard of personal danger contributed to the large measure of success achieved by the team of workers of which she was a member.

Not only did your daughter give her life for the national cause; she died also in her efforts to save life and property, which is an object denied to most of us in these times. This must be a source of consolation in your sorrow.

With deepest sympathy

Yours sincerely, Chairman, SAC.'

Fred Hards, the jovial driver, who became Jack's closest friend and confidante, working alongside him and handing him his tools in their darkest hours, lost his life doing something he believed was worthwhile with someone in who he had complete faith. Fred lived his life as a good, hardworking, fun-loving, caring husband, father and friend. He was buried in Elmers End Cemetery, Kent, in Grave 18216, Section 12. His grave can now only found with some difficulty. The man buried in the same plot during the 1950s does not share the Hards' name. It was Fred's wife who purchased the plot so no one is sure who the other man is, his family were probably not very wealthy. The ministry tried to push for some compensation for the family. Richard Hards (Fred's son who was only 3 years-old when he lost his father) applied and received, in error, a Defence Medal through the Home Office in the 1980s, so he has a ribbon on which to attach the oak leaf. It was sent in error because the employees of the Ministry of Defence were not included in the list unless they were carrying out such duties as firewatching.

It is important to remember that Fred Hards and Beryl Morden were killed whilst doing their job, they were not people killed in an air raid who happened to have a particular profession. In 2012, Terry Hissey from the Civil Defence Association managed, after a number of attempts, to get the Commonwealth War Graves Commission to amend Fred and Beryl's records to read:

Frederick William Hards

Additional Information

Son of Jack Hards, of 44 Colesburg Road, Beckenham: Husband of

Elizabeth Florence Hards of 9 Clarina Road, Penge. Worked and died with Charles Henry George Howard, Earl of Suffolk and his secretary Eileen Beryl Morden with the Experimental Unit, Ministry of Supply. Died at Belvedere Marshes. Posthumous Commendation from His Majesty King George VI for brave conduct in Civil Defence.

Commemoration

and

Eileen Beryl Morden

Additional Information

Of 29 Queensborough Terrace, London, W2: Daughter of Mrs E. E. Morden, of 34 Borough Road, Dunstable, Bedfordshire, and of the late W. H. Morden: Worked and died with Charles Henry George Howard, Earl of Suffolk, and Frederick William Hards with the Experimental Unit, Ministry of Supply: Died at Belvedere Marshes: Posthumous Commendation from His Majesty King George VI for brave conduct in Civil Defence.

Commemoration

The stunning stained-glass window in the church of St. John the Baptist, Charlton, (the earliest reference to the church was probably 1763, the registers are complete from 1661) was dedicated by Frederick Cockin, Bishop of Bristol, at a special service on the afternoon of Monday, 15 September 1947, as a memorial to Jack. The cost of the window was raised from the parish and included a significant donation from the Howard family. The window incorporates scenes of Jack Howard's adventures. Below the image of St. George is a panel depicting a bomb disposal squad at work and an inscription; below the image of St. John Nepomuk (Patron Saint of Silence), is a panel depicting a laboratory scene and contains the following inscription:

> He loved the bright ship with the lifting wing;
> He felt the anguish in the hunted thing;
> He dared the dangers which beset the guides
> Who lead men to the knowledge nature hides.
> Probing and playing with the lightening thus
> He and his faithful friends met death for us.
> The beauty of a splendid man abides.

By the KING'S Order the name of
'Frederick William Hards,
Van Driver,'
Experimental Unit, Ministry of Supply

was published in the London Gazette on
18th July 1941
as commended for brave conduct.
I am charged to express His Majesty's
high appreciation of the service rendered.

Winston S. Churchill

Prime Minister and First Lord
of the Treasury

Certified Copy.

Fred Hard's Commendation.
(*Courtesy of Richard Hards, his son*)

The words had been written by John Masefield, OM, when he first heard of the Earl's death.

Masefield was pleased that Lady Suffolk accepted his poem and he wrote saying that he hoped his few lines would help her through this dark time. The Countess accompanied by her son Michael, who had inherited his father's title, attended a ceremony at Buckingham Palace, on 14 October 1941, to receive her husband's George Cross medal from King George VI.

On 22 February 1966, Mimi, the Countess of Suffolk & Berkshire, one of England's most adored stage performers and accomplished dancers of her time, died in King's College Hospital, Denmark Hill, North London.

Charlton Park experienced many changes throughout its long life. In the Second World War it was used as a hospital, its patients ferried in by Red Cross ambulances. A few years later, large numbers of US troops were camped in huts and under tents erected around the park, it being a major assembly point before D-Day. This delighted Jack's children who were given Hershey bars, chewing gum and canned fruit by the soldiers. After the war, the house was leased to Wings, a private school for girls with the emphasis on riding, but it closed after a short time and the house fell into a sorry state of disrepair.

Period & Country Houses Limited, owned by C. Buxton, arranged with the 21st Earl of Suffolk to restore the mansion. The company was granted a ninety-nine year lease in May 1976 and the house was converted it into luxury apartments. Sadly, the Long Gallery was divided vertically but the spectacular ceiling can still be partially seen in three of the apartments. The restoration required a tremendous amount of work at the time; the house is now run by a management committee.

Lord Suffolk, the 21st Earl, a substantial landowner, had retained the farmland surrounding the house and is still extremely passionate about his family's historic home.

Appendix

Dr Gough's plea for exceptional favourable and compassionate treatment in the matter of compensation and pensions and so on for the dependants of the late Earl of Suffolk, Miss Morden and Mr Hard on their work of the utmost national importance was met with every assurance that everything possible was being done to achieve just that, but not all shared his view. (The Howards were more or less penniless. Paying death duties and taxes was a very effective way of breaking up large estates. Sadly, all Jack had left at the end of the day was his Earldom. It was his mother who bailed them out and that eventually got too much for her so she returned to the USA.)

Many were angry about the men who were killed. Why had they been so close to the bomb when it went off? Why were Beryl and Fred there? William Wells heard that the Earl was using acid in order to destroy the clock mechanism of the Type 17, and that Atkins was only five yards away with the headphones when the bomb exploded. Some thought the Earl too adventurous, too much of a showman, to be in bomb disposal. John Hudson said they were all very thankful to have Suffolk off their chests, but were very sorry he took a lot of their chaps with him when they should have been much further away.

It is known that the Earl was in the process of recovering the Type 17 fuse and that the sterilizing process had begun, indicating he had not yet attempted to extract it. His record of keeping the safety of Lieutenant Godsmark's men was also known so it is deemed that the explosion of 'Old Faithful' was extremely unexpected. Lord Suffolk did what was right.

The noise from the lorries could have muffled any sound of the ticking, or perhaps the batteries on the clock stopper were low because that would have affected the strength of the magnetic field which stopped the moving parts by magnetizing them. It could be that even though the clock stopper had stopped the clock running, it may not have held back the firing pin if the clock had almost finished its run (but then that could not have been the case because a metal plate presents a hole to the firing pin and if not lined up it would not release the striker). If the bomb was knocked hard when trying to remove the base plate, the firing pin could easily move to fire (that could have happened, and often did. It would also re-start a clock that had stopped running). The magnetic clock stopper was used on the Type 17 fuse but it was not a permanent solution because as soon as the clock stopper was removed, the clock restarted.

The Type 50 fuse was extremely sensitive in that it had to be dealt with before the clock stopper could be introduced to the ticking Type 17. In which time the clock may have run down and the bomb exploded. When the Type 50 fuse underwent tests it was revealed that a movement of 0.006in (0.15mm) in a time of 0.025 seconds was enough to activate the fuse. Some of the answers must lie with the men who put the bomb there on Belvedere Marshes in the first place, but of that there is no record.

The Ministry of Supply was under no illusion as to the surprises the enemy would introduce or to the consequences of heavy aerial attack on the country which was clearly impending. Throughout this work, the need for utmost urgency – regardless of conventional methods – was clearly recognized; the award by the Prime Minister of first priority to all research, development and production involved in dealing with unexploded enemy bombs was sufficient to show the realization of the position at the highest level.

After careful discussion with the Deputy Secretary of the MoS and the army, it had been decided to set up a Directorate of Scientific Research experimental unit whose primary work was to investigate and make trial of new methods using actual enemy UXBs, and it was Lord Suffolk who volunteered for the work. As accurate records of all experiments were paramount, a shorthand typist was required and Miss Morden – who had been associated in France and subsequently with Lord Suffolk in his official liaison duties – freely volunteered for the new duties. A special van was hired and equipped; the driver, Mr Hards, was quite fearless, and Dr Gough spoke highly of the service he rendered to the work and to the ministry, which was entirely outside anything that could be expected of him. Together with a specially trained BD squad, the unit proved to be an outstanding success, and every new development was immediately tried out on bombs of sizes varying from 50kg to 1,800kg.

Subsequent reconstruction of the operations conclusively showed Lord Suffolk took every possible precaution and the actual cause of the detonation of the bomb was a complete mystery, and it was certain from eye-witnesses' accounts that no attempt was made to remove the fuses when detonation occurred: the preliminary operation of emptying the bomb was in progress. Dr Gough emphasized the following points:

1. The duties of the civilians involved were absolutely outside anything which the MoS, as employer, could expect under the original and normal terms of employment.
2. The work was of an extremely hazardous nature, even using every available scientific and technical aid.
3. The work was voluntarily undertaken in the first place by Lord Suffolk and Miss Morden and Mr Hards and subsequently continued by them in full knowledge of the risks and dangers involved.
4. From his personal observation on a number of occasions, while Lord Suffolk was fully aware of the hazards, he never took any unnecessary risk himself, nor allowed his team to be exposed to any more danger than could be avoided.
5. The information and experience gained by the work of the experimental unit was an essential and most potent factor in making possible the solution of many vital problems of BD and the production and issue to the services, in an amazingly short time, the new equipment which so greatly facilitated the work of BD squads, thus saving many lives, valuable property and essential industrial production and public services.
6. Finally, the experimental unit was never intended to be, and has never been employed, as a BD Unit.

Dr Gough recommended the George Cross should be awarded to the late Charles Henry George Howard, the late Miss Eileen Beryl Morden and the late Mr Fred Hards. He also invited sympathetic consideration of the cases of Miss Morden and Mr Hards who constantly shared the dangers and the hazards and, like Lord Suffolk, displayed continuous bravery and indifference to death.

A.T. Sumner's note, dated 14 May 1941, indicated he had made arrangements with the Home Office to visit the Erith mortuary in the company of Mr Walsh, where they examined the remains and any articles salvaged. Certain remains were definitely identified as belonging to Lord Suffolk and he formally signed documents of identification. It was not possible to identify the remains of any other men killed in the accident by way of remnants of jumpers, scarves, coats, boots etc. But fragments of articles of clothing were identified as belonging to Lord Suffolk, to Miss Morden, Fred Hards and the soldiers.

A memorandum, dated 23 May 1941, written by Mr Gray involved everyone in bomb disposal: experimental work on bombs had been somewhat forgotten due to what had taken place on that fateful day, although new items would surely become available. The immediate future would see:

New fuse-pocket trepanner

Heat effect on fuses (steam jet)

Shooting fuses

Acid cutting

Also mentioned were the following investigations carried out by Lord Suffolk's experimental unit:

Thermite method of bomb disposal

Initiated and carried through by Suffolk himself and is now an accepted method for disposing of the bodies of bombs. A very large number of tests had been made and many partial explosions had occurred. It reflected great credit on Suffolk that this dangerous job was carried out without mishap, as the dangers attending the method had to be ascertained by trial.

Washing out the explosive

The washing out by high-pressure water – although leading to no practical result in the end – meant a great deal of experimentation with filled bombs. Suffolk frequently employed mechanical means of loosening the filling to facilitate the washing out: a very dangerous operation.

Plastic explosive

This work was completed in collaboration with Dr Soper under remotely-controlled conditions. This was a very tricky business and was again an exploration of unknown territory.

Trepanning a fuse pocket
This work called for the same qualities as the other trials. It was, however, carried out under the direct supervision of Mr Gray. The danger in this work was probably greater than was realized at the time.

Shooting the fuse
Experiments also controlled by Mr Gray. The first firing was made on an unexploded bomb by Lieutenant Godsmark using remote control and the bomb went off. Later tests were all made on empty bombs on Mr Gray's instructions.

Acid cutting
Work was proceeding in collaboration with Dr Martin of the Government Laboratory at the time of Suffolk's death. Filled unfused bombs were used.

There were many non-programmed episodes relating to the procuring of specimens of bombs and fuses. For example, the Earl had once disappeared, as he was apt to do on many occasions, this time to Bury St.Edmunds. He returned with a 250kg AP bomb – the first they had seen.

The outstanding feature of Lord Suffolk's work was experimenting with new and untried methods on filled bombs which necessarily involved dangers that could not have been assessed beforehand. This continued from last autumn until the time of his death with much valuable experience gained. It was difficult to dissociate Suffolk from the group that worked with him, especially Miss Morden and Mr Hards, but there was no doubt where the inspiration came from and its source should be recognized. *Nature*, a scientific journal, and *The Times* newspaper wrote in a similar vein to Dr Gough asking for more or less the same thing.

Dr Gough received, apart from many requests from the media and amongst a magnitude of correspondence, a letter from the London Power Company Ltd., dated 14 May 1941:

'I little dreamt when I wrote to you that we should so soon mourn the loss of His Lordship and his gallant comrades. My workshop staff all feel that they have lost a pal...'

Convinced there was some urgency in publicly recognizing the work done by The Holy Trinity, in respect of the three gallant people, Dr Gough thought if the George Cross could not be given to Miss Morden and Mr Hards, then they should receive the George Medal? The secretary of Lord Chatfield's Committee commented on their work that exposed them, voluntarily and continuously, to imminent danger. Mr Andrew Duncan earnestly hoped the committee would agree to award the George Cross to each of them. But, came the reply, the George Medal could not be awarded posthumously. Therefore, it was advised that Lord Suffolk be given a George Cross, and for the other two a Commendation, the only alternative posthumous award.

It was suggested that the file be sent back to the minister for a decision. It was doubtful whether the Chatfield Committee would be prepared to make simultaneous awards of the George Cross to the three individuals who comprised the BD Experimental Unit in spite of the fact they all faced the same danger. On the other hand, the only other available award for Miss Morden and Mr Hards, a Commendation, seemed an inadequate recognition of their work. Suggestion was made that the matter be taken up with Sir Robert Knox.

On 25 June 1941, Sir Robert Knox at Treasury Chambers, Whitehall, received an official submission on recommending the award of the George Cross to the late Lord Suffolk and his two assistants, and that this kind of bravery was almost in a class by itself. On 15 July 1941, King George VI approved the George Cross for Lord Suffolk and Commendations for Beryl and Fred, the notice appeared in a supplement to *The London Gazette* on Friday, 18 July 1941.

Beryl's mother and Fred's wife each received similar letters from Lord Beaverbrook dated 16 July 1941:

'I write with deep pleasure to tell you that the courageous conduct of your late husband/daughter while engaged in the service of this ministry is to receive a Commendation in the supplement to *The London Gazette* on Friday, 18 July.

'The public recognition to be given to his/her bravery and devotion to duty is a fitting tribute to one who gave his/her life for his/her country and that the safety of others might be preserved.

'And it will, I hope, be some comfort to you in your sad loss in which I ask you to accept my profound sympathy.

Yours sincerely

Beaverbrook'

The families of Beryl Morden and Fred Hards expressed their appreciation at the time of the personal contact they had received from the Minister. A note was placed on file that Mrs Hards had young children, and that both families found themselves in difficult financial circumstances.

P. A. 'Sandy' Sanderson, the curator of the EODTIC, in his extracted account of the accident at Belvedere Marshes, put forward his own opinion based on his experience and research into Second World War German bomb fuses and Render Safe Procedures:

'Specimens of enemy bomb fuses that could be recovered (in reasonable condition) were urgently required for intelligence purposes that eventually led to the scientific methods that were later applied.

'In the case of the German Type 17 electrically-initiated mechanical (clockwork) time-delay fuse, a variation of this fuse, a Type 17A, had recently begun to be employed, there is some debate as to whether the clock stopper would be effective in its then state of development against the mechanism of a Type 17A. The recovery of good potential working examples of this variation would have been required for testing... It was his personal conclusion that the 250kg bomb was fitted with a Type 17 (possibly a Type 17A) mechanical (clockwork) time fuse and probably a discharged Type 50 (anti-disturbance type). The Type 17 had definitely run for some time when it was being examined by Lord Suffolk, hence the telephoned request for the clock stopper and the electric stethoscope from 25 BD Coy HQ.

'The equipment was in place and most likely operating, the base plate had been removed; this would have exposed the main explosive fill for steaming out when the detonation occurred. It is possible that the clock stopper had either failed or had been unable to hold the clockwork of the fuse that, by this stage, had a very short period in the mechanism left to run, as no warning of any ticking seems to have been given by Staff Sergeant Atkin. I do not believe that the fuse was ticking at the time when the clock stopper was applied and positioned on the bomb the team believed it had stopped.

'Lord Suffolk, as the commander, would not have allowed the number of personnel into the immediate area to assemble and start the steam boiler and other procedures if he had considered it to be an immediate hazard.'

For his efforts in the war, Paul Timbal was awarded the *Croix des Évadés* 1940-1945 and the *Médaille Commémorative de la Guerre* 1940-1945. Captain Paulsen of the SS *Broompark*, accompanied by his wife, arrived at Buckingham Palace to receive the OBE for his war efforts. While they were there an air raid sounded so they all went down to the palace bomb shelter where they were served tea and biscuits by Queen Elizabeth. Later, Paulsen's wife told everyone in the family that 'she was very nice'.

In 1940, James Chadwick forwarded a file on the work of Kowarski and von Halban to the Royal Society. He asked that the papers be held, as he felt they were not appropriate for publication during the war. In 2007, the file was discovered during an audit and when opened it was found to contain details on how to control the chain reaction; also it described how to produce plutonium from uranium and therefore an atomic bomb.

Lew Kowarski and Hans von Halban travelled to the USA to work on what became known as the Manhattan project. After the war, von Halban became deputy director of CERN (see: *The Suffolk Golding Mission – A Considerable Service* by R. V. Martin, Brook House Books, 2014).

Lew Kowarski, when interviewed in the USA in 1969, said that it was 'a typical British muddle'. He did admit that a lot of infiltration was going on and had noticed signs of fear, but agreed that it was justified.

Paul Timbal was also well aware of the British concern about the possibility of fifth columnists being within the group. Timbal's story became known in 1942, when a Federal grand jury in New York served an indictment charging a number of German officials and several individuals with conspiracy to trade in diamonds, alleged to have been taken illegally in Antwerp. Timbal, at the time, was head of the New York branch of *Banque Anversoise SA*, Antwerp. In 1954, he became a director and president of the French-American Banking Corporation; a director of *Banque Diamantiere Anversoise SA* and also a director of the Alaska Industrial Corporation.

Paul Timbal died in Brussels during 1971, at what was thought to be the age of 70.

Baron Ansiaux and Timbal continued to be important figures in the Belgian banking industry after the war. Despite Lord Suffolk's best efforts, Capitain Bichelonne and others who greatly helped the mission were refused permission to leave France in 1940. Bichelonne died in hospital in Germany during 1944 in mysterious circumstances. Had he survived he would have been put on trial by the French as a collaborator supplying French slave labour to the Germans.

Miss Marguerite Nicholle died on 17 July 1998.

After the Earl's death, Felix, the Polish-born waiter at Kempinski's, still prepared a table for him every evening: 'It's like in the church, you know, when you light a candle to the memory of someone who is no longer there.'

Major Ardale Golding was promoted to Colonel, and retired from the army in 1956. He died in Nantucket, Massachusetts, USA, on 26 May 1992.

Malcolm McColm, the son of Captain William McColm, master of the Mount Stewart, served in the RAF during the Second World War as a Squadron Leader at RAF Bodney, near Watton, Norfolk. He was captured by the Germans after bailing out of a Bristol Blenheim bomber. He made seven attempts to escape before being sent to the infamous Colditz Castle, where he shared a room with Wing Commander Douglas Bader.

When Captain Olaf Paulsen retired from J & J Denholm for a second time after the war, the company employed him as a night watchman in their warehouse.

In 1973, BBC Television produced a four-part series, *The Dragon's Opponent*, a dramatization of the Earl's eventful life written by Colin Morris. In this the captain (Paulsen) of SS *Broompark* was portrayed as being a drunk. This caused great offence to the Paulson family as it was a complete figment of the writer's imagination as Captain Olaf Paulsen was tee-total. Later, the family received an apology from Colin Morris and the BBC.

Sergeant Brian Moss wrote in his diary that the Earl had been dealing with a bomb the casing of which was distorted, by hitting a steel girder that made it almost impossible to unscrew the locking ring and remove the fuse. Jack had begun hitting the ring with a hammer and chisel. All the team (or so he was told) were standing nearby by, except one who was some distance away and lived to tell the tale despite being seriously injured by the blast. Just before Doctor Michael Moss, the Sergeant's son, left Halifax, Nova Scotia, his mother found something of great value in one of his father's toolboxes. The family had previously searched, unsuccessfully, for it and presumed it lost. It looked so insignificant that it could have easily been thrown away – it was his father's brass Crabtree discharger. (The diary of Sergeant Moss remains unpublished to date.)

Bibliography

A Brief History of Civil Defence, edited by Tim Essex-Lopresti. www.pdffactory.com. Retrieved April, 2008.

Balchin, N., *The Small Back Room*, p. 63-64, Collins, London, 1946.
Baronage of England, George Olms Verlag AG; Facsimile of 1675-76 edition (December 1977).
Bayles W. D., *The Incredible Earl of Suffolk. The Story of the Old Radleian*, published in the U.S. on 28 November and 5 December, 1942.
Bexley Archives, Earl's remains claimed for burial. National Archives, AVIA 22/1221.
Blackett, P. M. S., *Biographical Memoirs of the Royal Society*, p. 86, Royal Society of London, 1955.
Boyd, A.K., *Radley College 1847-1947*, Basil Blackwell, Oxford, 1948.
Brenan, G. & Statham, E. P., *The House of Howard* Vols I & II, Hutchinson & Co., London, 1907.
Brown, M. & Harris, C., *The Wartime House. Home Life in Wartime Britain 1939-1945*, (new ed.), The History Press Ltd, England, 2005.
Burke, J., *A General and Heraldic Dictionary of the Peerage and Baronetage of the British Empire*, 4th edition, London.
Burke's Peerage and Gentry, http://www.burkes-peerage.net/. Retrieved August, 2008.
Burton, S., National Monuments Research Centre, Swindon, 2009, U.K.
Butler, M. Author of pamphlet on St. John the Baptist's Church, Charlton, U.K.

Cancer Bill, Hansard, 15th March 1939, http://hansard.millbanksystems.com/lords/1939/mar15/cancer-bill. Retrieved January, 2010.
Captain Henderson J.M., *Captain Olaf Paulsen, Mâtelot Extraordinaire*, ex-Director of Denholm Ship Management (Christmas ed.), 1976.
Cashford, N. MBE, RNVR, *All Theirs!*, p. 24, ALD Design & Print, Sheffield, 2004.
CDA Journal dated 12 April 2003, No.2. ISSN 1479-6856.
Ransted, Chris, *The Death Of An Earl*, After The Battle, Number 146, 2009.
Clarke, R., *The Greatest Power on Earth*, Book Club Associates, London, 1981.
Comer, B & Even-Zohar C, *Financing The World's Most Precious Treasures*, Tacy Ltd, Diamond Industry Consultants, Ramat Gan, Israel, 2009.
Country History of Wiltshire, Wiltshire & Swindon District Council, Chippenham.

Dahl, P. F., *Heavy Water and the Wartime Race for Nuclear Energy*, IOP Publishing Ltd., London, 1999.

Daily Mirror, *Earl Killed by Bomb*, 1941.

Daily Mirror, *Earl to Marry Actress*, 1934.

Daily Mirror, *Son for Mimi Crawford*, 1935.

Danger UXB, Channel 4 Documentary, 2 one-hour specials, 6th March, 2001.

Dictionary of National Biography, Vol. 10, p. 71-72.

Domesday Book, text translated by J. Morris, Chichester, 1975-1992.

Dr Peniston-Bird, C., Blitz: *A Pictorial History of Britain Under Attack*, Caxton Editions, 2001.

Durham, F.J. (as told to Doug Hay), *You Only Blow Yourself Up Once*, iUniverse, 2003.

Earl of Suffolk, Ministry of Supply liaison officer in France; Evacuation from France with French scientists and Equipment, National Archives, 22/2288A

Edinburgh University Journal, *Earl of Suffolk & Berkshire (1906-1941) Tribute*, by Professor Emeritus Neil Campbell, OBE PhD DSC FRSE. (Irene Ferguson, University Archives).

For New Tobacco Land, The Brisbane Courier (Qld. : 1864 - 1933), Saturday 14 November, p. 16, 1931.

Letters from Marguerite Hyde Paget (Leiter) to her husband, National Archives XOMN/A/1/5, 1915-1926, OMN/A/1/5.

Foster, S., Archivist, Winchester College, Hampshire, England.

Gardiner, J., *Wartime Britain 1939-1945*, Headline Review, England, 2005.

Garfield, S., *We Are At War*, Ebury Press, (new ed.), 2006.

Gawler, J., *Lloyd's Medals 1836-1989*, Hart Publishing, Toronto, 1989.

Green, T., *The World of Diamonds*, Wiedenfeld & Nicholson, London, 1981.

Goldsmith, M., *Joliot, Frederic–Curie, A Biography*, Beechman Publishing Inc., Woodstock, N.Y., 1976.

Hare-Scott, K., *For Gallantry, The George Cross*, Peter Garnett Ltd., Autumn, 1951.

Hebblethwaite, M., One Step Further, Book S to V, Chameleon HH Publishing, Witney, 2007.

Hissey, T., *Come If Ye Dare*, Civil Defence Association, Derbyshire, 2008.

http://chsmedia.org/media/fa/fa/M-L/LeiterLevi.htm, Retrieved October, 2008.

Hutchinson, R., *House of Treason*, Weidenfied & Nicholson, U.K., 2009.

Interesting Women of the Nobility. http://forum.alexanderpalace.org/index.php?topic=8984.0. Retrieved September, 2008.

Jappy, M. J., *Danger UXB*, Channel 4 Books, London, 2001.

Laureys, E., *Diamond Masters (Meesters van het diamante. De Belgische diamantsector tijdens het nazibewind)*, Lannoo, 2005.

Levine, J., *Forgotten Voices of the Blitz and the Battle of Britain*, pages 321-339, Ebury Press, London, 2006.

London Can Take It, Winston Churchill, (vol. Alone), p. 318-320.

Lord, W., *The Miracle of Dunkirk*, The Viking Press, USA, 1982.

MacKay, H., *The Long Dead*, published Andrew Melrose Ltd., London, 1915.

Macmillan, H., *The Blast of War 1939-1945*, Harper & Row Inc., New York, 1968.

Major Hartley A.B., *Unexploded Bombs*, Cassell, London, 1958.

Major Hogben, A., *Designed to Kill*, Thorsons Publishing Group, U.K., 1987.

Mantle, J., *Ship to Shore*, J & J Denholm 1866-1991, James & James Ltd., London, 1991.

Mason, K., *Charlton Park: A Short History*, published privately in 1996.

Mason, M., Greenhill, B & Craig, R., *The British Seafarer*, Hutchinson/BBC in Association with The National Maritime Museum, U.K., 1980.

The Death of Members of Jack's team, National Archives 22/2454.

Morning Bulletin (Rockhampton, Qld. : 1878 - 1954). Wednesday 24 February, p.7, 1932.

My Elizabethan Brother, the Earl of Suffolk, by The Honourable Greville Howard, as told to Peter Browne, The Reader's Digest, vol. 95, 571, 1969.

Nature, 141, 1003-1003 (04 June 1938) | doi:10.1038/1411003b0.

Newby, E., *Learning the Ropes*, John Murray Publishers Ltd., U.K., 1999.

News Chronicle, *He Robbed the Gestapo of Untold Wealth*, February 9th, 1943.

Ondaatje, M., *The English Patient*, Macmillan Publishers, U.K., 1993.

Owen, J., *Danger UXB*, Little, Brown, U.K., 2010.

Peer Bled by Moneylenders for 40 Years, Bankrupt by Extravagance, London, The Mail (Adelaide, SA : 1912 - 1954), p. 2, Saturday 29 July, 1933.

Phelps, S., *The Tizard Mission*, Westholme Publishing, U.S.A., 2010.

Picard, J.-F., *La République des Savants. La Recherche Française et le CNRS*, Paris, Flammarion, 1990.

Queensland's Earl Seriously Ill In Hospital in London, June 19. The Courier-Mail (Brisbane, Qld. : 1933 - 1954) p. 12, Thursday 20 June, 1935.

Radley College, (Clare Sargent, Head of Library & Archives), Archives Album 25 – The Vyvyan Hope Album, 1920s–1930s.

Richardson, E. M., *The Lion and the Rose (The Great Howard Story)*, vols I & II, Hutchinson & Co., London, 1922.

Robinson, J. M., *The Dukes of Norfolk*, Chichester, 1995.

Share Farming, The Brisbane Courier (Qld. : 1864 - 1933), p. 18, Thursday 26 November, 1931.

Southall, I., *Softly Tread the Brave*, Peter Garnett Ltd., Autumn, 1951.

State Digital Library of Queensland, 2008.

Supplement to *The London Gazette*, Friday, 18 July1941.

Sunday Times (Perth, WA,: 1902 - 1954), Saturday. *Earl's Country Seat, Circumstances Necessitate Smaller House LONDON*, First Section, p. 5, Sunday 30 July, 1933.

Suzanne Foster, Archivist, Winchester College, Hampshire, 2009.

Swindon & Wiltshire Council Archives, 88/1/139, 2008.

The Australian Associated Press, *Earl Gave Life to Save Life*.

The Craxford Family Genealogy Magazine, http://www.craxford-family.co.uk/themepurple/crauart4.php

The Girl In The 8.21, National Archives AVIA 22/2288A.

The Daily Mirror, *The Pond's Method*, 1927.

The Daily Mirror, *Work and Dance to Keep Slim*, 1928.

The Daily Star, *Lady Curzon's Wish*, Vol. 5, No. 153, Dhaka (SR Shaheed DOHS Banani, October, 25, 2004).

The Dragon's Opponent, BBC series 1973. Written by Colin Morris, Directed by Gerald Blake, www.ftvdb.bfi.org.uk/sift/series/27473 (BFI Film & TV Database). Retrieved May, 2008.

The Hartford Courant, *Suffered Terribly in British Columbia*, 1909.

The House of Lords, *Tribute to the Earl of Suffolk*, May 1941.

The National Archives, London, Files W24499, AVIA 22/2288A, AVIA 22/2454, AVIA 22/3201 & CUST 106/884; BT 381/1672 the Official Log and Articles of Agreement of the *Broompark*.

The New York Times, *British Peer to Wed Miss Mimi Crawford*, 1934.

The New York Times, *Countess of Suffolk Breaks Ribs in Fall*, 1924.

The New York Times, *Earl of Suffolk and Berkshire is Killed by Bomb at Age of 35*, 1941.

The New York Times, *Earl Quits London Gayeties to be an Australian Cowboy*, 1926.

The New York Times, *Saving Secrets From Foe Credited to Lord Suffolk*, 1941.

The Saturday Evening Post, *The Incredible Earl of Suffolk*, W. D. Baylis,
28 November 1942.

The Saturday Evening Post, *The Incredible Earl of Suffolk*, W. D. Bayliss,
5 December 1942.

The Sunday Dispatch, *Earl Raided the Bank Vaults - Foiled Invading Germans*, May 1945.

The Sunday Dispatch, *Thanksgiving Sunday*, May, 1945.

The Sunday Times, *Letter to the Sunday Times*, A. V. Golding (ret.), March 20th, 1960.

The Sydney Morning Herald, *The Mount Stewart*, 30th November 1923.

The Sydney Morning Herald (NSW: 1842 - 1954), *Earl of Suffolk, Nine Years in Australia*. p. 14, Saturday 11 March, 1933.

The Times, *Boy Earl's Shooting Accident*, 1920.

The Times, *Cancer Bill*, 1939.

The Times, *Charlton Park, Malmesbury, Wilts, To Let*, 1933.

The Times, *Lord Suffolk: A Friend's Tribute* by HJG, May, 1941.

The Times, *Lord Suffolk's Obituary*, May, 1941.

Tobacco Lands, The Brisbane Courier (Qld. : 1864 - 1933), p.8, Wednesday 29 July, 1931.

Townsville Daily Bulletin (Qld : 1885 - 1954), *Earl of Suffolk Visit to England. LONDON, July 25*, p. 4, Thursday, 27 July, 1933.

Turner, E.S., *The Phoney War on the Home Front*, Michael Joseph Ltd., London, 1961.

Waltham, C., *An Early History of Heavy Water*, Department of Physics & Astronomy, University of British Columbia, Canada, 2002.

www.bbc.co.uk/ww2peopleswar/user/47/u752247, WW2 People's War, BBC Retrieved May, 2008.

www.bombdisposalclub.org.uk/BD_history. Retrieved July, 2008.

http://www.bombfusecollectorsnet.com/page29.htm. Retrieved January 2014.

http://www.craxford-family.co.uk/themepurple/crauart4.php. Retrieved March 2013.

www.en.wikepedia.org/wiki/Norwegian_heavy_water_sabotage. Retrieved July, 2008.

www.en.wikepedia.org/wiki/Thermite. Retrieved August, 2008.

www.gc-database.co.uk/receipients/SuffolkBerks. Retrieved May, 2008.

www.hansard.millbanksystems.com/commons/1939/sep/21/ministry-of-supply. Retrieved May, 2008.

www.clutch.open.ac.uk/schools/emerson00/rss_page1.html. Retrieved August, 2010.

www.fas.org/irp/world/uk/mi5/history.htm. Retrieved August, 2010.

www.mi5.gov.uk/output/world-war-2.html. Retrieved August, 2010.

www.nndb.com/people/442/000102136/. Frances Drake. Retrieved July, 2008.

www.robertmorris.edu/news_oldradiusfall04.pdf. Retrieved July, 2008.

www.unihistories.com/officers/RNUK_officersH. Retrieved August, 2008.

www.unihistories.com/officers/RNVR_officersH.html. Retrieved October, 2008.

https://docs.google.com/viewer?a=v&q=cache:DIdn8U- www.scotspgc.qld.edu.au/attachments/Clocktower%2520417%2520-%2520From%2520Scots%2520College%2520to%2520Colditz%2520Castle.pdf+captain+william+mccolm&hl=en&gl=uk&pid=bl&srcid=ADGEESju83sm7nLUhAXsTg-NI6OVHf2M3b9oCNStxJCjC1yFrJMw1bIQaIugm5AxkAuxhokzDfzfZGlzPq6KzeP_qyvs1CcWKyWTh8xGjc0j7CQKu0ccldXkpZePEC4GR2ApJQU6yVvw&sig=AHIEtbRKZEk3gb2Apq0uqiaV5lxcc-ctQQ. Retrieved February 2012.

www.wikipedia.org/wiki/Dewoitine_D.520. Retrieved August 2012.

Yates, J. & King, S., *Dunstable and District at War*, The Book Castle, Bedfordshire, 2006.

Index